VOICE OF THE OTHER

VOICE OF THE OTHER
Understanding Marginal Identities

Vulli Dhanaraju

GenNext Publication

ISBN: 978-93-5324-100-1

Price : ₹ 1150

First Published in 2016

Published by

GenNext Publication

5, Ansari Road,

Darya Ganj

New Delhi-110002

Mob: 9811692060

E-mail: gennext@hotmail.com

Printed at : G. Print Process, Delhi

Cataloging in Publication Data—DK

Courtesy: D.K. Agencies (P) Ltd. <docinfo@dkagencies.com>

International Conference on "Contesting Self and Other: Identities of Caste, Tribe and Gender" (2015 : Assam University)

Voice of the other : understanding marginal identities / [editor], Vulli Dhanaraju.

pages cm

Papers presented in the International Conference on "Contesting Self and Other: Identities of Caste, Tribe and Gender" organized by the Department of History and Department of Anthropology, Assam University (Central University), Diphu Campus, Assam, India during 27-28, March, 2015 in collaboration with Maulana Abul Kalam Azad Institute of Asian Studies (MAKAIAS), Kolkata, India and Indian Council of Social Science Research (ICSSR), New Delhi, India.

ISBN: 978-93-5324-100-1

1. Marginality, Social—India—Congresses. 2. Marginality, Social—India, Northeastern—Congresses. 3. Ethnicity—India—Congresses. 4. Ethnicity—India, Northeastern—Congresses. 5. Women in development—India—Congresses. 6. Women in development—India, Northeastern—Congresses. 7. Marginality, Social, in literature—Congresses. I. Dhanaraju, Vulli, editor. II. Assam University (Silchar, India). Department of History, organizer. III. Assam University (Silchar, India). Department of Anthropology, organizer. IV. Title.

HN690.Z9M26 2015 DDC 305.560054 23

For

My Inspired Teacher
Dr J. Krishna Prasad Babu

Contents

Forward

The Pride of Identity Politics

- ***To speak is assume culture*-Franz Fanon**

The Voice of 'Other' is about marginality, identity and self assertion of subordinated communities. From late 1980s onwards we are hearing the protest voices of dalits, women and tribals. Dalits are protesting against Brahminical social order. Women are fighting against patriarchy. Tribals are fighting for livelihood along with ethnic cultural rights. Each social group finds its own site of oppression and structural violence. For dalits, it is caste and gender in case of women. The shared social experience of respective social group is playing vital role in shaping their identity. Identity signifies the political activity and theorizing founded in the shared experiences of injustice of a social group. Identity formation is a reflection on their suffering and also a move towards freedom. Identity refers to the capacity for self reflection and awareness of self. It is a kind of selfhood. Identity constitutes in and through making stance of morality. Through the assertion of identity public, they are demand social recognition. In other words, identity means celebrating ones dignity and pride of collectivity. However, these contemporary struggles are not providing the new world views to understand our social reality but also compelling the academic world to critically reframe their social theories.

Experience plays a crucial role in evolving beliefs, social systems and knowledge. The dominant social groups are always in privileged position and pushing others to margins or make them subordinate to them. The privileged strategically design their own methods and social practices to keep the system status quo by not allow any dissent from other. The power holds a key role in regulating the hegemonic social system. The assertion of other is creating a new situation by contesting the dominance and hegemonic social relations. The assertion of identity is always in relation or response to the dominant, hierarchical, oppressive and exploitative social and political structures. The experience of the other is enriching the epistemology by interrogating the dominance.

Identity politics suggests a special form of agency-self conscious 'collective agency' The collective agency enacted in a moral space. Identity constitutes in and through making stance of morality. Collective identity explains 'how structural inequalities get translated into subjective discontent.' Identity makes the sense of social world. Thought and action are fused as a subject, self or person in persuasion of freedom to be. The identity politics are not only critical about existing political theories and provides the new inputs to political theory. The dominant political theories are either revised or rejected. The identity politics are critical about both liberal and Marxist theories. The modernity mediated by the liberal theory is under scrutiny. The politics of universalism of liberal theory and the politics of difference of post modern/communitarian theories are renewed the political discourse in the back drop of identity politics. Identity politics are critical about liberal theory of universal, which is not prepared to acknowledge the specific problem. Identity politics are equally critical about economic reductionism of Marxism. Identity politics are not only brought in view of marginalised discourses but also articulated the rich concrete social life, which is not part of dominant political discourses. As Sonia Kruks rightly articulated that the demand of identity politics is not for inclusion within the fold of "universal humankind" on the basis of shared human attributes; nor is it for respect "in spite of" one's differences. Rather, what is demanded is respect for oneself *as* different.

The demand of recognition is the basic human need. The recognition/non-recognition influences the identity. Non-recognition causes damage/pain and oppresses people. As Charles Taylor in *Politics of Recognition* says that, "equal recognition is not just the appropriate mode for a healthy democratic society. Its refusal can inflict damage on those who are denied it .... The projection of an inferior or demeaning image on another can actually distort and oppress, to the extent that the image is internalised." Our identity is partly shaped by recognition or its absence, often by the 'misrecognition' of others, and *so a person or group of people* can suffer real damage, real distortion, if the people or society around them mirror back to them a confining or demeaning or contemptible picture of themselves.

The idea of freedom and justice are driving forces of identity politics. The identity politics defined both these concepts in novel form rather confining to existing theories. Collective dignity, Pride and self respect of the community are defended and highlighted in their political discourse. The concepts of social justice and self respect are inextricably linked. The disrespect for a group or individual has the consequences in rebuilding the strategies of respect. Moral worthiness is an important criterion in demanding respect for a social group or individuals. It is generally regarded as human beings are possessing moral worth and an inherent dignity, which is worth defending. All human beings are entitled to expect human respect by allowing their dignity as human being. In case of dalits, the human dignity is undermined by the caste system. In case of Women, patriarchy has undermined the modesty of women. The liberal theory believes that human beings have intrinsic moral worth regardless of how unworthy they might be in other ways. Reflexive self-respect is the way in which others treatment of us affects the way we feel about ourselves. The inherently unequal relationship affects the individuals/groups self-respect. To be constantly under another's dominion is to be reminded of one's own powerlessness and this must undermine the sense of ones own moral worth. The existing relationships in a society, provides the foundation for one's self respect. Self-respect is not simply a reflection of the respect we receive from others, although of course that is important. It is also about how we feel about ourselves. It is partly about maintaining a set of norms or values. The moral standards allow us to construct ourselves as persons worth respecting. This is an evaluative element of social practice.

Charles Taylor considers the debates of merit of identity politics are as philosophical questions about the very nature of subjectivity and the self. He argues that the modern identity is characterised by an emphasis on its inner voice and capacity for *authenticity* – that is, the ability to find a way of being that is somehow true to oneself. In their projection of authentic self, dalits are departure from the earlier notions of politics of recognition and liberal idea of equality. Their demand is not just for inclusion within the fold of universal human kind or to get sympathetic note of their difference from the others. Rather, demanding respect for dalit *as* different with pride and self assertion. The shared experiences of caste oppression and the alternatives commonly persuaded to overcome this are crucial for understanding the politics of dalit identity. Dalit identity rests on the unifying claims about the meaning of politically laden experiences of diverse individuals of untouchable communities. Dalit identity based on the assumptions of self dignity, respect, inward strength and democratisation of cultural life and social practices. The social imaginary in Dalit intellectuals ignites the sense of identity to recapture their own history, which is marginalised so far. The dalit self is embedded in indigenous cultural tradition. It has its own version of modernity that is different from both western liberal modernity and brahminical modernity of India. Indeed, it had a potential to mediate both liberal and communitarian politics..

The identity politics has its own significance in contesting the dominance and adding new vision to understand reality. But at the same time, there is a problem to make it as a grand narrative by not allowing other discourses in due course of time. It is apt to remind the words of Kenyan writer Ngugi Wa Thiango in the context of identity politics: 'It was not a question of substituting one center for the other. The problem arose only when people tried to use the vision from any one center and generalize it as the universal reality.'

I'm sincerely appreciating Vulli Dhanaraju for refreshing the marginalised discourse by bringing into centre of academics. This work has its significance by adding the issue of ethnicity/ tribal identity along with issues of caste and gender. The exclusive section on literature is an extension of articulation and performance of voice of unheard and unrepresented social groups in literary and cultural traditions.

P. Kesava Kumar
Professor
Department of Philosophy
University of Delhi
Delhi-110007

Preface

The voice of 'other' is crucial in the discourse of marginal identities. The voice of the 'other' highlights how many societies create a sense of belonging, identity and social status by constructing social categories as binary opposites. It has been discussed in the construction of marginal identities in India However, the concept of the voice of other' has been the subject of much academic debate in the study of marginal identity struggles in India. In keeping view of this the marginal identities have been undermined due to the globalisation and social network revolution that enabled the marginalised communities to look into their own identities and resisting the power and hegemony of the agencies in the name of social identity movements in the twenty first century. The marginal identities have all arisen is some way from a redrawing of the 'otherness' and every day personal experiences in the society. This book used the concept of the 'voice of the other' in order to understand the contested nature of marginal identities and its relation with the state and other hegemonic institutions.

The book also addresses the concept of marginalisation in understanding of various identities in Indian society. Marginalisation is often described as a social process where people are referring to the periphery or 'margins' of the society. It is defined as processes, in which individuals or communities are socially excluded and denied access to participate in social and political processes which are basic to integrate with the society. Marginalisation stalls a person, a group, a section or a community to enjoy rights, privileges, opportunities and resources that are normally available to members of a society. It may therefore be considered as an inharmonious relationship between those who marginalise as compared to those who are being marginalised.

In this context, the term, 'marginality' is used in this book in order to understand the depressed and socially excluded sections, estranged by others such as Brahmanism in mainstream society, exploitative nature of non-tribals in northeast and patriarchy in Indian society.

This book also covers six papers on literature and language in understanding of marginal identities. The marginal literature generally talks about the issues that seem to be strange or unfamiliar with present social context. Queer theory is one of the important parts of marginal literature. It gives dimensions that are totally different from the canon (other literature). The word 'marginal' refers to the 'dismantle' of the traditional customs or culture. Generally, marginal literature represents the life of the people who do not accept the social rules and regulations, rather build their life which goes against the norms of the society.

The book is divided into four thematic sections covering 17 papers by scholars, social science researchers and other experts on the theme. The four thematic themes are *Caste and Marginality, Ethnic Identities and Marginality, Gender and Marginality and, Literature, Language and Marginality*. Each section has covered main theme of the book. Thus, the readers will find this book dealing with voice of other in the study of marginal identities in Indian society.

Vulli Dhanaraju

Acknowledgments

For preparing of this edited book I am very thankful to the contributors who presented their papers in the International Conference on *"Contesting Self and Other: Identities of Caste, Tribe and Gender"* organised by the Department of History and Department of Anthropology, Assam University (Central University), Diphu Campus, Assam, India during 27-28, March, 2015 in collaboration with Maulana Abul Kalam Azad Institute of Asian Studies (MAKAIAS), Kolkata, India and Indian Council of Social Science Research (ICSSR), New Delhi, India. Without these contributors' of this book cooperation and support this book would not have been reality in this form.

I wish to admit my gratitude to the Maulana Abul Kalam Azad Institute of Asian Studies (MAKAIAS), Kolkata, India and Indian Council of Social Science Research (ICSSR), New Delhi, India for collaboration and financial assistance in organising of the International Conference at the Department of History and Department of Anthropology, Assam University (Central University), Diphu Campus, Assam, India. I extend my gratitude to the Assam University (Central University), Diphu Campus, Assam, India for giving an opportunity to organising the International Conference at the Diphu Campus.

I am very grateful to Professor P. Kesava Kumar, Department of Philosophy, Delhi University for accepting my request to write a forward to this book. Interacting and engaging with him in various occasions has been a great learning experience and source of intellectual enrichment.

I wish to express my deep sense of gratitude to my teacher, Professor Y. A. Sudhakar Reddy, Centre for Folk Culture Studies, University of Hyderabad, India who has guided me to develop this book. Despite his busy schedule, he gave so much time for discussion and shared his ideas which helped me to develop this book. His erudition and characteristic unassuming style provided inspiration and encouragement for me. Without his exceptional generosity and scholarly support, this book would not have been possible.

I am deeply indebted to my favorite and lovable teacher, Dr J. Krishna Prasad Babu, Associate Professor and HoD, Jawahar Bharathi Degree College, Kavali, Nellore, Andhra Pradesh who took keen interest in my career and gave valuable suggestions to pursue my higher education. He is the person who inspired me to read history very fascinatingly during my graduation days at college. My indebtedness to him could not be expressed in words. I am dedicating this book to him.

I owe an intellectual debt to Dr B.C. Dash, Associate Professor, Department of English and also one of the contributors of this book for his invaluable ideas and insights in many conversations with him during preparation of this book. I also extend my gratitude to Professor Chinna Rao Yagati, JNU, New Delhi, Dr B. Eswara Rao, University of Hyderabad and Chittibabu Padvala, IIT Mumbai for their intellectual support and encouragement in completing of this book. I also extend my gratitude to Dr Kh Narendra Singh, Associate Professor, Department of Anthropology, Assam University, Diphu Campus for his cooperation and support in organising International Conference as one of the coordinators of the conference.

I also thank the entire faculty and staff of the Department of History, Assam University, Diphu Campus, Assam, India for all the academic and administrative support. Words fail to express my gratitude to Dr R.K. Bijeta, Guest Faculty, Department of History, Assam University, Diphu Campus. She has always gone out of her way to help me what she is known for unfailing support without reservations or conditions throughout, and without a shred of tiredness.

I also extend thanks to the Research Scholars in the Department of History, Assam University, Diphu Campus particularly, Ms Rupali Rongpipi, Ms Junmoini Hansepi, Ms Nukshirenla and Rashmi Engtipi for their assistance in proof reading of this book. Like any other works this book is collective endeavour. My friends and students have always encouraged me and generate inspiration to expand new ideas that constantly helped me in preparation of this book in the present form.

This endeavour would not have come to fruition but for the support that I have received from my family members especially my mother and my sisters.

No words are left to express my gratitude to the GenNext Publication, New Delhi for their keen interest in the publication of this book.

Vulli Dhanaraju

List of Contributors

1. **Nil Ratan Roy,** Associate Professor, Department of Education, Vinaya Bhavana, Visva-Bharati (A Central University and an Institution of National Importance), Santiniketan, West Bengal.

2. **Mallikarjun Ch,** Research Scholar, Centre for Folk Culture Studies, University of Hyderabad, Hyderabad.

3. **Kartik Chandra Sutradhar,** Assistant Professor, Department of History, Netaji Subhas Mahavidyalaya, Haldibari, Cooch Behar, West Bengal.

4. **Keisham Ingocha Singh,** Assistant Professor, Department of Anthropology, Kha – Manipur College, Kakching, Manipur.

5. **Sanjib Goswami,** Senior Researcher, Institute of Social Research, Swinburne University of Technology, Australia

6. **Uttam Kr Pegu,** Assistant Professor, Department of Mass Communication and Journalism, Tezpur University, Assam.

7. **Ankur Goswami,** Research Scholar, Jawaharlal Nehru University, New Delhi.

8. **Vulli Dhanaraju,** Assistant Professor, Department of History, Assam University (Central University), Diphu Campus, Diphu, Assam.

9. **R.K. Bijeta,** Guest Faculty, Department of History, Assam University (Central University), Silchar, Assam.

10. **Sunanda Sahu**, Assistant Professor, Department of Anthropology, DHSK College, Dibrugarh, Assam.

11. **Lakhimi Nath,** Research Scholar, Assam University (Central University), Silchar.

12. **Devastuti Sharma,** Assistant Professor, Department of English, Assam Women's University, Jorhat, Assam.

13. **T. David Jeyaraj Franklin,** Assistant Professor of English, Gandhigram Rural Institute – Deemed University, Gandhigram, Tamil Nadu.

14. **R. Senthil Kumar,** Assistant Commissioner, Kendriya Vidyalaya Sangathan, Chennai Region, Tamil Nadu.

15. **Bishnu Charan Dash,** Associate Professor, Department of English, Assam University (Central University), Diphu Campus, Diphu, Assam.

16. **Maibam Monoranjan Singh**, Asst. Professor, Department of Anthropology, D.M.College of Science, Imphal, Manipur.

17. **Indira Priyanka Veernala,** Senior Researcher, Centre for Translation Studies, University of Hyderabad, Hyderabad.

18. **Suranjana Barua,** Assistant Professor (English), Humanities and Social Sciences, Indian Institute of Information Technology (IIT), Guwahati, Assam.

Introduction

Vulli Dhanaraju

The voice of 'other' has been the subject of much academic debate in the study of marginal identity struggles in India. The marginal identities have been undermined due to the globalisation and social network revolution that enabled the marginalised communities to look into their own identities and resisting the power and hegemony of the agencies in the name of social identity movements in the twenty first century. In this context how do we understand the concept of identity in understanding of the voice of the other? There are several broad categories which are used normally in social science discipline. The people use different identities in contemporary India such as national identity, cultural identity, political identity, linguistic identity, gender identity, ethnic identity, regional identity, religious identity, etc. The formation of identity is essentially a question of perception by the other. Our identity lies in a manner in which we are perceived by others. This implies, when applied to marginalised communities, that the formation of identity is dependent upon their perception by the non-marginalised groups. These group markings, within which an individual normally defines himself, can and does change over different historical periods or as societies evolve in relation to each other.

Thus, identity formation must be viewed as a dynamic process which changes with historical changes. But, the identity formation among the marginal communities is not an accidental affair. It has evolved through several forces in the past. However, reconstruction of their history is very difficult task, precisely because they have had no written records by themselves. Whatever records are available, they are written by others, with different interests and compulsions. These are mostly divorced from the subjective conditions of the marginal people.

I

The voices of the other identities are crucial in understanding of nature of identity struggles in India. This is because the representation of different marginalised groups is controlled by groups that have cultural/political hegemony. In order to understand the notion of the other, we need to put a critical analysis in which social identities are constructed. Rather than talking about the individual characteristics or personalities of different individuals, which is generally the focus for psychology, sociologists focus on social identities[1]. Social identities reflect the way individuals and groups internalise established social categories within their societies, such as their cultural (or ethnic) identities, gender identities, class identities, and so on. These social categories shape our ideas about who we think we are how we want to be seen by others, and the groups to which we belong. The concept of the 'self' has long been salient in feminist philosophy, for it is pivotal to questions about personhood, identity, the body, and agency that feminism must address. That is why Simone de Beauvoir's[2] work quoted in highlighting the distinction between men and women that "He is the subject, he is the absolute-she is the other". To be the other is to be the non-subject, the non-person, the non-agent-in short, the mere body. In law, in customary practice, and in cultural stereotypes, women's selfhood has been systematically subordinated, diminished, and belittled, when it has not been outright denied. Since De Beauvoir's[3] the notion of 'the other' as a construction opposing and thereby constructing "the self", the concepts of 'the other', 'othering', and 'otherness' have taken root in areas of thought and inquiry ranging from nursing science to cultural geography[4]. De Beauvoir's 'other' was not an entirely new idea, however, as she acknowledged herself, but was heavily influenced by Hegel's[5] dialectic of identification. Zygmunt Bauman[6] writes that the notion of otherness is central to the way in which societies establish identity categories. He argues that 'identities are set up as dichotomies'. Such as woman is the other of man, animal is the other of human, stranger is the other of native, abnormality the other of norm, deviation the other of law-abiding, illness the other of health, insanity the other of reason, lay public the other of the expert, foreigner the other of state subject, enemy the other of friend.

Thus, this discussion on the 'other' highlights how many societies create a sense of belonging, identity and social status by constructing social categories as binary opposites. This is visible in the social construction of marginal identities in India. It is argued that no group ever sets itself up as the one without at once setting up the other over against itself.

II

Marginalisation is often described as a social process where people are referring to the periphery or'margins' of the society. It is defined as processes, in which individuals or communities are socially excluded and denied access to participate in social and political processes which are basic to integrate with the society[7]. Marginalisation stalls a person, a group, a section or a community to enjoy rights, privileges, opportunities and resources that are normally available to members of a society. It may therefore be considered as an inharmonious relationship between those who marginalise as compared to those who are being marginalised has argued that the term 'marginalised' may be used synonymously with the term 'oppressed' in comparison to an 'oppressor' as Paolo Freire used in his famous 'Pedagogy of Oppressed', 'proletariat' as used by Karl Marx, 'subaltern' used by Gramsci, 'powerless' as elaborated by Michel Foucault.

In view of the above , the term, 'marginality' is used in this book in order to understand the depressed and socially excluded sections, estranged by others such as Brahmanism in mainstream India, exploitative nature of non tribals in northeast India and patriarchy in general in the context of identities of caste, tribe and gender respectively in Indian society.

Caste based marginalisation is one of the most deplorable issues in India today. This discrimination entails social and economic exclusion, segregation in housing, denial and restrictions of access to public and private services and employment, and enforcement of certain types of jobs on Dalits, resulting in a system of modern day slavery or bonded labour.

Caste and marginality are central part of Hindu ideology. No historian / scholar could challenge to ignore this reality in Indian society. The caste ideology has undergone significant changes in different historical periods. Modern and post modern scholars/ historians have also revealed the hegemonic ideology of Hinduism for exclusion of marginal sections in history.

However, caste is the most debatable issue that has enthralled and divided scholars who have wished to study this system of stratified social-hierarchy in India. There is an enormous body of academic writing and political polemic on the issue. Dalit or lower caste voice in contemporary India is varied and different, intervened and related. It is sometimes difficult to talk about one Dalit group without mentioning the other. Within the Dalit political discourse, Dalit identity is constructed of different categories'. At the same time, Dalit idenity contains meanings that circulate between different discourses within socio political space in India. The Dalit identity movement is embedded in India's socio-political context and holds its 'ideology of Ambedlar. Ambedkar's contribution to the Dalit movement becomes its guiding force. His was a committed personality for the liberation of Dalit voice in particular and for the nation-building and social transformation in general. His writings are full of serious analysis of the caste-ridden Indian society and of the Hindu social system. He also gave the most desired direction for modernisation and development by framing the Constitution of Free India and served as the first Indian Law Minister for in the Nehru Cabinet. Lastly, he equipped an alternative vision in Constitution that gives equality, liberty and fraternity by embracing of Buddhism. Hence, the Constitution symbolises the success of Dalit struggle and institutionalised the philosophy of Dr Ambedkar. The Constitution is also important as a legal base and often referred to in their rhetoric.

Hardtmann[9] describes several Dalit identities (voices) that are from different geographical spaces in India: the Dalit Christian discourse from South India, Dalit Buddhist discourse from Maharashtra and Dalit political discourse from Uttar Pradesh with BSP as main political body. In view of that we can also find another alternative marginal discourse (voice) come from Madiga community of Scheduled Caste of Andhra Pradesh and Telangana. Since 1997 they have been raising the issue of classification of

Scheduled caste reservation under the banner of *Madiga Reservation Porata Samithi* (MRPS). This discourse challenged dominance of mala community in distribution of reservation among the Dalits in Andhra Pradesh and Telangana. However, they failed achieve their goal as they dreamed when they started movement for the classification of reservation based on population due to political reasons.

In view of that, the Dalit identity voice has its own historicity and regional base. The history of marginality is perceived by Dalits from the perspective of their suffering and oppression by the dominant Hindu castes.. The difference from before is that now they are engaged in social action and are struggling for a change. The history takes shape and becomes reality' and voice of the Dalit activists' perceptions comes from the ideology of Ambedkar's movement in India during the pre- and post-independence period. It divides Dalit history into two periods, one being archaic and mysterious, vague and of an endless suffering, and the other one of self-awareness and struggle, although still, full of pain. However, the entire Dalit movement is believed to form one Dalit discourse (voice) in Indian socio-political space under the ideology of Ambedkar.

However, social scientists have often revealed it that the caste and identity movement has undergone significant changes during different historical periods especially during the post-independence. Various sociologists have brought our attention towards the mobility persisting within the caste system. It has also been said that in different historical phases the socio-economic context are responsible for the changes occurring in the caste system, and it is through articulation with this alone that the changes take place in the internal structure/ideology of the caste system.

III

Secondly, Unlike the Dalits, the tribals are a product of marginalisation based on ethnic politics. The tribals like the Dalits face structural discrimination within the Indian society. In India, the Scheduled Tribes population is around 84.3 million and is considered to be socially and economically disadvantaged. Their percentages in the population and numbers however vary from state to state. They are mainly landless with little control over resources such as land, forest and water. They constitute a large proportion of agricultural labourers, casual labourers, plantation labourers, industrial labourers etc. This has resulted in poverty among them, low levels of education, poor health and reduced access to healthcare services. They belong to the poorest strata of the society and have severe health problems

Nonetheless, the tribal identity voice in India is largely a product of colonial ethnography. Though the early sources for information about the tribals were the accounts of travellers, administrators and Christian missionaries, a systematic study of these people in India begins with the establishment of the Asiatic Society of Bengal. Anthropological studies in India until independence were confined to the study of tribes and were geared largely to the need of colonial administration, with its years of experience in governing the 'nature' and some administrators realised fairly well the importance of anthropology in all works relating to the people under their charge. The following section briefly discusses the idea of other in the construction of tribal identity.

Tribal voice is mainly focus on ethnic identity. This means that ethnic homogeneity, along with other factors, characterises a tribe. Tribe represents a historical continuity and exclusiveness. Groups which had been living together without losing or dilute their specific characteristics were formed into tribe. The formation of the tribal identity, as indeed that of tribes, was a product of territorial, economic, ecological and technological isolation. In other words, human groups of a similar ethnicity which remained isolated than the rest of the world through geography, or the use of a specific primitive technology or through economic specificity were formed into a tribe and came to acquire a tribal identity.

After independence national state faced the issue of ethnic politics and identity movements in India. Almost all the major regions of the country have witnessed ethnic movements. They take the forms of movements for regional autonomy, for creation of separate states, demand for secession or insurgency. These manifestations of ethnic movements are also called self-determination movements. In several cases ethnic movements give rise to conflicts or riots on the lines of ethnic divide based on some of the markers such as tribe, language, religion, etc.

The self-determination movements actually question the nation-state building model which was introduced by the Independent India. The most common issues which account for the tribals' ethnic mobilisation are: perceived or real threat to their indigenous culture and economy including the natural resources like mineral, forest and modern market opportunities by the outsiders; their discrimination by the state, especially at the central levels and its representatives such as central government employees, army, police, etc. Let us make out the nature of ethnic politics in northeast India in the following section.

Northeast India as a single region has the largest number of the tribal population in the country. They follow different religions especially Christianity, Budhism, Hinduism and indigenous religious tenets. They can further be divided between the plain and hill tribes. Almost all state of northeast India has witnessed one or the other forms of ethnic movements. It is important to note that ethnic issues of Northeatast India are related to the geographical factors and its regional dimensions. Though there are differences among different tribals of northeast in terms of their cultural practices, they share common experience of deprivation due to their regional location. A large amount of literature exists on the northeast which seeks to explain the ethnic problems of the region. But there are wide differences in the discourse on explaining the ethnic issues of the region. And the divide in the discourse also reflect on the basis of the formation of the ethnic identities and the movements in the regions. The main problems of the northeast region are insurgency, autonomy movements, ethnic conflicts, riots, etc., It has been explained by mainly two perspectives: first, the 'modernisation/development/nation-state building' perspective and; second, the 'federation-building perspective'.

The followers of the first perspective mostly argue that the problems of the Northeast are related to the issues of 'nation-state building'; conflict between the new middle classes, especially among the tribals of the region, which has emerged as a result of the modernisation/development/transition democratisation with the traditional leadership; inability of the system to meet the rising aspiration of this group.

The second perspective is essentially the critique of the first one and came from the voice of non-tribal communities of the northeast. They argue that problems of the northeast India arose because the Indian state overlooked the perspective of the people of the region in their quest for 'nation-building'. In order to build 'nation-state' the central government adopted 'step motherly' treatment towards the northeast; ignored the 'periphery' and the smaller nationalities; shown arrogant attitude towards them; have been indifferent to the human rights violation in the region. The need for a 'Federation-building' perspective has been most prominently underlined by Sanjib Baruah[10] in his books *India against Itself: Assam and the Politics of Nationality* and *Durable Disorder: Understanding the Politics of North-East India.*

However, the second perspective too neglected the authentic voice of the tribals who have been struggling against nation building voice from the perspective of the tribals of the northeast. Now we need to address the voice of the other in the context of autonomous movements in the northeast India from their perspective. That is the reason this book covers five papers in order to understanding the ethnic politics and identity formation in northeast India.

IV

The voice of 'other' is also crucial in the discourse of gender. The concept of the 'other' highlights how many societies create a sense of belonging, identity and social status by constructing social categories as binary opposites. This is clear in the social construction of gender in Western societies and how socialisation shapes our ideas about what it means to be a "man" or a "woman." There is an inherently unequal relationship between these two categories. Note that these two identities are set up as opposites, without acknowledging alternative gender expressions. In the early 1950s, Simone de Beauvoir[11] argued that 'Otherness is a fundamental category of human thought'. Thus it is that no group ever sets itself up as the one without at once setting up the other over against itself. Gender identity is in sense of self-associated with cultural definitions of masculinity and femininity. Gender identity in the sense arises out of a complex process of interaction between self and others.

In recent times, the feminists processed their ideology and perceptions through postmodernist and poststructuralist discourses and shifted their concern from women centered or women stand point to postmodern feminism wherein the emphasis is on difference and critique of sameness. They deconstruct the gender and power relations transforming or reconstructing social values and institutions.

In Indian patriarchal system, cultural ideas have been used as a tool of the powerful in making of gender relations. Men in general have constructed ideologies that define women as inferior to justify their inferior treatment. Culture is so powerful that operates gender identity. Feminist scholars have recognised that Indian women are disadvantaged by widely shared gender ideologies of Hindu culture that restrict women's movements outside the home and limit women's interactions with their husbands within the homes. Accounts such as women' subordinate economic position, the rigid boundaries of a caste system, or joint-family living, all these Hindu social structures help to form gender ideology. Hindu men and women confront every day the structure of gender inequality. It is evident that men realise the advantages that gain by controlling women and that they consciously act and talk to maintain those advantages.

V

This book also covers six papers on literature and language in considerate of marginal identities. The marginal literature generally talks about the issues that seem to be strange or unfamiliar with present social context. Queer theory[12] is one of the important parts of marginal literature. It gives dimensions that are totally different from the canon (other literature). The word 'marginal' refers to the 'dismantle' of the traditional customs or culture. Generally, marginal literature represents the life of the people who do not accept the social rules and regulations, rather build their life which goes against the norms of the society.

The marginal literature fundamentally contests the ideological, economic and political structure of dominant class/ caste which silences the voice of the subalterns, makes them invisible and declares their narratives to be unworthy of record and transmission. Such a contestation is the most visible in marginal literature that contextualise individual identities within the larger socio-political, economic and historical critique. Amongst the projected multiplicity of voices in the mainstream history, this literature inserts and activates the voice of the marginalised to expose the speciousness of its projections. The multiplicity of the voices/narratives (as is claimed by the mainstream historiographers) is in fact, a monologue emanating from the same hegemonic space. These voices, when put together, form the central narrative of history. The self literature contested with the so called official literature by engraving the personal autobiographies.

VI

The book is divided into four thematic sections covering 17 papers by scholars, social science researchers and other experts on the theme. The four thematic themes are Caste and Marginality, Ethnic Identities and Marginality, Gender and Marginal Identities and Language, Literature and Marginal Identities. Each section has covered focal theme of the book. Thus, the readers will find this book critical understanding of multiple voices while study of Indian society.

SECTION-I
CASTE AND MARGINALITY

The first section entitled, 'Caste and Marginality' deals with caste identities from historical perspective along with changes in occupation in Indian society. This section is consisting of four papers. Nil Ratan Roy's paper, *Social Movement of Dalits in Bengal with Special Reference to Namasudra* deals with Namasudra Movement in Bengal. The Namasudra community agitated for over thirty years for change of their nomenclature. It is interesting to note that during (1911-1931) most castes of Bengal including Baidhyas and Kayasthas demanded change of caste nomenclature. The relation between the Chandals and the high caste Hindu was so strained and ill feeling ran so high that in 1911 they represented to the British Govt. for grant of treatment of the caste on par with the Muslims and demanded separate privileges. In the present paper an attempt has been made to highlight the main fact behind of the Namasudra movement in Bengal. Mallikarjuna's paper, *Untouchability as Social Exclusion: Historical Perspective*' discuss that caste' as a social category got crystallised in the *varna-jati* matrix over a very long period of time and it became an essential feature for identity for any social group that differentiates itself with the other group. In this paper he argues that the complex phenomenon of social exclusion in the form of untouchability is traced from the historical times. The untouchables were not a homogeneous unit. Their division into several hierarchical castes under the influence of the dominant caste ideology thwarted the development of any bond of unity among them or with the landless Sudras. In due course, "the notion of pollution as an enduring feature of social life - an important characteristic of caste - was institutionalised as untouchability in the law books". Kartik Chandra Sutradhar's paper, *Evolution of the Rajbanshi Society of North Bengal: Question of Identity Crisis* examined the identity crisis among the Rajbanshi Society of North Bengal. The Rajbanshis were the indigenous people of the greater part of North Bengal and lower Assam in the pre- colonial and colonial period. There are many debates among the origin or ethnological identity of the Rajbanshis. The main debate was whether Rajbanshis were originated from Mongoloid race or Aryan race. This debate has been going on even today. It is argued that whatever the identity of the Rajbanshis, they were the people like semi- tribes, simple in habit. Many characteristics of their society, customs, usages as well as physiological structure prove that the Rajbanshis originated from non-Aryan race. It is true that the people of higher caste Hindus coming from East Bengal and South Bengal treated the Rajbanshis as inferior caste, many times called them *'Bahe'* or *'Banku'* and suppressed them extensively in many forms. The same treatment is continuing even today. Keisham Ingocha Singh's paper, *The Marginalised Potters of Nongpok Sekmai in Manipur* deals with the issue of marginality among the potters of Nongpok Sekmai, a pottery village in Manipur. Marginality is an issue of today because it involves thousands of people throughout the world. People or groups are found marginalised on the basis of their occupational trade, cultural minority, ethnic affinity and other social factors. In India, rapidly growing economy due to technological development, globalisation and social network has meant a better life for many people, but not for everyone. The caste which is associated with occupational attribute in Manipur has a tremendous change due to these factors. As a result, many people are marginalised. Among them, the Artisans and craftsmen may be mentioned. They are the people using the traditional technology for their occupational traits. Because of the unfit contestation with the modern technology, their trades and crafts are now disappearing. As a result, they loss their traditional occupational traits and thereafter challenge their identity. Pottery, an ancient craft that used to be the measure of a country's civilisation, is now also dying.

SECTION-II
ETHNIC IDENTITY AND MARGINALITY

In the second section four papers are included. This section is entitled as 'Ethnic Identity and Marginality'. One paper deals with historical understanding of tribal identity in India. Rest of the papers are discussing about ethnic nationalism and conflict in order to understanding of marginality in Northeast and Jharkhand. Sanjib Goswami's paper, *'Assam as a Settler State: Contextualising Identity and Social Conflicts Within: A Colonial – Settler Colonial Paradigm'* analyses colonial constructions of identity in northeast India. It traces how colonialism moved from references to a civilising mission for elites onto projects aiming to define and manage differences between populations. It does so by outlining the ways in which identities in Assam were constructed under indirect rule and how, crucially, these constructions were later incorporated into the Constitution of postcolonial India. The ongoing unrest in India's northeast is thus contextualised in its historical dimension. In this context this paper presents an alternative interpretation based on appraising a settler colonial system of relationships. A settler colonial relationship is different from a colonial one. It envisages socio-ethnic triangulation, and a settler desire to achieve greater political autonomy, to remain dominant over both indigenes and migrants, and to build cultural and economic bonds that maintain settler solidarity and cohesion. This alternative interpretation will help new understandings of the social conflicts in Assam.. Uttam Kr Pegu's paper, *'An Anatomy of Ethnic Conflict and the Mass Media in Assam'* investigates media reports on identity and ethnic assertions in northeast and the increasing debate on the ethics of reporting ethnic conflict. Given the belief that the media can mould peoples' opinion, it is worth examining how the media communicate ethnic conflict. It is argued that if the media could support forces that lead to conflict, it seems logical to examine how it could contribute towards mitigating conflict and foster peace in the region. In this context this study interrogates the ethical issues relating to the fundamental techniques of news reportage on conflict and the wide range of professional responsibilities of journalists which are grounded in economics and the politics of sensationalism which thrives the media industry particularly in India. Finally, it shows how the media could communicate ethnic assertion with greater sensitivity and conscientiousness and how individual journalists and the mass media could collectively address the ethical complexities of communicating conflict. Ankur Goswami's paper, '*Tribal Movement as 'Nationalism'- Analysis of the Jharkhand Movement*' explores the idea of 'otherness' in the tribal movements in the context of Jharkhand movement. This paper mainly proposes that be it the 'white' colonial, the upper class industrialist or the Indian State, they have been the 'other' for the tribals of Jharkhand. Tribal movements of central India have been generally analysed through the identity politics based on regionalism paradigm. Unlike the movements of Kashmir, Punjab or Assam which are categorised as national or sub-national movements striving to form a separate political community, the tribal movements of central India have supposedly shown no such orientation and even an analysis from this perspective is absent. In this context this paper argues that the basis of Jharkhand movement lied in the shared cultural and collective memory of the various tribal communities and their collective action during the colonial period as expressed the *Santhal Hool* or the *Brisa Munda* movement. It can be said that there did exist a sense of common identity among the various tribal groups and they did constitute a nation. Thus the paper tries to understand, whether that the Jharkhand movement can be called a nationalist movement striving for a separate political community, which was reflected in its initial demand of political autonomy. Vulli Dhanaraju and R.K Bijeta's joint paper, '*Historical Understanding of Tribal Identity in India*' proposes that understanding of contemporary tribal identities requires a basic appreciation of the historical processes that have been determined the course of successive changes in socio-cultural, economic, ideological and political life of the tribes. Keeping in mind the vastness of the Indian sub-cultural multitudeness of those people, one can only generalise that the historical experiences would be as variable for different people as their interaction with their ecology and the neighboring cultures from time to time. In this context this paper assesses the nature of tribal identity formation by exploring various historiographies in various historical contexts.

SECTION-III
GENDER AND MARGINALITY

In the third section three papers are included. This section entitled as 'Gender and Marginal Identity'. Two papers highlighted the issue of marginality among the women in Assam. The third paper deals with position of women through the writing of Mahasweta Devi's *Rudali* (1979). Sunanda Sahu's paper , '*Status and Identity of Tea Garden Women: A Case Study of Tamulbari Tea Estate in Dibrugarh*' deals with the women of Tamulbari Tea Estate of Dibrugarh with an objective to find out the actual scenario of the identity and status of the women in the present context. This paper tries to make an attempt to get a brief idea about the status and identity of Tea Garden women. Majority of the women in Tea Garden are engaged in Tea Plantation works. They are considered as most potential labour force of the Tea Industry. This paper argues that Men and Women are like two wings of a bird which only in unison can take a lofty flight. Therefore, both the wings have to be developed equally for progressive development of a society. In a patriarchal society like India the scenario is not the same because the role of male is considered more important than the female. These gender inequalities give importance to the study of Identity and status Women. Women play an important role in the upliftment of society. Status is primarily a position in a social structure which involves rights, duties and reciprocal expectations of behaviour. Lakhimi Nath's paper, '*Social Inclusion of Tribal Women through Social Development: A Study of Tribal Women Empowerment in Assam*' emphasises the social inclusion of tribal women through their social development in Assam. The status of women in a society is often described in terms of their level of income, employment, education, health and fertility as well as their roles within the family, the community and society. They are one of the largest socially suppressed and discriminated groups. Tribal women generally face certain kinds of domestic violence and social exclusion. Therefore, it is very important to bring positive changes in the lives of tribal women. Empowerment of women is a concept that has developed in connection with improving their status. Empowerment is only possible when a socially depressed and excluded section of the society can be brought into the system of social inclusion through social development. Social inclusion simultaneously incorporates multiple dimensions of well-being. It is achieved when all have the opportunity and resources necessary to participate fully in economic, social, and cultural activities. Devastuti Sharma's paper, '*Sanichari's Odyssey: The Stratagem of Identity Assertion in Rudali*' highlight the short fiction of Mahasweta Devi's *Rudali* (1979) is Sanichari, a woman born on and named after the 'accursed' Saturday (*Shanivaar*). She lives in the village of Tahad where the majority of the inhabitants belonged to 'lowly' *Ganju* and *Dushad* castes. *"Like the other villagers, her life too was lived in desperate poverty."* She is a victim of a tripartite Marginalisation involving gender, caste and class. Sanichari is, simultaneously, a woman, a low caste Ganju, a bonded labour and belongs to the subordinate occupational class of professional mourners (rudali). In this context this paper aims at examining how Sanichari manipulates the exploitative feudal system to her advantage and works her way to empowerment and emancipation. She dismantles hegemonic power structures and rises from being a voiceless Subaltern to being her own self with independence and agency. Sanichari is not individuated but is representative of an entire community of socio-economic 'Others'.

SECTION-IV
LITERATURE, LANGUAGE AND MARGINALITY

The fourth section deals with 'Literature, Language and Marginal Identities' in understand of marginality through the cram of marginal literature and language in Indian society. In this section six papers are included under two parts. Three papers of the first part deals discuss the nature of marginalisation in study of subaltern/peoples' literature. The second part focuses on how the language is a source of identity formation among the marginalised communities. David Jeyaraj Franklin's paper, '*Parallel Struggles; Paralleling Identities: A Reading of Two Native Novels*' proposes that native literature has the ironical distinction of being the newest literary expression produced by the oldest communities of the world. Throughout the history of humankind, native societies have shied away from literary expression of their existential experiences, especially in the written form. This has changed in the recent times, especially in the 20th century when the native communities started representing themselves through the written word despite their fascination for oral literatures and the folk form. These texts are genuine representations of their experiences, drawing upon characters, incidents, identities, and questions from their own lives. Native American writer Louise Erdrich and Tribal Indian author *Kocharethi* Narayan are two examples of such experiences represented through the print form. Though received with differing reactions and responses, these writers have something in common: the experiences and the corresponding creative expressions. *Tracks* and *Kocharethi,* masterpieces in their own right, present an interesting proposition when read in consonance. In this context this paper attempts to parallel the native identities through the parallel struggles encountered by the respective communities in the 20th century. R.Senthil Kumar's paper, *Fluid Identity and Floating Societies in Amitav Ghosh's The Hungry Tide'* focuses the story of the marginalised refugees who became homeless owing to the partition of India. The shadow lines of new states from 1947 tossed them place to place: from Bangladesh to neighboring Bengal, from Bengal to a refugee re-settlement colony in Dhanbad. In this context Amitav Ghosh's *The Hungry Tide* is a novel that deals with a plethora of characters that are rendered homeless. Even the so called privileged in society admit the fact that behind the façade of their translated world of titles and designations, the emptiness of loss of home linger on. While they could negotiate their space in the postcolonial world by their political connections and bribes, the really disadvantaged such as the Dalit settlers, the Muslim Minority and the refugees fail miserably to make the state keep its election promises and become mute players in the drama of colonial brutality. This paper argues how the conflict of the 'self' and the 'other' leads to fluid identities in their changed habitats at three levels: nature, people and the state. Bishnu Charan Dash's paper, *The Voice of the 'Other': Situating Sahityarathi Lakshminath Bezbaroa's Subalterns at Sambalpur* have taken the concept of the 'other' which has been conceptualized by various social scientists for the study of the writings of Bezbaroa from subaltern perspective. This paper tends to argue in the light of Partha Chatterjee's observation how the subalterns of Sambalpur (West Odisha) like Kolhs, Gandas and Mundas have been otherised during the World Wars by the colonial setup- caste Hindus and the cruel Zamindars (Gauntias) of Sambalpur. In his short stories written at Sambalpur such as *'Ratan Munda', 'Dasamantar', 'Bhaira', 'Barichowa'* and *'Maganiyar Buddha'*, the Sahityarathi Lakshminath Bezbaroa has narrativised the subalterns of Sambalpur who have been crushed and exploited by the moneylenders, Zamindars , upper caste Hindus and various centres of power and politics. However, Bezbaroa's subalterns like Ratan, 'Dasamantar and Maganiyar Buddha are not altogether voiceless and they have been projected as 'aggrieved subalterns' often interrogating hegemonic power structure with a 'spirit of resistance' (Edward Said).

Maibam Monoranjan Singh's paper, *Language loss among the Thangal Tribe of Manipur*, deals with intermarriage and the declining use of the local dialect as means of communication among the Thangal tribe of Manipur. With the exception of Thangals inhabiting Tumnoupokpi and Thangal Surung villages, the local dialect has become near to extinction among the rest of the Thangals. A mixed dialect has emerged as the lingua franca which is threatening the original. The Thangal, formerly identified as Koirao, is a small Scheduled Tribe population of Manipur. They are now clustered in 11 villages in Senapati District of Manipur. Though clan exogamy is the general rule, many women from neighboring communities or tribes are found to have been recruited into the Thangal tribe through marriage. Also on the rise is the number of Thangal women marrying outside the group and taking refuge at Thangal villages. In this context this paper argues that intermarriage has resulted in intermingling of cultures. Each marriage partner brings to marital union a list of what to do or not do what to say or not say, in a marriage. These individual lists learned in different cultural or racial environments can be differed so much that misunderstandings and conflicts become unavoidable. The most distinct change brought in by marriage among the Thangal is observed in the local dialect. Indira Priyanka Veernala's paper, *'English Medium Education and Dalit Emancipation: Some Reflections'* argues that English medium education is the key factor for promoting the equality which is important in the Indian social context. English is the Language of liberation for Dalits. In this context this paper argues that the upper castes have been handling the contradiction between English and mother tongue language quite carefully. But when it comes to teaching English to the Dalits they have been arguing that English is the responsible for the obliterate the mother tongue. It has not been proved in reality. But their children study in the foreign universities and occupy the good positions in India. The Dalit society are very keen to let their children study English medium because Dalits thinks feels that who have been educated in English they get the good opportunities in the globalisation. They consider English as the important factor for their social mobility in the world. Suranjana Barua's paper, *'Othering in Self-Ascription: A Case for the Linguistic 'Selfie'*, deals with identity' as an academic notion has been studied across the social sciences from various perspectives: while sociological perspectives such as the social identity theory have often concentrated on categorization, group identity and group behavior, psychological perspectives have tended to concentrate on the (sub/un-)conscious processes of individual identity formation. In this context this paper treads the middle ground in attempting to look at linguistic self-ascriptions of individuals from psycho-social and also cultural perspectives. In examining speech extracts of young Assamese speakers, this paper tries to analyse self-ascription along multiple axes of gender, class and geographical distribution to emerge with a composite picture of these individual 'linguistic snapshots' vis-à-vis others.

Thus, the 'voice of other' plays an important role in order to understand the marginal identities. The post modern social scientists and cultural theorists also used the concept of the voice of the other in analysing contested social identities. This book also used these concepts in order to understand the contested nature of marginal identities and its relation with the state and other hegemonic institutions.

References

1 Richard Jenkins, *Social Identity (Key Ideas),* Routledge,2008.

2 Simone de Beauvoir, *The Second Sex'*, Penguin Books, Harmondsworth, 1977. Available online at www2.cddc.vt.edu/marxists///reference/subject/ethics/de-beauvoir/2ndsex/introduction.htm

3 Simone de Beauvoir, *The Second Sex'*, Penguin Books, Harmondsworth, 1977.

4 For Full details se in Lajos Brons, *Othering, an Analysis*, http://www2.hu-berlin.de/transcience/Vol6_No1_ 2015_69_ 90.pdf, accessed on 20th June,2015.

5 G.W. F.Hegel, *Phenomenology of Mind*, translation of Hegel (1807) by J. B. Baillie, Harper & Row, London, 1967.

6 Zygmunt Bauman, *Post-modernity and its Discontents*. Polity Press, London, 1998; http://othersociologist.com/otherness-resources/, Accessed on 19th May,2015.

7 Shalu Nigam, 'From The Margins: Revisiting the Concept of `Marginalised Women', http://www.countercurrents.org/nigam030914.htm, accessed on 16th October,2015.

8 Ibid.

9 Hardtmann, Eva-Maria, *The Dalit Movement in India. Local Practices, Global Connections*, New Delhi: Oxford University Press, 2009, p.88.

10 Sanjib Baruah, *India Against Itself: Assam and the Politics of Nationality*, Oxford University Press, New Delhi, 1999; *Durable Disorder: Understanding the Politics of North-East India,* Oxford University Press, 2005.

11 Simone de Beauvoir, *The Second Sex'*, Penguin Books, Harmondsworth, 1977.

12 Queer theory is a field of Post-Structuralist critical theory that emerged in early 19990s in order to discuss the voices of the marginal communities and gender identities.

I

Caste and Marginality

1

Social Movement of Dalits in Bengal: With Special Reference to Namasudra

Nil Ratan Roy

Introduction

The word 'Dalit' comes from the Sanskrit root *dal*- and means 'broken, ground-down, downtrodden, or oppressed'. Those previously known as Untouchables, Depressed Classes, and Harijans are today increasingly adopting the term 'Dalit' as a name for themselves. 'Dalit' refers to one's caste rather than class; it applies to members of those menial castes which have born the stigma of 'untouchability' because of the extreme impurity and pollution connected with their traditional occupations. Dalits are 'outcastes' falling outside the traditional four-fold caste system consisting of the hereditary Brahmin, Kshatriya, Vaishya and Sudra classes; they are considered impure and polluting and are therefore physically and socially excluded and isolated from the rest of society.

Dalit is a designation for a group of people traditionally regarded as untouchable in India. Dalits are a mixed population, consisting of numerous social groups from all over India; they speak a variety of languages and practice a multitude of religions. There are many different names proposed for defining this group of people, including Panchamas ("fifth varna"), and Asprushya ("untouchables") etc. The Government of India recognises and protects them as Scheduled Castes people. The term Dalit has been interchangeably used with term Scheduled Castes, and these terms include all historically discriminated communities of India out-caste and Untouchables.

At present Dalits represent a community of around 170 million in India, constituting 17 per cent of the total population. One out of every six Indians is Dalit, yet due to their caste identity Dalits regularly face discrimination and violence which prevent them from enjoying the basic human rights and dignity promised to all citizens of India. Caste-based social organisation extends beyond India, finding corollaries in Nepal, Pakistan, Sri Lanka, and Bangladesh, as well as other countries outside of South Asia. More than 260 million people worldwide suffer from this 'hidden apartheid' of segregation, exclusion, and discrimination.

Genesis of Caste in India

The Caste system has got its origin in the Indus Valley Civilisations and flourished as early as 2500 BC. The term 'caste' has been widely used to describe ranked groups within the rigid systems of social stratification an especially those which constitute the society of Hindu in India.

Mr. Nesfield described the origin theory of Caste in India in the following ways- "A Caste is a marriage union, the constituents of which were drawn from different tribes (or from various other castes similarly formed), in virtue of some industry, craft or function, either secular or religious, which they possessed in common. The internal discipline by which the conditions of membership in regard to marital and convivial rights are defined and enforced has been borrowed from the tribal period which preceded the period of castes by many centuries, and which was brought to a close by the amalgamation of tribes into a nation under a common specter. The differentia of caste as a marriage union consists in some community of function, while the differentia of tribes as a marriage union consisted in a common ancestry, or a common worship, or a common totem, or in fact in any kind of common property except that of a common function. Long before castes were formed on Indian soil, most of the industrial classes, to which they now correspond, had existed for centuries, and on a rule most of the industries which they practiced were hereditary on the male side of the parentage.

According to Sir H. Risley, "a caste may be defined as a collection of families or groups of families bearing a common name which usually denotes or is associated with specific occupation, claiming common descent from a mythical ancestor, human or divine, professing to follow the same professional, callings and are regarded by those who are competent to give an opinion as forming a single homogeneous community."

The practice of Casteism in the society was very much serious when the Aryan people came to the India. Before the Aryan people the Indus Valley Civilisation was prevailed in India. The Indus Valley Civilisation is most probably a genuine gradual growth on Indian soil but an importation by immigrant foreigners establishing a colony in India. The sudden almost explosive rise of this Civilisation and its spontaneous growth may have several causes. The great fertility of the soil caused the population to increase rapidly. Though initially the population of the Indus Valley Civilisation may have been a uniform race, it did not remain so, for the skeletons found in the cemeteries of the sites show a mixed racial composition. Since the chronology has been revised and the end of the Civilisation fixed at about 1750 BC, the old hypothesis has been revived that the Aryan invaders.

Status of Dalits and their Movement in India

As it has mentioned earlier that Dalits refers to one's caste rather than class; it applies to members of those menial castes which have born the stigma of 'untouchability' because of the extreme impurity and pollution connected with their traditional occupations. Dalits are 'outcastes' falling outside the traditional four-fold caste system consisting of the hereditary Brahmin, Kshatriya, Vaishya, and Shudra classes; they are considered impure and polluting and are therefore physically and socially excluded and isolated from the rest of society. But in some writings it has also been found that the 'Sudra' the forth category of people of the society during the Vedic period were suffered a lot from various aspect of the society and were considered as dalit later on. They were considered as the lower group people because they are the Non-Aryan; just they have adopted Aryan culture and religion. They are considered as the lower because they have come from the feet of the Creator (God) mentioned in the hymn of Purushasukta.

The Sudras were treated very badly in that society so far as their social status in concerned. This class represented domestic servant, approximately very nearly to the position of slaves. The Sudra is described as "the servant of another", "to be expelled at will", and "to be slain at will". The Panchavimsha Brahmana defines this position still more precisely when it declares that the Sudra, even if he be prosperous, can't but be a servant of another, washing his superior's feet being his main business. Yet, according to the same work some of the king's ministers were Sudras. The milk to be used for fire obligation was not allowed to be milked by a Sudra. He is declared to be unfit for sacrifice was being offered. The Shattapatha Brahmana goes to the length of declaring that the Sudra is untruth itself. Illicit connection between an Aryan male and a Sudra female is mentioned, and uneasiness felt by the Sudra husband whose wife is a mistress of an Aryan is also hinted at. In this connection we may mention that Vasishtha quotes a Brahmana text to the effect that a woman of the black race, meaning the Sudra people, was meant only for enjoyment and not for furtherance of any higher motives.

Among the four Varnas, the old distinction of Aryan and Shudra appear predominantly as Dvija and Shudra, through the old distinction is occasionally mentioned. The first three Varnas are called Dvijas (twice born) because they have to go through initiation ceremony which is symbolic of rebirth. This privilege is denied to the Sudra who is therefore called 'ekajati' (once born). It is well known that in the story of Ramayana Rama is represented to have killed a Sudra who was practicing austerities. The Sudra was regarded to be so despicable, that a Brahmin when, out of sheer necessity, he had to make up the Sudra's occupation, was asked not to mix with them. So, it is clear that the Sudra could not perform a sacrifice, could not listen too or recite the Vedic text, nor could he practice austerities. He was categorically denied the right of initiation and consequently the first stage of individual life the studentship. Sudra had no right to perform any of the important sacraments. As he couldn't kindle the sacred fire, his marriage was certainly not regarded as a sacrament, intended for the fulfillment of religious duties but only as a sexual union.

The Mahabharata says that the Sudra can have no absolute property, because his wealth can be appropriated by his master at will. If the master of a Sudra has fallen into distress, the latter shall be at the disposal of the poor master. The king is enjoyed to appoint only persons of the first three classes over villages and towns for their protections. Sudra trying to hear the Vedic texts shall have his ears filled with molten tin or lac; if he recites the Veda his tongue shall be cut off, and if he remembers it, he shall be disremembered. If he assumes a position of equality with twice born men, either in sitting, conversing, ongoing along with the road, he shall receive corporal punishment. A Sudra committing adultery with woman of the first three castes shall suffer capital punishment, or shall be burnt alive tied up in straw. If he intentionally reviles twice-born men or criminal assaults them, the limbs with which he offends shall be cut off. A Sudra committing adultery with an Aryan woman shall have his organ cut-off and his property confiscate. According to Kautilya, a Sudra calling himself a Brahmin shall have his eyes destroyed by poison or shall pay the heavy fine of eight hundred 'ponas'. If he violates a Brahmin female he shall be burnt to death. If he intentionally reviles or criminally assaults a Brahmin the offending limbs shall be cut.

Kautilya prescribes differential rate of interest for debts according to caste, a Brahmin being charged two per cent a Kshstriya three per cent, a Vaishya four per cent and a Sudra five per cent. It shows that how the Sudra were being treated in that contemporary society. Though they are very poor so far as their socio-economic condition is concerned still they had to pay highest interest. According to Dharmashastra, in the case of eating and drinking, if one had received food or beverage from a Shudra, he was ordered to do prayasitta by suppressing his breath seven times a day for seven days. Any Sudra male who had sexual relations with a twice born woman would be heavily punished by having his genital severed and his wealth confiscated, and if the woman has a husband or patron of some kind, these a fore mentioned punishments will be followed by death.

So, it is found that the Sudra people suffered a lot for a long time. The Sudras had no place within the Aryan society. They had no any right even. They were servants to be disposed of at the master's whim.

The Dalits or scheduled castes movement, in the familiar sense of organised resistance of the ex-untouchables to caste oppression, may not be traced beyond colonial times. However, in a wider sense of the struggle of lower castes against the hegemony of Brahminical ideology, it has to coexist with the history of caste itself. The broad framework of caste remaining the same, the Dalit movement could also be seen in a historical continuum with its previous phases. In another sense, it could be taken as the articulation phase of the numerous faceless struggles against the iniquitous socio-economic formation ordained by the caste system that has occupied vast spaces of Indian history. By any reckoning it seems to have done well in identifying its friends and foes, putting in place its strategies and tactics and more importantly, carving out a space for itself in every sphere. It kept pace with the changes taking place in socio-political sphere during the colonial times and thus displayed significant learning during this phase. However, it could not do so thereafter when it had to consolidate its gains particularly in the context of substantial changes that befell during the post-independence times.

Social movement of Dalit can be called as a collective agitation of Dalits against the exploitation both in the form of class, caste, creed, cultural and social exploitation in the society. This exploitation is due to the discrimination followed by age old caste hierarchical tradition in the Hindu society. This hierarchy has been the cause for oppression of Dalits in each and every sphere of society since centuries. It has subjected the Dalits to poverty and humiliation. Dalit movement is a struggle that tries to counter-attack the socio-cultural hegemony of the upper castes. It is a movement of the masses that craves for justice through the speeches, literary works, dramas, songs, cultural organisations and all the other possible measurers. So it can be called as a movement which has been led by Dalits to seek equality with all other castes of the Hindu society.

The Dalit movement erupts like a volcano all over India around 1970. The Dalit movements are called by different names in different states of the country such as-

1. Ad-Dharm Movement in Punjab
2. Namasudra movement in Bengal
3. Adi-Dravida movement in Tamil Nadu
4. Adi-Hindu movement in Kanpur
5. Pulaya movement in Kerala
6. Untouchable movement in Maharashtra, and
7. Dalit movement in Karnataka

Movement among Namasudra

The etymology of the word 'Namasudra' which is not mentioned in any of the pre-nineteenth century Medieval Bengali literature, is extremely, uncertain colonial ethnologists like James Wise and Herbert Risely believed that it was derived either from the Sanskrit word '*namas*' or adoration or the Bengali word '*namate*' i.e. below or underneath. In the first case it would mean those who were bound to show obeisance even to the Shudras. In the second case, the word would perhaps mean a lower grade of Sudras, a status the Chandalas of Manu had gained promotion to. But these two explanations appear to be highly improbable in view of the new sense of self respect associated with the Namasudra identity. The Namasudras themselves were also confused about the meaning of the term. Sashi Kumar Badoi Biswas thought that the word could mean two things: namaskar or paying obeisance to and tyaja or to be avoided. If the word was used in the first sense, then it would mean those who paid obeisance to the Sudras (Shudrang namati). But if it was in the second sense, then it would mean avoided by Sudras (Namah Shudrena). None of the meanings, however, seemed to be acceptable to him, though he failed to arrive a definite conclusion. According to another Namasudra commentator, Naresh Chandra Das, the word means the Sudras who were paid obeisance to an explanation which seems to be the most plausible of all.

The late nineteenth century colonial explanation for this geographical anchorage of these people was their tribal origin, as territoriality was believed to have been a salient feature of the tribals. However, what constituted a 'tribe' in the Indian context has been a subject of controversy among anthropologists. In general, until the 1940s, many believed that a tribe was a 'self-contained' unit, and being a stage in an evolutionary process, the tribes gradually fused into the general Hindu society and were transformed into castes. The Namasudras ideally fitted into this explanatory scheme, which was initially developed in the colonial context of the late nineteenth century with a marked racialist bias. The Chandals of Bengal, as the Namasudras were referred to before their more respectable caste name came to be accepted, were described in the early twentieth-century *jatimala* literature as the non-Aryan autochthonous people of the land. The theory certainly appears to have been derived from the late nineteenth-century racial ethnology of the colonial officials like Herbert Risley, who divided the Indian population into two racial types, the Aryan and Dravidian, and held that a tribe was a development out of race, while a caste was a development out of tribe. In typology the Namasudras (Chandal) appeared as 'tribal', who had gradually embraced Hinduism, accepted the Hindu social organisation and thus had hardened into a caste. James Wise, shortly before him, had observed in a more racialist tone that the Chandals were a 'Dravidian tribe' who, driven before the Aryan invaders, or later persecution, sought shelter in the marshy forests of Bengal.

The different synonymous of the Namasudras are Chandal, Charal, Namasud and Namah. In the census of 1901, at which caste names and caste precedence were scrutinised and registered rather minutely, the Chandalas of Bengal, who were otherwise known as Namasudras though the Namasudra people were considered as Chandal in earlier text of India, but that can't be confirmly accepted. Because it is only Ballal Sen then lord of Bengal considered the Namasudra people as Chandal and untouchable.

As is widely known, the term Chandal is derived from Sanskrit *Candäla*, a representative term for the 'untouchables' which has been used even in old Japanese in the form of *Sertdara*. The Namasudras, densely distributed in the southern part of East Bengal, numbered 2,087,162 according to the1911 census, constituting the biggest community among the 'untouchables'. The Rajbansis in north Bengal (2,049,454) and the Bagdis in West Bengal (1,041,892) came next to them. All three castes were of tribal origin. The Namasudras and the Rajbansis are considered to have been transformed 'at a comparatively recent date'. The Namasudras are assumed to be Hinduised tribes 'who were driven into the marshes of the interior by successive waves of invasion'. They have been despised by the caste Hindus and forced to live in separate quarters on the outskirts of villages. So far as it is known, the oldest colonial document recording the movement of the Namasudras is dated at 1873. In this incident, an affluent Namasudra peasant named Dwarkanath Mandal, who lived at Mushlundpore in the *bil* area spanning in the southwestern part of Faridpur planned to invite 10,000 people of every caste to his father's *sraddha* ceremony in 1872. The Kayasthas responded to this invitation with insulting answers and instigated other castes not to accept it. The offended Namasudra headmen including Dwarkanath Mandal agreed in protest neither to give any service to other castes and the Muslims nor to allow their women to visit *hats* and *bazars.* This agreement was forced upon their fellow caste men with the threat of excommunication should violation occur. This movement had spread to the adjoining Bakharganj District by the next spring. The protestors told the Magistrate of Faridpur who came to inspect the movement (a kind of 'strike' in Pradip Sinha's wording) on the spot that their object was 'to obtain a better position in place of being the despised and degraded class' they were 'in the eyes of their neighbours'. In his report on this Chandal movement, the British Magistrate referred to them as 'Nomoshudros' in the bracket after mentioning their common name Chandals. Though it is not clear only from this remark that since when they had called themselves Namasudras, their socially elevating movements apparently began to quicken before the 1870s. At this point of time, however, Namasudras remained as their self designation and they were commonly called Chandals.

During the British period also Namasudra people were considered as Chandal or Charal; which the Namasudra people opposed and started agitation against so called higher caste people. The year of 1872 was a very important in India. Before 1872 some states and some districts were sending annual census statistics. The British Govt. however undertook first of all India census in 1872. This census recorded every caste and tribe of India. The govt. as a matter of policy went by the advice of the pundits regarding caste determination. It is worthwhile to mention that classification of castes and tribes by district magistrates were generally impartial, while the pundits and the native officials often failed to overcome caste prejudices and their enumeration cannot be considered objective. Sometimes they misled the census commissioner. It goes to the credit of the district magistrate, they on many occasions differed from the native census officers. Even British census executives were presumably influenced by the native officers. The striking indigenous Bangas (Namasudra) the most memories people of East Bengal nerve accepted the slang 'Chandal' which the Aryan brought it from Aryandom and slapped on them. This tribes were formerly dominant and it only because they lost their political supremacy and have fallen under the Yoke of the Brahmanas, that they have sunk to their present position.

The deep-seated grievances of the Namasudras found expression in the form of caste struggle which influenced the course of the national movement. True nature of their agitation can be traced from various factors that shaped the course of movements viz. traditional domination of the upper castes, colonial impact, and sectarian identity can clan fraternity of the Namasudra. The Namasudras, mainly inhabited in the district of Faridpur, Backergumge, Dacca, Jessore, Mymensingh and Khulana of East Bengal, became the supporter of the British Raj to elevate them socially and economically. The educated section of the Namasudras protested against the social disabilities imposed upon them by the caste Hindus. First protest in the form of organised movement began in 1872 against the misbehaviour of the upper caste Hindus. They organised strike in protest against the refusal of an invitation of a rich Namasudra by the upper caste Hindus at the instigation of some Kayasthas. This incident hurt the Namasudras who, accordingly, held a meeting and resolved that they would not serve under other castes and accept food cooked by other castes excepting the Brahmins. They also decided not to send their women to markets. Though their first organised movement ended in failure it prepared the ground for later movements. This movement of the Namasudras united different sections of the community and provided solidarity to their caste organisation. They became conscious of the strength and weakness of the movement. They came to realise that without the help of the British Government they would not be able to fulfill their demands. Meanwhile they started mobilising mass support for the change of their caste name. The British officials did not turn a deaf ear to the demands and aspirations of the Namasudras for a long time. After 1881 census, the Assistant Commissioner of Sylhet W.C. Machpherson issued a notice on 9.9.1882 endorsing the demands of the Namasudras that they should be referred to as Namasudas in all officials' correspondence. Similar attitude was reflected in the administrative reports of F.B. Peacock, the Commissioner of the Presidency Division.

Despite the good intensions of the British Officials the new caste name of the Namasudras was not used by the caste Hindus. The Namasudras leaders, however, carried on struggle against social injustices and humiliating treatment of the upper caste Hindus. The internal organisation of the Namasudras was strengthened through meetings, caste associations and religious gatherings where they stressed the need for education, self respect and self reliance for their rise in social scale. In their struggle against socio-economic injustices they remained united and class indifferences could not cut across caste lines. The agitation of the Namasudras for honourable appellation in place of the despised one assumed a new dimension in view of the swadeshi movement. The nationalist leaders, under political compulsion, supported their movement for socio-economic upliftment. Indeed they vied with government to get the support of the Namasudras to strengthen national movement. In 1907, few representatives of the Namasudras, under the leadership of Guruchand Thakur and at the instance of Dr Mead, the Australian missionary, met Lieutenant Governor of Bengal and Assam and apprised him of the social injustices imposed upon them by calling them 'chandal' which was highly derogatory for their social status. As a result of their concerted efforts the derogatory epithet was removed in 1901 census and they came to be regarded as Namasudras.

During the period of national movement the Namasudras did not question the legitimacy of the British rule as they thought that it would serve a providential purpose elevating them socially, economically and politically. So they found nothing wrong in pursuing the policy of appeasement with British rulers. On the other hand, British Government considered it high time to execute its policy of 'divide and rule' playing the depressed classes against the upper castes. In this circumstance the Namasudra leaders refused to take part in the national movement. They dissociated themselves from the anti-partition movement in Bengal and opposed it on a number of occasions.

The agitation of the Namasudras, however, cannot be identified as separatist movement for what they demanded was not political separation but the fulfillment of their genuine demands. Thus, movement for rise in social scale and their political aspirations are historical forces to be reckoned with.

Indeed their movements made the nationalist leaders aware of the real meaning of freedom which induced them to take the initiative in removing the social disabilities of depressed classes and became successful in involving a section of depressed castes into the main stream of national movement.

It is interesting to note the gradual transformation of the Namasudra movements from caste struggle against social injustices to a movement for separate political identity. Initially the Namasudras began their struggle against social disabilities and put up great efforts for the upliftment of their caste through dissemination of learning. Caste consciousness and political awareness of the Namasudras led them to form caste associations which later on turned into political organ for extracting their demands. While fighting against the Zamindars the Namasudras made common cause with the Muslims. Gradually their movement drifted away from agrarian issues and turned into a politics of reservation and institutional benefits.

Conclusion

From the above discussion it is observed that Dalits or scheduled caste population constituted around 17 per cent population of the country. It is also concluded that the Dalit movement which was born to achieve its aims of bringing equality and peace and prosperity to the people has not achieved its goal, may be due to the fact that it had became a reactive element. The protests or the strikes are happening only when exploitation come to light through newspapers. A few programmes are arranged, only during the birth day of Ambedkar, and the day of his Parinibbana (death day) on 14th of April and 6th of December respectively. Otherwise, the movement and the organisations are inactive without any protest or agitations, till they come across any new atrocities. But one has to agree to the point that the Dalit movement as created awareness in the society and it gave self-respect to the poor Dalits. It really created an identity to the people. This movement opened the eyes of upper caste educated masses about their wrongdoings, and their unjustified atrocities on the weaker sections of the society. People came to know about their strength and they had come to know that the practice of untouchability is punishable according to the law. The Namasudra in India are considered themselves as very strong group among any other scheduled castes groups. Because of their social movement they could remove the term untouchable and chandal from them and became Namasudra in the society.

References

1. Bandyopadhyay, S. *Caste, Politics and the Raj: Bengal 1872-1937*, Calcutta, 1990.
2. Biswas, A. K. *The Namasudra of Bengal,* Blumoon Books, New Delhi, 2000.
3. Biswas, R.K. *Namasudra Movements in Bengal (1872-1947): A Case study of the transition from caste struggle to political identity,* (an unpublished thesis from Jadavpur University), Kolkata, 1998.
4. Biswas, U.N. *The Strike,* NCMB Memorial Trust, Kolkata, 2004.
5. *Census of India, 1901,* Vol.VI, Part I, pp. 3956, 459, Vol.VIA, Part II, Table XIII.
6. Ghatak, N.K. Namasudra of Bengal through the Ages, *Bulletin of the Cultural Research Institute Vol. XVII, No. 3-4,* Govt. of West Bengal, 1987.
7. Ghuyre, G.S. *Caste and Race in India,* Popular Prakashan, Bombay, 1996.
8. Kothani, H. *Caste System, Untouchability and the Depressed,* Manohar, 1997.
9. Sarkar, G. *Jatitattwa Sangraha*, (Bengali) Hiranmoy Sarkar, North 24 Paragana, West Bengal, 1995.
10. Sarkar, S. *Namasudrai Parsav Bipra,* Khulna Press, Khulna, Bagladesh, 1382, (Bengali Year).
11. Singh, K.S. *The Scheduled Castes*, Oxford University Press, Delhi, 1995.

2

Untouchability as Social Exclusion: Historical Perspective

Mallikarjun Ch

Historically, society in India is formed on the paradigms of Varna, the ritual ranking and *jati*, the actual status which got transformed as caste determined on the basis of one's profession. Each caste group got segregated in a distinctive cultural unit that functions on the norms of purity and pollution and identity. The very notion of maintaining purity from pollution by different castes is to construct one's own distinctiveness from the other, i.e. the identity. Thus, social exclusion, on one hand, pertains to cultural practices for culture is for identity and identity is for incorporation and legitimation of one's own positioning in respective social groups, and on the other hand, it reinforces one's own group's cultural behaviour by which any violation is considered as social offence leading to excommunication. Again re-entry (inclusion) is allowed after expiatory rituals. Thus, the identity at personal as well as at social realms contributes for social exclusion and inclusion and thereby reinforce cultural values and norms of respective caste groups to keep themselves pure and away from pollution.

In India social exclusion is historically construed on purity and pollution basis. The social formation based on ritual ranking and actual positioning of a social group created hierarchies. These hierarchies are both vertical and horizontal for each social group in relation to the other. These social groups are termed as 'castes' and some of the castes are socially excluded and included depending upon the need of the society from time immemorial. In this paper the complex phenomenon of social exclusion in the form of untouchablity is traced from the historical perspective.

I
Concept of Social Exclusion

The concept of social exclusion as an academic endeavour is of recent origin. Though it is an ontological phenomenon in almost every culture across the globe, it gained attention with 'globalisation'. Globalisation is the process by which existing political, cultural and economic boundaries are being superseded and the world is becoming more and more interconnected by bringing cultures into contact. Globalisation also encouraged recognition of relativism, and reflexivity in terms of human rights and civil liberties. As a result, a spurt in consciousness of the communities hitherto left behind in advancement has become an occurrence. This situation led the academia to coin the term 'social exclusion' to denote the plight of certain communities as socially distanced, marginalised, and inadequately integrated. There are many devices that different cultures adopted to implement social exclusion. For instance, extermination and ostracism is applied in the Asian cultures such as India; exile and abandonment is used in European cultures such as the British; marginalisation, and discrimination is adopted in American Cultures and; shaming and segregation is implemented in African Cultures.

The concept of social exclusion is now widely used in discussions about the nature of disadvantage, and there are ongoing initiatives to promote social inclusion among those with mental health problems. Such people were labelled "social problems" and were not protected by social insurance, particularly the young, the elderly, and the disabled and single parents. Social exclusion initially referred to a process of social disintegration, a progressive rupture of the relationship between the individual and society. It later extended to incorporate those suffering multiple deprivations in worst affected locations. The unfavourable inclusions with unequal treatment may carry the same adverse effects as unfavourable exclusion. It is viewed as an umbrella concept for measures and policies for combating unemployment, dependency and poverty.

However, social exclusion is a contested concept, with multiple meanings. In social science literature the concept of social exclusion is defined as 'the process through which individuals belonging to some groups are wholly or partially excluded from full participation in the society in which they live'.

II
Concept of Untouchability in Ancient Literary Texts

The ancient and medieval texts, both orthodox and heterodox religious canons mentioned socially segregated professional groups like, *pulkasas*, and *svapacas* that stayed away from ritually ranked *jatis*. These literary sources suggests how religious, ritual, political, and economic concerns are inextricably intertwined in depicting the picture of untouchability in terms of social groups fixed in professional hierarchies designed on the norms of *sauca / suci* (purity/pure) and *asauca* (pollution). The condition of personal purity (*suci*) was concerned with the 'competence' (*adhikara*) of a master to act with respect to his domain. Acts of purification increased or restored a person's competency. Seen from the perspective of the ritualism of the law books, *adhikara* highlights the interdependence between the purity that is demanded of a competent human agent and the auspicious results that follow from such pure actions in the form of wealth and power. The basic polarity here is that between human and divine agency. Human agency has limited power but possesses a moral-ritual potency that is generated by actions that are either in accordance with *dharma* (good potency) or *adharma* (evil potency). Divine or cosmic agency is all-powerful, but it is so in response to the moral-ritual potency of human acts. What divine agency returns in the form of human conditions of existence whether fertility or infertility, health or disease, wealth or poverty happens according to the *dharmika* quality of human acts. Reduced to its essence, it is a relation between 'visible' (*drsta*) human endeavours, on the one hand, and the other 'invisible' (*adrsta*) connections that guarantee that such endeavours bear fruit in the form of fertility, health, and wealth. As such, it logically follows that the economically and politically oppressed are considered inherently inauspicious. Unintentional poverty is itself a sign of inauspiciousness. According to the definition of the *Suddhikaumudi* a sixteenth-century digest of purity rules, purity is the state of 'being fit for performing the rituals that are known from the Vedas' that is to say, purity is a prerequisite, a 'felicity condition' of ritual action. Ritual, in turn, is a paradigmatic human activity.[1] The untouchability as per the law books pertains to *adhikara* (competence) and distinction between purity and pollution.

Untouchability has always consisted of a complex of several different avoidances. The segregation of untouchable groups was not absolute but negotiable on two grounds; (i) to receive certain services characterised by the removal of impurity from personal and common domains and (ii) to avoid the polluting influence entailed by these services. It was also likely the case that the services that were demanded from untouchable groups consisted increasingly of unskilled manual labour, and the regulation of contact with these groups therefore served as a method of isolating and preserving such an unskilled labour force. As a result of expanding trade and urbanisation, such artisans had gradually gained economic influence (Sharma 1990: 199-201, 262-68).[2] Through careful observance of the rules of untouchability and social segregation, a similar upward mobility of untouchable castes could be prevented. The achievement of the aforementioned ends necessitated both interaction (inclusion) and segregation (exclusion) at the same time. The emphasis was, therefore, not so much on strict exclusion but rather on what went on along the boundary between the untouchables and the twice-born and on the many ways in which this boundary could be crossed from both sides. In Patanjali's commentary (from around 150 BCE) on a rule in Panini's grammar for the interaction between the *candalas* and the upper *varnas*, the exclusion of the *candalas* is defined not by segregation from villages and settlements (which was not demanded at this stage) but by the rule that food vessels used by the *candalas* could not be used by others even after the vessels had been washed (*Mahabhasya* 1.475.2-10). This rule that the avoidance of the exchange of food vessels (*apapatratva*) was also applied in the law books. (*Manusmrti* 10.51)[3] explicitly designates the *candalas* and the *svapacas* as *apapatras*. Medhatithi, the ninth-century commentator on this text, discussed how food could be distributed to the *candalas* and the *svapacas* in such a way that there would be no exchange of food vessels: either it had to be given in earthen vessels which were thrown away afterwards, or in vessels held by a third person or placed on the ground, or in broken vessels. Patanjali's discussion, as well as the later elaborations in Manusmrti and its commentaries, shows how exclusion and segregation boil down to pragmatic questions regarding the regulation of concrete transactions. The concern was with safeguarding and regulating a necessary interaction and not with prohibiting it altogether. In this sense, the untouchables were in an ambiguous position. They did not stand outside the community of the four *varnas* but at its margins. From this vantage point, they were in a position to perform tasks that were necessary for the ritual and political constitution of the community by disposing of the impurity that was fatal to the competencies of its members. For this service, they in turn might have received food.

There is some evidence in the Vedic literature that untouchability as a minimal but distinct complex of avoidances was first practiced within the domestic sphere, particularly in connection with menstruation, before it was projected onto interactions at the demographic level (*Taittireya Brahmana* 3.7.1.9; *Taittireya Samhiat* 2.5.1.5-6; Kane 1968-77, 2: 803). Although a clear distinction between the two cases the temporarily untouchable persons in the family and the permanently untouchable groups in the villages is not absent in later texts (*Visnusmrti* 5.104-5)[4]. One should understand them in their totality. P.V. Kane (1968-77, 2: 803)[5] holds that the underlying notions of untouchability are religious and ceremonial purity and impurity. A man's nearest and dearest women relatives such as his own mother and wife or daughter are untouchable to him during their monthly periods. To him the most affectionate friend is untouchable for several days when the latter is in mourning due to death in the family (1968-77, 2: 170). In the law books this is apparent by the manner in which quite different untouchable categories are classified together and rules of avoidance are treated across such categories. Two early (250 150 BCE) eight lists of untouchable persons and things became normative for later similar lists. One is *Baudhayanadharmasutra* 1.5.9.5, which reads: "A Brahmana who has touched a memorial tree (in memory of dead persons), a funeral pyre, a sacrificial post (for binding the victims),. [or] a seller of the Veda (who stipulates certain wages before giving instructions in the Vedas) should enter the water with his clothes on". Even in the *Gautamadharmasutra* 14.30 it is stated that: "In case of touching an outcast, a woman in confinement, a menstruating woman, [and] a person who has touched a corpse or any of these, a man should purify himself by bathing with his clothes on". Apart from the persons and things listed in these two texts, animals form a third group. Taken together, and including the other ancient *Dharmasutras*, persons include: the, representing the permanent untouchability of the lowest castes; the woman in confinement; the menstruating woman; the dead person; the person who touches a dead person; the outcast (*patita*), that is, the severe violator of moral laws, such as a Brahmana-killer and the Veda seller. Among animals only the dog is particularly associated with the *svapacas* (literally dog-cookers), as mentioned in the early texts (*Apastambadharmasutra* 1.5.15.16; *Baudhayanadharmasutra* 1.5.11.39; *Gautamadharmasutra* (14.32; *Vasisthadharmasutra* 23.33). Among objects nothing else is mentioned besides those items mentioned above in *Baudhayanadharmasutras* 1.5.9.5[6]. On the avoidances to be observed with *candalas* are as follows according to the same early texts (*Dharmasutra* texts):

Avoidance of Physical Contact

(1) Avoidance of sexual contact (*Baudhayanadharmasutra* 2.2.4.12-13; *Vasisthadharmasutra* 23.39- 1).
(2) Avoidance of touch or Avoidance of contact through the senses (*Apastambadharmasutra* 2.1.2.8; *Baudhayanadharmasutra* 1.5.9.5; *Gautamadharmasutra* 14.30; *Vasisthadharmasutra* 23.33).
(3) Avoidance of contact through sight (*Apastambadharmasutra* 2.1.2.8).
(4) Avoidance of contact through hearing (during recitation) (*Vasistha dharmasutra* 23.34).
(5) Avoidance of contact through speech (*Apastambadharmasutra* 2.1.2.8). Avoidance of contact through things exchanged.
(6) Avoidance of contact through food (*Baudhayanadharmasutra* 2.2.4.14; *Vasisthadharmasutra* 20.16-17).
(7) Avoidance of contact through exchange of food vessels (*Apastamba dharmasutra* 1.1.3.25, 1.5.16.30, 1.7.21.I7).

(8) Avoidance of contact through gifts and Avoidance of contact during religious activities (*Baudhayanadharmasutra* 2.2.4.14).

(9) Presence of a hindrance to recitation (*Apastambadharma sutra* 1.3.9.15; *Gautamadharmasutra* 16.19; *Vasisthad-harmasatra* 13.11).

(10) Glance of a spoiling the *sraddha* food (*Gautamadharmasutra* 15.24).

Categories of Impurity

Haradatta on *Gautamadharmasutra* (2.5.1) identified four categories of impurity. One category consists of persons who undergo *asauca*, the period of purification after the death of a relative. The other three are: the suspension of the right to perform rituals, of the possibility for others to partake of one's food, and of receiving one's gifts. All these criteria had long been attached to the *candalas*. Commenting on *Parasarasmrti* (2.6.24), Madhavacarya quotes two verses attributed to Devala that clearly take the list in *Gautamadharmasutra* (14.30) and it is parallel to *Manusmrti* (5.85).

Dharmasastra model of Untouchability

"A man who has touched a *svapaca*, an outcaste, a cripple, a fool, a corpse burner, both parents undergoing the impurity of childbirth, a woman overtaken by menstruation, or the dogs, cocks, and hogs of the village is purified as soon as he has bathed fully, including his head, and with his clothes on. A little further he quotes *Caturvimsatimata* (another incomplete text; Derrett 1973: 39)[7], which has a list similar to *Baudhayanadharmasutra* (1.5.9.5). The memorial tree and the Veda-seller are omitted, but instead it includes the temple priest (*devalaka*), whose prestige is very low from the point of view of the Veda-learned *sastra* authors. A relation to the state is suggested in *Atrismrti* (P.V. Kane 1968-77, 2: 384), which adds the 'barbarian' foreigner (*mleccha*) to the list. *Vijnanesvara* on *Yajnavalkyasmrti* (3.30)[8] quotes other *smrtis* which extend the lists further; for instance, a priest who sacrifices for a whole village, the seller of the soma plant, and the shadow of a *svapaka*. And we could go on finding peculiar additions. *Atrismrti* makes crows, camels, and jackals untouchable to women during menstruation. In addition, there are certain situations that render people momentarily untouchable to each other. According to *Parasarasmrti* (2.7.20c-22b), a person who is eating or who has not yet cleaned himself after the meal is impure (*ucchista*) and untouchable to others in the same situation. With respect to untouchable castes, it is more significant that *Caturvarga cintamani* (p. 38) lists sixteen groups, most of which are occupational (Kane, 1968-77, 4: 115n264). They are: washermen, leather workers, dancers, reed and bamboo workers, fishermen, Medas (several polluting occupations; see Kane 1968-77, 2: 92), Bhillas (mountain people), goldsmiths, Sauvikas (possibly Sauvidas: attendants on women's apartments), blacksmiths, stone cutters, barbers, carpenters, oil grinders, butchers, and wine dealers. All these groups are labelled as '*candalas* living in the village', and the text specifies what this means in terms of avoidances: Wise people avoid looking at, touching, or talking to these persons. Moreover, they do not wish to hear them speak or to see them during the time of bathing, eating, or performing *japa, homa*, and worship. The sun is to be looked at in case of seeing them, and a man should abandon his meal if these things happen during that time. In case of talking with them, he should wash both ears well with his hands, and having finally talked with a Brahmana, he is freed from the defect (*Caturvarga cintamani* : 38-39). The avoidances follow the paradigm of the *Dharmasutras* in distinguishing between what happens in ritual contexts, during which the results of pollution are more serious (even hearing is damaging), and at other times. This proliferation of occupational untouchable groups as listed in *Caturvarga cintamani* is remarkable in that it moves beyond the previously delimited unskilled services of the workers at the cremation grounds and serving as executioners and scavengers (Manusmrti 10.55-56). The *Vaikhanasa smarta sutra* (10.14) includes seven occupations of the so-called 'low-born' (*antyaja*), that is, washer man, leather worker, dancer, reed and bamboo worker, fisherman, Meda, and Bhilla (Kane, 1968-77, 2: 70). Not only do the untouchable categories proliferate, the complex of avoidances is also extended during the medieval period (from about sixth century CE). Added to the list of avoidances in the ancient *Dharmasutras*, we find rules that clearly segregate the *candalas* from the villages and cities (*Vaikhanasasmarta* sutra 10.14). It is stressed, however, that this segregation only pertains to their place of living, not to work. On the contrary, the texts deal increasingly with how to contact with the *candalas* inside the village. This is paralleled by more detailed descriptions of the duties of the *candalas* within villages and cities. The image presented in the *Vaikhanasasmartasutra*, dated to the fourth century (Kane, 1968-77, 1: 260) and probably even later. According to J. Duncan Derrett (1973: 39) it is an example of the fully elaborated stereotype of an untouchable village: "*candala* is begotten by a *Sudra* on a Brahmana woman. He wears ornaments of lead or black iron, a leather thong tied round his neck, and a cymbal fixed to his girdle. He wanders from place to place and is excluded from all rites. In the morning, he removes the dirt on the road and elsewhere in villages and other places and takes it outside. He should dwell far away outside the village together with his own kind. After midday he cannot enter a village. If he does, he has to be punished corporally by the king. Otherwise the king incurs the guilt of murdering a learned Brahmana" (*Vaikhanasasmartasutra* 10.14). Other occupations for the *candalas* mentioned in earlier texts include hunting, working on the cremation grounds, executioner (*Manusmrti* 5.131, 10.55-56; *Visnusmrti* 16.11, 23.50; *Yajnavalkyasmrti* 1.192), and security functions such as guarding frontiers (*Arthasastra* 2.1.5), searching for robbers in the villages (*Naradasmrti* 14.25), and participating in certain military units (*gulma*) (*Katyayanasmrti* 681). Commenting on *Manusmrti* (10.55), Medhatithi (ninth century; Derrett 1973: 49) gives us a parallel picture of the *candalas* on duty in the larger city as follows:

"During the day they walk about on business, that is, either on their own business, such as buying and selling, or on the king's business, for instance when there is a public show or a festival in the town. At such occasions, they should be marked according to royal order by such marks as the thunderbolt, and so on, which are ordered by the king, or by the axe or hoe, which they carry on their shoulders for the purpose of executing criminals. Along with the increasing need for the *candalas* presence within villages and cities, rules regulating the spatial limits of contact became more complicated. *Parasarasmrti*, for instance, does not at all prescribe where the *candalas* have to live. Instead it gives detailed instructions about how to purify the house of a Brahmana if *candala* has stayed inside it without his knowledge (*Parasarasmrti* 2.6.34-38b; Aktor 2000: 144-48). Thus, the sphere of possible contact comes closer. This is reflected in the way in which the avoidance of touch itself proliferates. Apart from direct touch, there are detailed rules about contact through common facilities, such as roads and beds (*Parasarasmrti* 2.6.23), particularly when food is involved (Brahmanas eating fruit from a tree touched by the *candalas* in Atrismrti 178-83b). Even without any material medium, untouchability is extended to pollution at a distance that is precisely measured out: If a Brahmana happens to get closer to *candalas* than four *yujanas* (about three and a half meters), he has to take a bath (*Parasarasmrti* 2.12.54-55; *Mitaksara* 3.30). Some texts, as previously mentioned, also prescribe the untouchability of the shadow of a *svapaka* (*Atrismrti* 288c-89b), although this is controversial, since shadows in general are declared pure according to the authority of *Manusmrti* 5.133, *Visnusmrti* 23.52, and *Yajnavalkyasmrti* 1.193. Note also the duty of the *candalas*, mentioned in the quote from *Vaikhanasasmartasutra* above, to make him visually and audibly known by wearing, for instance, a leather thong and beating a cymbal. Another important avoidance is the restricted access to the wells and other water sources of the high castes. It is not that the *candalas* are explicitly prohibited from drawing water from the common well but that the twice-born are warned against drinking water from wells dug by the *candalas* or water which has come into contact with their pitchers (*Mitaksara* 1.192; *Parasara smrti* 2.6.25-29). Apart from these proliferations of untouchable characters and avoidances associated with them, one can also see a differentiation of various situations that aggravate the pollution of untouchables. As noted, the impurity after eating was one such situation. Parallel to this are the rules that prescribe specific purification in the case a man has been touched by a *candala* while he is still impure after defecation (*Parasaramadhaviya* 2, 1: 110, 2, 2: 143). For menstruating women, in particular, the preoccupation with purification is overwhelming. Detailed rules are given which account for every possible combination of the *varna* in case menstruating women happen to touch each other (*Pararasmrti* 2.7.11c-15b). And if such a woman is touched by *candala*, then there are specific penances depending on which day of the menstrual cycle the incident occurred, the first day being considered the worst (*Parasaramadhaviya* 2, 1: 162; Leslie 1994). Thus, various types of untouchability are combined.

III
Dimensions of Untouchability

Basing on law books two dimensions of untouchability are identified for avoidance in social participation. They are: (i) spatial pattern (ii) purity and pollution pattern.

(i) All the untouchable characters like cripples, *candalas*, criminals, menstruating women, death of kin relatives, foreigners are distributed according to the different spatial spheres of activity and competence in which the high-caste male householder pursues his goals. At the centre of the sphere is one's own body. This is a domain of its own because the ritual competency of the householder as an agent within larger spheres depends on the state of his body. But first and foremost he is the master of a home with family, livestock, and so on. Homes are organised in village communities of transacting occupational groups or in larger urban centres like the royal city. All these form part of the king's territory, the country that is his personal domain. In spatial terms *candalas* is a phenomenon.

(ii) There is the pattern by which all these untouchable categories are distinct from other categories that merely denote impurity. This is the pattern in terms of a distinction between purity and auspiciousness, between human agency and types of agency that are beyond the human domain. These extra human domains are particularly related to human prosperity, since prosperity cannot be guaranteed by human agency alone. Whether one's wife delivers a son or a daughter, whether the rains fall as expected, and whether one's enemies are successful in their attacks are all matters in which divine agency has a determining role.

Candala as a Phenomenon

From the perspective of law books, the untouchable categories are organised in relation to those spatial domains, through within which householder operates (the body, the home, the village, the town and the country). These include that type of *Candala* that is the result of a *sagotra* relation, in which the partners belong to the same lineage (Parasaramadhaviya 2, 1: 306)[9], and that outcast (*patita*) who has 'violated his guru's bed' (that is, who has had sexual relations with one of the wives of the preceptor, a relation which tends to be incestuous, since the guru is one's own father, either in fact or by interpretation). However, as the *patita* in general is segregated from the village and not simply from the house, the case of this latter sinner is ambiguous. In any event, the untouchability rules of the home reveal that the power of the master of the house depends upon his duties in terms of kinship. The untouchability of the home brackets off elements that, although they are intimate parts of the kinship sphere, are seen as negative, critical, or illegitimate in relation to the proper kinship expectations of high-caste householders. The untouchables of the village or town are the *Candalas* (and similar groups, such as *svapacas* or *pulkasas* these terms seem more or less interchangeable) and people who have become *patitas* due to severe sins. The permanently untouchable (the *Candalas*, for instance) are part of a set of practices that are related to the prosperity of the village or town communities. These communities depend on occupational transactions between its various groups. Although all professions are in fact integral parts of this interaction, some are not recognised as contributing to it in any other sense as a necessary evil (just as defecation is not recognised as part of the sacrifice/food cycle but only as a waste product caused by it). In a similar vein, the professional function of the *Candala* is to remove the most polluting waste that is produced by the villagers in their homes and through their work, particularly in connection with cremation and litter in the streets (*Vaikhanasa smarta sutra* 10.14). In villages that fall under royal jurisdiction, the *Candala* is also responsible for the imprisonment and execution of criminals, although this service might have been centralised in larger urban centres (*Manubhasya* 10.55; *Manusmrti* 10.56). All these jobs comprise a low status, negative aspect of the professional life that makes a community prosper. Although they are necessary for the welfare of the community, these jobs are associated with inauspicious forces, such as death and crime, and are therefore not recognised as part of a common sphere of mutual transactions. In fact, the *Candalas* are explicitly excluded from the common sphere of mutual transactions. *Apastambadharmasutra* 1.7.21.5-6 forbids

Brahmanas to make any transactions, such as trade with *patitas* and *apapatras* (the *Candalas*, *Svapacas*, and other untouchables), even during critical times when Brahmanas are allowed to live by trade with other groups. Similarly, *Manusmrti* 10.53 states that the *Candalas* and *Svapacas* should only make transactions among themselves. The *Candalas* are, therefore, not seen as making use of 'transactions' within a larger, mutual social economy but as providing obligatory services that must be carried out by people who are spatially segregated from the villagers. As an occupational group in the professional life of the village or city community, the position of the *Candalas* is structurally analogous to that of the menstruating woman in relation to kinship or saliva in relation to nutrition: a necessary part of the actual paradigm, but segregated from the ritualised version of it. In the technical sense of *Gautamadharmasatra* 21.4-5 an outcaste (*patita*) is a person who, after committing severe sins, is deprived of the right to perform and to benefit (in the sense of stereological rewards) from the rituals and work that follow from his birth and initiation as a twice-born. That is to say, it is a person who, for a period of time, has lost the *adhikara* for the activities that pertain to his *jati* (not only in the sense of 'caste' but also of kinship), including, it seems, the economic rights connected with it (Derrett, 1962: 39-40; Kane, 1968-77, 3: 616). But the *jati* itself, that is, the membership in these groups, is not lost if the sinner is willing to undergo the prescribed penance. During this observance the sinner has to live outside the village and is untouchable (*Apastambadharmasutra* 1.10.29.8; *Baudhayanadharmasutra* 2.1.2.18; *Gautamadharmasutra* 14.30). Loss of *jati*, that is, excommunication, only happens if the sinner refuses to undergo the penance (Hardatta on *Gautamadharmasutra* 20.1; *Manubhasya* 11.181; *Mitaksara* 3.294; P.V. Kane, 1968-77, 2: 388, 3: 615). In other words, unlike the *Candalas* who are permanently confined to the periphery or altogether outside of the village or town community (and are further restricted by avoidances when they work inside of it), the *patitas* have not completely lost their affiliations to their homes inside these areas. But precisely because they retain such affiliations, the *adhikaras* that apply to them, first of all the right to stay in their home, are bracketed by segregation until their sins are expiated. This is because the invisible effect of sins is not a private affair. Although such effects are not shared among individuals, they still affect people's communities. Sins are not transferred from one domain to another, for instance, from one individual to single members of his family, but their very presence within larger domains, like one sinning member within the family or criminals within the state, hinders the ritual integrity (and hence the prosperity) of these larger domains (that is, family and state). Accordingly, it is the family that has to perform the excommunication ritual (*ghatasphota*) *Gautamadharmasatra* 20.2-7; Kane 1968-77, 2: 388). If the sinner refuses to go through the penance, and the king (the lord of the state) has to make sure that such an obstinate sinner is branded on his forehead as an additional punishment. He is now a permanent outcast, totally excluded from all association with other people (*Manusmrti* 9.236-39; Kane 1968-77,4: 71-72).

Speaking in terms of spatial areas, one can therefore make a distinction between *patitas* who undergo penance outside their villages, still connected to them by a slender bond, and excommunicated, branded *patitas* who have severed such connections through their obstinacy and are commanded to 'wander over the earth' (*Manusmrti* 9.238) without location. The *Vijnanesvara* (on Yajnavalkyasmrti 2.294) applies the same distinction between expiated and unexpiated sin in the case of a twice-born male who has had sexual relations with a *Candala* woman but refuses to undergo the penance. He is not only liable to pay a fine for the crime itself but is further branded with a mark shaped like the female organ. The physical branding is even carried into future births. Madhava (in his digression on the *karmic* effects of sin, *Parasaramadhaviya* 2, 2: 209-10) quotes some verses attributed to *Visnudharmottarapuruna* to the effect that sinners who refuse penance and also escape the king's punishment are reborn as animals, and even when they attain human births, they will be marked by bodily defects (P.V. Kane, 1968:77, 4: 153n356). The implication of both the branding and the bodily defects is clear. Sins that are not removed by penance or punished by the king must become physically visible. Unexpiated sins should not be hidden within the ritualised spheres of communal life. Such sins destroy the rituals by which these spheres are preserved (*Manusmrti* 7.20-21): they obstruct the cosmic cycle that connects sacrifices, cosmic agents, and prosperity. They do this both by their immediate destruction of the conditions of sacrifice (the welfare of the Brahmanas, in particular) and by their invisible effects on the larger domains of which the sinners form a part.

Whereas the Candalas and *patitas* who undergo penance are related to the village, the *mlecchas* are defined in relation to the state, but not merely as geographical outsiders. The notion of untouchability is only meaningful inside common domains. There is no point in segregating people as untouchable if they are not part of such domains. Therefore, the untouchability of *mlecchas* should not simply be seen as a demarcation towards an outside 'other' but as recognition of a shared domain either in the sense of interaction or in terms of a hegemonic appropriation of the world. The land of the Aryans, *Aryavarta*, has a privileged place in the world as the land of dharma. This implies 'a unique ritual, religious and sociological statuses' among other peoples and other countries (Halbfass, 1988: 177). These other peoples of the world are regarded as incomplete or negative exemplars of *dharma*. The absence of the *varna* system (*Visnusmrti* 84.4) and the rituals prescribed by *sruti* and *smrti* means that the *mlecchas* are regarded as subordinate in this world order. They have no place in *Aryavarta*, and if they nevertheless reside there, this weakens *dharma* (Halbfass, 1988: 177)[10].

Medhatithi (*Manusmrti* 2.23) holds that the integration into the caste system of the conquered foreigners, who as a caste will be regarded as the *Candalas*, that is, untouchables. Barbarians beyond conquest, on the other hand, are also beyond the *varna* system. The implication of these texts is that, ideally, integration would mean subordination in relation to *dharma* in the sense of accepting the duties assigned to them as untouchable castes and that the ritual and political integrity of the country depends on this. The general pattern that emerges from this exposition is the following: A ritualised agent and a ritualised sphere of agency is one that is conducive to prosperity. Prosperity has different aspects according to each particular sphere: food for the body, fertility for the home, wealth or welfare in relation to village and city communities, common merit in relation to moral norms of action as part of the same community domain, and, similarly but on the larger scale of the state, subjects who are unified by their acceptance of a common social norm (the caste system) and a minimal common code of action. The ritualisation of each sphere implies privileging and segregating single elements, and untouchability is the mark of segregation applied to elements that are in reality indispensable or unavoidable within single spheres but charged with inauspicious possibilities. More than any other category in the complex system of untouchability, the *Candala* therefore represents the total phenomenon.

Untouchability vs. Panchama Varna

The nature of untouchability practised in relation to the *Candalas* and their economic plight in the *Buddhist Jatakas*, which are posterior to the *Pali* Canon and often coincide with the *Manusmriti*, are as severe as had been prescribed by this lawgiver who is generally regarded as the symbol of the ugly face of Brahmanism even though the *Candalas* are found pursuing several callings including those of a corpse carrier, remover and cremator, hangman, sweeper, night guard, public performer and hunter. The *Nesadas* who engaged in hunting and fishing (there are occasional references to their villages, chiefs and guilds), the *Pukkusas* who were hunters and refuse-cleaners, the *Venas* who were bamboo-workers and also possibly hunters, and the *Rathakaras* who built chariots for war, are portrayed as sharing the status and penury of the *Candalas*. It is significant that the professions of the basket-maker, leather-worker, potter, weaver and barber had a better rating in contemporary Brahmanical works; The *Grihyasutras (Vivekananda Jha :1997,f.n.39 &40)* of Boudhayana and Bharadvaja prescribed even *upanayana* for the *Rathakara*; and the caste of bamboo-worker and basket-maker, *Buruda*, came to be looked upon as untouchable only in the early medieval Smriti. The emphasis that both Buddhism and Jainism laid on non-violence evidently coloured their attitude and perception towards many of these castes which were obliged by their wretched material condition and needs of subsistence and livelihood to engage in activities involving violence. In the case of the *Candalas* the primitive dread of dead human bodies which they handled aggravated the degree of pollution.

The basic fact is that caste had come to play an important role in economic life and it developed strong roots in occupations in the birth-based hierarchical class society of early India and few movements of protest against injustice involved in its intrinsic inequality had power to change this ground reality or to offer any viable and enduring alternative. That Brahmanism, Buddhism and Jainism ideologically contributed to the irreversible process of the development of caste and untouchability instead of resisting.

Caste actually solidified with the hardening of class relations in north India between 600 BC and AD 200, and untouchability, too, originating in pre-Mauryan times, got accentuated by AD 200. Since most of the castes which were initially reduced to the level of untouchables were those which had little share in the distribution of wealth, power or prestige. Untouchability has to be viewed as the extreme manifestation of the institutionalised inequality of both caste and class. The untouchables were remained as a part of the Indian caste and class structure. There has been a lively debate as to whether the untouchables are part of the four-*varna* structure or they constitute the fifth *varna*. The reality about their being distinct from the *Sudra* is incontrovertible. Without subscribing to the five-*varna* theory, Kautilya explicitly distinguishes the *Candalas* from the *sudras.*[11] It is however, equally true that almost the entire corpus of Brahmanical literature in early India has vehemently denied the existence of the fifth *varna*. Like the *Dharmasutras*, Manu is categorical in this regard: "*brahmanah kshatriyo vaishyastrayo varna dvijatayah chaturtha ekajatistu shudro nasti tu panchamah*". It means that the Brahmana, the Kshatriya and the Vaishya are the three twice-born *varnas*; the once-born *Sudra* is the fourth. There is no fifth [*varna*]. So is the *Anushasana Parva* of the *Mahabharata* the phrase *panchamon adhigamyate* reveals that there is no fifth [*varna*]. The only well-known exception is Shankaracharya who in his commentary on the *Brahmasutra* (Vivekanada Jha, 1997:26-29)[12] in the eighth or ninth century describes the *Nishadas* as the fifth (varna) (*nishadapanchamap arigrihitah*). The *Samba Purana* dated between the sixth and eighth centuries also speaks of *panchamamsavarnikam* (*Ibid*: 26), which may be translated as "*varna* categories are five".

Hence in early India is concerned, the expansion of caste and untouchability from AD 200 to AD 1200 was an uninterrupted and continuous process. New groups, indigenous as well as alien, were absorbed at various levels of the social structure in different parts and ideology proved flexible and receptive enough to effectively cope with developing situations and historical cross-currents. The extent of social mobility, both upward and downward, was certainly remarkable, and the system, instead of cracking up under pressures all-round, got reinforced and firmly entrenched. By the early medieval period the untouchables comprised two broad segments. The first included the backward tribal communities whose original occupations and those acquired after integration with the mainstream were not enough to give them economic security. Virtually landless, they served as the cheapest source of servile labour in the countryside. With progressive improvement in the overall condition of the *sudras* and their displacing the *Vaishyas* as the bulk of peasantry along with other landed classes, the interests of the *sudras* and the untouchables often diverged. The second category of untouchables included several depressed artisan castes who had remained at the level of sudras until the sixth century AD but under the impact of certain feudal developments in post-Gupta times such as the decline of trade and commerce, decrease in commodity production, break-up of craft guilds and increasing immobility became closely integrated with the villages in a predominantly agrarian economy dominated by the landed classes.[13] With their hereditary skill and low wages, often in kind, they were another cheap and easily available source of exploitation. Neither of these categories of untouchables was a homogeneous unit. Their division into several hierarchical castes under the influence of the dominant caste ideology thwarted the development of any bond of unity among them or with the landless sudras and debilitated them for any fight for social justice on their own. Parashara, who composed his *Smriti* during this period, reflected this social change clearly when he prescribed a number of expiations especially for the sudras in case of their being polluted by the untouchables.[14] The availability of cheap landless labour and artisan products on an enduring basis has been underlined by Irfan Habib as the major contribution of caste from which the Muslim landed and ruling classes benefited as much as their Hindu counterparts.[15] In fact, social justice is by its nature closely linked with equality at the level of mundane existence and this was bound to remain elusive without some sort of tangible equality and justice at the economic level. This required a kind of socio-economic transformation which was outside the agenda of the religious movements in early medieval times. The transition from *vedic* ritualism to puranic theism which upheld *bhakti* ideology distributed the message of god irrespective of caste and creed. The precepts of *Dana and dakshina, tirthadarsana* formed the crux of *bhakti* ideology which gave ritual status to the donors. The sectarian cults of Saiva, Vaisnava and Smartha religions became ecumenical in their approach to the marginalised communities to incorporate them into the fold of society. Virasaivism propounded by Basava and *Viravaisnavism* advocated by Brahmanaidu in Andhra and Karnataka respectively embraced the *panchamas* who played vital role in the village rituals and offices. Brahmanaidu incorporated the castes like gollas and *panchamas* into the realm of Vaisnavism which combated the caste distinctions by converting them into Vaisnavites by suffixing the word *dasa* (the slave of god). Through Chennkesava cult he dismantled caste hierarchies and opened the gates of the temple at Machrla in Andhra Pradesh for the participation of *panchamas* in the temples. Further, he broke the barrier of the taboo of inter-dining and he got married a woman from *Panchama* community. The *Panchamas* were associated with the caste myths of the peasant communities like the Velamas and Reddis.

Recognising the formidable and inescapable reality of the hierarchical and nonegalitarian caste structure could not be uprooted or abolished wholesale, and seeking to reform the spirit of its working from within, it presented an idealised version of *varna* and declared itself in favour of eradication of untouchability. This was the legacy of Gandhi, who drew his inspiration from the *Gita* and launched an arduous campaign to eradicate untouchability for social justice of the untouchables from within the system. B.R. Ambedkar hypothesised two reasons for the origin of the Untouchable caste; these are contempt and hatred of broken-men (untouchable) as Buddhists by the Brahmans and the continuation of beef eating by the broken-men after it had been given up by others.[16]

Conclusion

The exclusivity of untouchability manifests itself in the law books on both the empirical level and on the more implicit level of ritualistic rationale. Empirically it appears that of all the many different avoidances that are involved in the untouchability complex only two are inclusive and valid in relation to larger sections as well. These are the avoidance of sexual relations (*agamyatva*) and the prohibition against eating the food of those avoided (*abhojyannatva*). All other avoidances such as the avoidance of touch (*asprsyatva*), of accepting gifts (*apratigrhyatva*), of conversation (*asambhasyatva*), of looking at (*adrsayatva*), of exchanging food vessels (*apapatratva*), of sharing wells, and of social 'mixing' in general, as well as spatial segregation (*bahyatva*), the suspension of the right to perform rituals (*karmanadhikara*), and the command to wear visible marks of untouchability apply exclusively in relation to persons within the class of untouchable categories, some to all the members of the class (the *Candalas* and menstruating women alike), and some to only certain members of the class. This empirical exclusivity can be explained by two factors, both of which are a part of the ritualisation of the personal and common domains within which the twice-born male householder operates. One factor is the special relation between untouchability and the central processes of prosperity that govern each domain (nutrition for the body, kinship for the family, and so on). The other factor is the elements intrinsic to each process that are charged with potential inauspiciousness and which are therefore bracketed off or segregated spatially in order to establish a ritual order of things (which in turn secures an auspicious outcome). Untouchability is related to these elements and in particular with menstruation, death, and crime. These distinguishing characteristics become apparent when untouchability is viewed from a holistic perspective as comprising not only the permanently untouchable *Candala*, who is rightly regarded as the prototype of later observed untouchable castes (Dumont, 1980: 52), but also the temporarily untouchable.

The holistic strategy may appear to privilege ritual-ideological explanations of untouchability at the expense of socioeconomic considerations (that is, the fact that the untouchables represent an economically exploited group). Although the *Dharmasastra* is not a very explicit source for the broader socioeconomic aspects of untouchability as a means of preserving a large unskilled labour force, it is possible that even on the ideological ritual level, matters of ownership, wealth, prosperity, and power are essential to the phenomenon.

References

1. Suddhikaumudi, (1905). (ed.) K. K. Smrtibhusana, Calcutta: Asiatic Society of Bengal, 1905:1.
2. Sharma, R S (1990) *Comprehensive History of India, IV, Part I*, People's Publishing House, New Delhi, pp. 199-201, 262-68.
3. Max Muller, F (2007), *"Sacred Books of the East"*, *"Laws of Manu"*. Translated by Georg Buhler, Motilal Banarsidass Publishers, Delhi,
4. Jolly, Julius (1881). "Institutes of Vishnu", The Asiatic Society Publications, Calcutta.
5. Kane, P V (1968), "History of Dharmasastra" Vol. I, 4, Bandarkar Oriental Research Institute, Poona, pp. 803.
6. Max Muller, F (2007), *"Sacred Laws of the Aryas"* (As Taught in the Schools of Apastamba, Gauthama, Vasishtha and Baudhayana), Translated by Georg Buhler, Vol. 2, Part – I, (Apastamba and Gauthama) Motilal Banarsidass Publishers, Delhi, Vol. 14, Part – II, (Vasishtha and Baudhayana), Motilal Banarsidass Publishers, Delhi.
7. Derrett, J Duncan M (1973), "History of Indian Law (Dharmasastra)", Wiesbaden.
8. Vidyarnava, Srisa Chandra (1918), "The sacred Laws of the Hindus", Vol. XXI, Apurva Krishna das Publishers, Allahabad.
9. Chandrakanta Mahamahopadyaya, Tarkalankara (1974), "Parasarasmrti Parasara Madhava", The Asiatic Society, Calcutta.
10. Halbfass, Wilhelm (1988), *India and Europe : An Essay in Understanding*, State University of New York Press.
11. *Sudra sadharmano va, anyantra chandalebbyah, Arthashastra, III.7.37.*
12. Jha, Vivekananda, *"Caste, Untouchability and Social Justice: Early North Indian Perspective"*, Social Scientist, Vol. 25, No.11/12(Nov-Dec, 1997).
13. R. S. Sharma, *History of Untouchables in India*, Patna University, 1972. 50; *Social Changes in Early Medieval India (circa AD 500-1200),* The First Devraj Chanana Memorial Lecture, 1969 (People's Publishing House, New Delhi, 1969), pp. 6- 9; *Indian Feudalism, c. AD3 00-1200*, 2nd edn. (Macmillan, Madras, 1980), pp. 43- 48, 53-55, 187-90, 220-22; *Urban Decay in India (c. 300-c. 1000)*

(Munshiram Manoharlal, New Delhi, 1987), pp. 135-36,154-55,158,165-67,177,182,184; B.N.S. Yadava, *Society and Culture in Northern India in the Twelfth Century* (Central Book Depot, Allahabad, 1973), pp. 141, 147, 163-72, 267-75);

14. Vivekanand Jha, "Stages in the History of Untouchables", *Indian Historical Review*, Vol. II, No. 1 (July 1975), pp. 28-31). The position has been discussed in detail in my unpublished Ph.D. thesis "Early History of Untouchables in India", Patna University, 1972).
15. Irfan Habib, *"Caste in Indian History"* in *Essays in Indian History: Towards A Marxist Perception* (Tulika, New Delhi, 1995), pp. 166, 171-72).
16. Chinna Rao, Yagati (2003), " *Dalits' Struggle for Identity*: *Andhra and Hyderabad 1900-1950*", Kanishka Publishers, New Delhi, pp. 35.

3

Evolution of the Rajbanshi Society of North Bengal: Question of Identity Crisis

Kartik Chandra Sutradhar

It should be mentioned here that the writing of the society of a community in the regional context is a herculean task because of the paucity of source materials and the lack of authentic books or writings by the renowned historians and scholars for their negligence to cast their eyes to the vulnerable areas. In spite of that I have tried my best to explore different aspects of the society, their evolution and the identity crisis of the Rajbanshis. The Rajbanshis were the 'son of the soil' and majority people of North Bengal, particularly in the districts of Jalpaiguri, Rangpur, Dinajpur and the plain areas of Darjeeling district and the Cooch Behar state. Other than North Bengal, Rajbanshis had been living in the other parts of Bengal and Assam. Swaraj Basu writes, "...the Rajbansis constituted the most predominant section of the local Hindu population in the northern districts of Bengal. Numerically they were the third largest Hindu caste in Bengal as a whole. The origins of Rajbanshis are shrouded in mystery and the basic debate is around the question of their association with the Koches. Whatever might have been their actual origin; there is no dispute about the fact that the Rajbanshis were the early settlers in North Bengal. They were a socially homogenous community, in the sense that there was no sub-caste among them."[1] Dr Charu Chandra Sanyal opined, "The above observations point to the fact that the Koches are non-Aryan in origin. Some of them adopted Hinduism and became Rajbansis. These Rajbansis later on claimed to be Kshatriya."[2] Swaraj Basu again writes, "The local situation also provided a sufficient ground for the Rajbansis' assertion of a Kshatriya identity and their endeavour to build up caste solidarity."[3]

There are many debates about the origin or ethnic identity of the Rajbanshis. The main debate was whether the Rajbanshis were originated from Mongoloid race or Aryan race. This debate was initiated from the starting of the census work from 1870 onwards by the British-India Government. In the census report Government has shown the Rajbanshis and the Koches in the same group. Here, one point should be mentioned that the Koches were originated from the Indo-Mongoloid race and they were treated as tribal community. In accordance with the Aryan culture, the non-Aryan people treated as 'Dasa', 'Dasyu', 'Kirata', and 'Nisada' which means the lower graded people in the society. The non-Aryan people had no prestigious or honourable position in the eyes of upper strata of the society of so called traditional Hindus or Aryan people.

So, when Rajbanshis were shown as a non-Aryan people that were Koches, they protested against the census report. This protest turned into a social movement called "Kshatra Movement". They demanded that Koches and Rajbanshis were not originated in the same human race. Koches were the tribal people and the Rajbanshi originated from Aryan race. In accordance with the social status of the Aryans, Rajbanshis held the second position that was "Kshatriyas" after the Brahmanas. They gave the description from different sources of the Hindu Shastras or mythologies that after defeating in the battle to the Parashurama they came in the Ratnapith that was the place beside the Trishrota or Jalpes, settled there and they were called "Bratyo Kshatriyas". This Kshatra movement got a new motion under the leadership of Thakur Panchanan Barma who led the movement throughout the North Bengal and Assam. Ultimately their demand became success and in the census report of 1911 Rajbanshis and Koches were shown separately. In spite of that debate it is not proved anthropologically that the Rajbanshis were originated from the Aryan race because their physical structure or biological features of their bodies are assimilated with the Mongolian stock of people. Naturally, almost all the historians and scholars and the British officials showed that the Rajbanshis originated from the Mongoloid race. Swaraj Basu pointed out, "…. In case of the Rajbanshi caste movement, we find that one of the main thrusts of their movement was to distance themselves from the Koches and to establish their superior social rank.[4] He also added that when the Rabhas in north Bengal tried to move upward in social hierarchy the Rajbanshi leaders did not support their movement"[5]. Sunder showed in his report, "The Rajbanshis or Koches predominate in the Duars. The last census returns shows their number as 123,439. They are now recognised as a distinct caste of Hindus, but generally the Rajbanshis of the Duars is a Hindu when suits him to be one and a Mech when he obtains pork and wishes to eat it."[6] Hunter also showed in his reports that the Koches and the Rajbanshis were the same communities. He wrote, 'The Koches, or the Rajbanshis as they are now called, may be briefly mentioned among the semi-aboriginal tribes, although they are now recognised as a distinct caste of Hindus. The Koch race first came prominently into notice about the close of the fifteenth or the beginning of the sixteenth century, when Hajo established the Koch Kingdom upon the downfall of the more ancient Hindu Kingdom of Kamrup."[7]

It is stated that among the Koches who were converted into Hindu religion called the Rajbanshis and who were converted into Islam called Muslim or Mahamedan. Hunter here pointed out that the name of Koch was abandoned by the converts who assumed that of Rajbanshis literally of the Royal Kinded. The Koch or the Rajbanshis form by far the majority of the Hindu population of Jalpaiguri district.[8] Whatever the identity of the Rajbanshis had, they were the people like semi-tribes, simple in habit. Swaraj Basu again writes, "As they were guided by the traditional Brahmanical cultural values, the Rajbansis, with a tradition and culture of their own, failed to get a respectable position in the status estimation of these immigrant upper caste gentry."[9] It is true that the people of higher caste Hindus coming from East Bengal and South Bengal treated the Rajbanshis as inferior caste, many times called them 'Bahe' or 'Banku'; on the contrary the Rajbansi people called the Bengali people coming from East Bengal or South Bengal as 'Bhatia'.[10] They were mainly habituated with agrarian cultivation. Almost all the people of Rajbanshis were uneducated in the colonial period. They would live in the villages. Their house was made mainly with the Bamboos and thrash and the economically solvent jotdars made their house with tin and wood. Generally in the house of the Rajbanshis four huts were seen. Sunder stated in his report "Among the Rajbanshis as well as Mahamedan there four huts in every homestead. These face North, South, East and West. Sometimes an extra hut called Darighar is also built and is used by friends who may be staying for a night so. In building a homestead cars is taken to have it bounded as follows whenever possible.[11]

North————— Betel nut trees
South ————— Compound
East ————— Water
West ————— Bamboos

In making the homestead of the Rajbanshis a proverb is prevailing in the Rajbanshi society which is followed by the Rajbanshis people at the time of making their house like this –

Uttare gua, dakshine Dhua,
Purbe Hans, pashime Bansh.

'Uttare gua' means in the north of the homestead there would be a betel nut garden, 'Dakshine 'dhua' means in the south of the homestead there would be blank field or farm house that means no trees would remain in the south. 'Purbe Hans' means in the east portion of the house there would be a pond and in the pond ducks would swim, 'Pashime Bansh' means in the western portion of the house a garden of Bamboos would remain.[12]

Food Habit

As the Rajbanshis people became Hindus, so they eat everything in accordance with the Hindu religion, but some special food or items are eaten by the Rajbanshis of which 'Chheka Shak' is one of the delicious food of the Rajbanshis which is cooked by different types of vegetables specially mixing with one kind of soda. Another delicious vegetable of the Rajbanshis is 'Lapha Shak'. Another delicious food is eaten by the Rajbanshis people locally known as Sutka and Sidal. Sutka means dry fishes and sidal is made by crashing of small dry fishes, spices, turmeric and chilly, all these are crushed in a husk locally called *chham* and Gain.[13] 'Pelka', one kind of delicious vegetable item to the Rajbanshis is one kind of traditional food which is mainly cooked by vegetables specially 'Lapha shak'. Dai and Chira is favourite to the Rajbanshi people. Rajbanshis like to eat very much pan and supari locally known 'Gua pan', 'gua' means raw betel nut. They honoured their guest by offering gua pan at the initial stage of receiving. Many of them always keep this gua pan in their pocket or small container, and gradually they eat this after some duration.

Later on, after huge number of people migrated in North Bengal, many indigenous foods were taken as the food of the migrated people; on the other hand the indigenous people were habituated with the food habit of the migrated people. Not only that, the indigenous people accepted the process of cooking and spices from the migrated people. Beside these, after independence and partition, the spread of education accelerated, many school, colleges, institution were established, as a result of which many indigenous people came under the education. They became educated and many of them got services, the number of employee increased day after day. These educated people went out of the house, settled into different places, started to live different places of the country, as a result of which they gradually became habituated with the food habit of multi-character dishes. The food habit of the educated people automatically influenced the other people of the villages. For example, many people of Rajbanshi community used burning fishes as their food, but the new generation people including educated people do not use various types of spices, simply they used turmeric, cumin, coriander etc. dusting in the traditional husking machine, nowadays they use various types of spices purchasing from market. In this regard Sitangshu Prosad Chakraborty stated, "Relating food habit they also habituated with modern food habit at present, particularly, the educated Rajbanshis and the Rajbanshis of urban areas use modern food instead of taking their traditional food habit such as pelka, chheka, sidal-sutki.[14]

It is found in the field survey that almost all of the indigenous people use modern type's food accordingly the global culture of food habit. Jagat Singh Barman stated that they eat everything in accordance with the Hindu food habit. Both of the veg and non-veg they take as their food which are available in the market and they purchased accordingly their financial capacity. They sometimes eat their traditional food like pelka, sutka sidal, chheka etc. But usually they use all the food which is eaten by other Bengali people. There are no vast differences between our food habit and the food habit of other Bengali people.[15] Kaitalu Barman of the same village told that they rarely use traditional food, generally they are habituated with the food habit like the other Bengali people. He also added that their children preferred the modern food than the traditional food.[16] I have also collect informations from many educated Rajbanshis who serve in various departments and dowelled in the town and my colleagues of Rajbanshi community talking with them directly where no differences have been found in their food habit between the Rajbanshis and other Bengali people.

Dress

Upendra Nath Barman stated, "It is known that the women of Rajbanshi community wear a dress called Buki (Bukali) and it was prevailing since ancient time. Apart from this the two parts of dress named Riya and Mekhla were used by the women. It should be mentioned here that the men of poor family wear small dhoti from the upper side of knee and the very poor men wear a piece of cloth called 'Nengti'. At the time of continuing social reforms movement Thakur Panchanan Barma propagated to wear dhoti instead of 'Nengti' and sari of women instead of 'Buki'.[17] Advance group among the Rajbansis whom we may refer to in the absence of a better term as the Rajbansi 'elites', followed the upper caste Hindus of the region in dress, lifestyle, marriage customs, and religious practices."[18] Charu Chandra Sanyal pointed out, "Discarding the traditional clothes, both men and women dressed in the fashion of the upper castes in society."[19]

All the indigenous people started slowly to wear modern dress like other people of mainstream. The young generation both male and female is habituated with the modern dresses they started to wear pant, shirt, shoe, etc. The girls and female wear churidar or salwar kamij, frok, sarees etc, not only that, presently, the female also wear the dresses of the male such as pant, shirt etc. The old men wear Dhoti, Punjabi also pant, shirts etc. Nowaday's almost all the indigenous people have been wearing modern dress, no differences are followed in terms of dresses between the indigenous people and the immigrated people. For the emergence of global culture no man can deny to accept the global culture. So, nowaday's no man can be identified of which community they belong with their dresses because of the abolition of traditional dresses except few instances and increasing the modern dress-habit.

Marriage

As the Rajbanshis belonged to Hindu community, so the marriage ceremony is performed according to the Hindu religion or Brahmanical references. Despite of that many traditional customs or rituals were to be followed at the time of marriage. A middle man locally known as 'ghatak' or 'ghatki' communicated between the guardians of bride and bridegrooms and information is sent time to time to both the parties. If both sides are satisfied and chosen each other the wedding is confirmed and fixed up the date of marriage.

The marriage ceremony of the Rajbanshis of the district is completed by three stages, namely pan tola, adhibas and marriage. The guests of bride are gone to the house of bridegroom and the new clothes and ornaments are wear to the bridegroom and blessed her. This occasion is called Pan Tola. In the second stage the following occasion are performed — turmeric was touched to the body of the bridegroom called adhibas and in the occasion called Naua kamani was performed. Then the Hargouri puja, Nandi mukhi shradhya and the last stage the main marriage ceremony is performed. Among the local customs or rituals of the marriage ceremony among the Rajbanshis a 'Mittar' or friend is to be selected at the time of marriage who remain as a friend or a relative of the bride in the whole life. Another custom is seen, a person who dropped water in the head of the bride and bridegroom at the time of marriage and related with them as their parents called 'Pani chhita Baap' and 'Pani chhita Mao'. They are also related with the bride and bridegroom in the whole life as their parents. Another custom in the marriage of the Rajbanshis which is not seen in the marriage of Aryan culture a Bairati played a vital role in the whole marriage ceremony. Polygamy was seen in the society of the Rajbanshis meaning of which that a Rajbanshi man could marry more than one. Widow Remarriage was also a common practice in the society of the Rajbanshis in the pre-colonial and colonial period where in the society of higher caste widow remarriage was a hard task. In this point of view, Rajbanshis were more liberal than the higher caste people.

Worships, Customs and Festivals

At present the Rajbanshis are Hindus. But originally they were Koches, an Indo-Mongoloid tribes believing in tribal culture, though it is debatable. It is assumed by most of the historians and social scientist that the Rajbanshis were converted to Hinduism from Koches. There were many Gods, Goddessess and Deities who were worshipped by the Rajbanshis. It should be mentioned here that there were many non-Aryan God and Goddess worshipped by the Rajbanshis as they were basically non-Aryan. After converted into Hinduism they worshipped Hindu God and Goddess. Among the non-Aryan deities there were Bisto Thakur, he was worshipped by the name of Jalthakur also. This worship was held in the month of Bhadra. He is a deity of water. The Brohma thakur is a deity of Agni or fire. Besides, there were Paban thakur or deity of air, Basumati thakur, Bisha hari thakurani, Mahakal thakur, the oldest Deity,, Gramthakur, Shib thakur, or Maheswar, Lakshi thakurani, Dharmathakur etc."[20] The worship of Banadurga is held in every year at the time of ekadashi of Durga worship at Bhandani in the village of Barnish near Maynaguri. This worship is performed in accordance with the Rajbanshi Mythology.The Devi's is immersion at the midnight of ekadashi according to the Vedic literature. There was a custom to sacrifice of goat and dove to the Goddess.[21] The worship of Ban Durga is held at the time of Ekadashi in every year at the Barnish village of Maynaguri in accordance with the Rajbanshi customs.[22]

Harihar Adhikary informed me, 'Late Hariprosad Basuniya was a zamindar. He introduced Kalipuja at first. The worship of Kali of the house of Hariprosad Basuniya was known as 'Hariprosad Basuniya Barir Puja' and later on it was known as 'Kal Singh Basuniya Barir Kalipuja'.[23] According to him, "The Basuniyas then had a total land of (80) eighty" Hals' (an unit of fifteen bigh as), comprising of the jotes of Betgara, Khagrabari, Naktabari (near Baksirdanga) and "Dhanda Simla" (near Nathula). It is also learnt that the former title of the Basuniyas was "Das". They came from the Gaibandha thana of Rangpur District (Now in Bangladesh). The title 'Basuniya' was probably given by the British.[24] The marriage of Rajbanshi society was like a social festival. Different types of customs and usages were performed at the time of marriage which were enjoyed by the relatives, invitees and the villagers.[25]

Kainagata

The worship of Kainagata is started from the previous Purnima. In this worship their forefathers are respected by sacrificing water oblation to their forefather by the Brahmana or Adhikary. *Nabanna*—this worship is observed at the time of collecting new crops. There is a custom prevailing among many of the Bengali Hindu families that they worship 'Nabanna' before eating new crops. Binapani Adhikari stated, "Baishakhi puja or worship is performed in the month of Baishakha (April-May). Bananas, Kandali etc. different types of fruits and flowers are given in this worship. Out of these, dahi (curd) and chira are also given. No Brahmana or priest is necessary to perform this worship; rather the priest of Rajbanshi community called Adhikary performed this worship.[26] Kali/Bishahari worship is performed by local priest known as Mareya or Ojha. It is significant that no Sanskrit mantra is uttered in this worship, rather the mantras are pronounced in local dialect or Rajbanshi language.This puja is sacrificed by the left hand.[27] Before performing the marriage ceremony the worship of Kulaguru, placed the east corner of the house is given and thereafter the worship of Bishahari is given. *Gochubona*-This worship is observed before growing plants of paddy in the land. At first land is prepared for growing plants of paddy, thereafter a worship called guchubona is performed in the lands. Few plants of paddy are poured these worships performed to their deity with rice, banana and other fruits. Masdal (one kind of beans), black arum and raw milk is given to the worship. *Jatrapuja*—this worship is performed in the day of Nabami of the month of Aswin (October) by giving sugarcane, lemon and other fruits and the next day, in the day of Vijoya Dasami the Jatrapuja is observed in the house. In this worship the essential instruments of the house including books have been worshiped". *Laxmi puja*—Laxmi puja is popular festivals of the Hindu Bengali. In every houses of the Hindu Bengali the Goddess mother Laxmi is observed. Like other Hindu Bengali people in the house of Rajbanshi community mother Laxmi is observed. The Rajbanshis worship with dai, chira, banana and other fruits. The trees of paddy is cut at the bottom, covered with banana leaves and kept in the kitchen"[28].

Different kinds of religious occasions are seen to be performed in the Rajbanshi society through the ancient period when rain is not seen in the rainy season as a result of which agricultural cultivation is affected. One of these festivals is 'Benger Biyo' (marriage of frog). This occasion is performed by women. A proverb is prevailing in the society of North Bengal that when frogs croak rain is falling. So for falling of rain Rajbanshi women perform the occasion of frog's marriage. Another occasion was held in the Rajbanshi society though it is not seen in the present day society that was 'Hudum Khela'. In this occasion women would go house to house in the dark of night being naked unfolding hair warning the male members of the house either they would leave the house or they would remain in the room shutting the door. The naked women in such a way entered the house and dance together in the courtyard and sang songs for falling rain.[29] According to W.W. Hunter, "A singular relic of old superstition is the worship of the God Hudum Deo.The women of a village assemble together in some distant and solitary place, no male being allowed to be present at the rites which is always performed at night, a plantain or young bamboo is stuck in the ground, and the women throwing off their garments, dance round the mystic tree, singing old songs and charms. The rite is more especially performed when there is no rain and the crops are suffering from drough."[30]

As the Rajbanshis were converted into Hindus which is referred earlier, they perform all the worship, festivals, occasions in accordance with the Hindu customs and mythology. But many of the customs, festivals and worships and rituals are found which is out of the Aryan culture. These cultures have been going on through the ancient period to the present day.

Language

George Abraham Grearson published his research report in "Linguistic Survey of India" in 1927 where he mentioned, "When we cross the river (Brahmaputra) coming from Dacca, we meet a well marked form of speech in Rangpur and the districts to its north and east. It is called Rajbansi and while undoubtedly belonging to the eastern branch has still points of difference which lead us to class it as a separate dialect."[31] He also wrote "The dialect is usually known as Rajbansi, from the tribe of that name already alluded to. It is also frequently called Rangpuri from one of the districts in which it is spoken. In the Darjeeling-Terai the dialect is influenced by the neighbouring Northern Bengali and has a special name, as a sub-dialect viz Bahe."[32]

The Rajbanshi language is a dialect of main Bengali language.[33] Provat Ranjan Sarkar stated that the language of Rajbansis of North Bengal as 'Rangpuri Bangla'.[34] Upendranath Barman stated that the Rajbanshi language is a pure Aryan language which was supported by different scholars like Hodson etc.[35] Charu Chandra Sanyal wrote, "The Rajbansis speak Bengali but it is a local dialect sometimes widely away from standard Bengali."[36]

Amusements

There are many dramas, songs, palatiya songs which were written and performed by the Rajbanshi language. The famous song of the Rajbanshi as well as of the indigenous Muslims of North Bengal and lower Assam is 'Bhwaoaiya' which is written and sung in Rajbanshi language. The 'Bhwaoaiya' songs are the themes of every aspect of the lives and hearts of Rajbanshi people. This song is divided into two categories namely 'Chatka' and 'Dariya'. These songs are composed on the basis of every aspect of the society, economy, culture, custom, religion, love, joy and pain taking place in everyday life of the Rajbanshis. Other famous songs of the Rajbanshis are 'Dotaradanga Gaan' and 'Kushan Gaan'. These songs are performed in different villages of North Bengal and lower Assam; these are performed particularly in the season of different occasions and festivals. These songs are composed on the basis of different Hindu Sastras such as Ramayana, Mahabharata and Purana. In the song, different 'Pala' or Play is performed on the basis of various aspects of the society, economy, religion and politics etc. In these songs the 'Gidal' plays the significant role. Beside the 'Gidal', the 'Dohari' and 'Chhokris' sing and dance jointly. The Gidal sings first, Dohari and Chhokris follow the song; after singing the Gidal explain the meaning of the song. The Dohari also explain it. Now-a-days, these songs and play are not seen sufficiently to perform. The people of present generation are interested to modern songs, Jatras, theaters and cinemas. In Dinajpur district one of the ancient dramas "Monai Yatra". The original writer of Monai yatra was Telenga Fakir, inhabitant of another writer was Najir Mahmud Sarkar. In Malda, Dinajpur, Bagura, Murshidabad districts of one kind of drama named Alkap was performed where evolved the various incidents of society and the story of the poor and distressed people. Another type of drama of Malda and Dinajpur districts was Gambhira remaining the story of various people and comedy.[37] Rangpur Bartaboho Patrika introduced a valuable literature and culture. Many informations and writings were published in this Patrika. It was patronised by the zamindar of Kundir of Rangpur district.[38]

In the post-colonial period for entering the modern culture indigenous people gradually accepted it. They accepted Baul, Bhatiali, Rabindra Sangit, Nazrul giti, Adhunik songs etc. Not only that nowadays the young generation people like Hindi songs, Adhunik songs, Hindi cinema instead of their traditional culture. It should be mentioned here that in spite of all these changes many indigenous people still now do not forget their traditional culture. They observed and preserved their traditional culture as their wealth and heritage.

Position of Women

Accordingly with the assimilation of Mongolian culture the Rajbanshi women hold the prestige and dignity in the society. The female were not inferior to the male. They had equal right and prestige in the society, moreover in many cases female had more honourable position than male. Females played a significant role in the Rajbanshi society in their everyday lives.

Females did their household works such as cooking, cleanliness of houses, look after their children, observes different types of worships and occasions in the scheduled dates of whole over the years, maintained various customs and ritual activities for well of their family. Out of the internal works of the family, females would go out of the houses for doing different types of works. They participated in the agricultural works in the field.

In this regard it is relevant to mention here that the female members of the jotdar families works in the land at the time of planting of paddy called 'amon dhan', though the jotdars were economically solvent. They thought it as an honourable work.

In the rich families or economically solvent families women confined themselves in the interior of the house; generally they would not come outside the house. When guest or people of outside would come to the house, they would sit in the sitting room locally known as 'Dari Ghar', where discussions were continued and they were honoured by serving them tea and betel nut called 'Gua Pan'. The women prepared the food or tea but they would not serve it because would not go to Dari Ghar; these were served by the male members of the house. Here, one point should be mentioned that after coming of guest in the house and sitting in the Dari Ghar at first they had been served betel and nut called 'Gua Pan', then other foods were served. Nowadays most of the Rajbanshi families accepted the modern culture, as such the serving of gua pan is not seen; the system of Dari ghar is not also seen in most of the houses of the Rajbanshis.

In the Rajbanshi society there was no dowry system in the traditional system of marriage. Bridegroom or his parents or guardian would not get any kind of dowry from the parents or guardian of bride, rather the father or mother or guardian of the bride would get money or wealth from the side of bridegroom at the time of marriage for which a proverb is heard still now in the Rajbanshi society that the father or mother calls the marriage of his daughter as 'Becheya Khaowa' meaning of which selling of their daughter, once as they would get money from the bridegroom at the time of marriage, so it was treated as selling their daughter. It is mentioned in the book of Subha Jyoti Roy "Ordinarily, the girl has to be paid for by the bridegroom party; the amount paid is called pan, or bride's value .... the common expression indicative of marriage is byacheya khaya meaning the selling of the girl. When a man cannot pay for a girl, he has to work in his would- be father- in- law's house as a servant, and serve out a probationary period, before he can claim the hands of the bride."[39] But, nowadays this custom is not seen in the Rajbanshi society, rather the dowry system has been prevailing among the Rajbanshis. But the word 'Beche Khaowa' is still heard in the society, particularly in the village area. As the Rajbanshis converted into Hinduism, so they accepted the ritual customs and they have been leading their lives in accordance with the Hindu Shastras or ideology in spite of maintaining many traditional customs and rituals. Regarding marriage they also accepted the Hindu laws to perform their marriage system. Subha Jyoti Roy writes, "More important than the replacement of the bride-price with dowry, or the changes in the marriage rites to more brahmanical forms, was the changed attitudes towards marriage itself which had important implications for the attitudes towards women. In the second decade of the twentieth century under the influence of the Kshatriya movement, 'protection' of married women and widows from the 'marauding' Muslims was to assume great significance".[40]

Another point is significant in relation to the Rajbanshi women that widow remarriage was prevailing in the Rajbanshi society where it was banned in the higher caste society for which Ishwar Chandra Vidyasagar fought to prevail the widow remarriage in the colonial period. Like different groups of non-Aryan people including tribal people and Muslims Rajbanshis were habituated with the widow remarriage. H. N. Chowdhury writes, 'Strictly speaking the term "widow marriage", as applied to a form of connection among the Rajvanshis, is a misnomer. The union between a widow and a man among the native Hindus in this State is no marriage at all and no ceremony is performed on the occasion'.[41] He again writes, "The lower classes of the people do not always consider the marriage tie as inviolable as it should be. Case of the same girl being married twice are not therefore rare; it often happens that a married girl is detained by her parents or other relatives for affecting a second marriage, and the husband is not allowed any access to her. This practice is not confined to the Rajbanshis alone but obtains among the Musalmans as well."[42] Subha Jyoti Roy pointed out in this regard, 'If a widow agreed to live with a man the arrangement went by the name of gao gach. A widow could also enter the house of a man with the purpose of living with him, in which case she was the pachua wife of the man. Finally, a man could enter into the house of a widow and live with her, becoming a dangua. Also, contrary to the practice in other parts of Bengal, widows were not prohibited from eating non-vegetarian food.'[43]

Identity Crisis

In the wave of time many changes have been taken place in the Rajbanshi society balancing with the multi-dimensional culture of the world, as a consequence of it many crises and problems, crisis of their ethnicity, linguistic and traditional culture have seen in the Rajbanshi society. These crises and problems were started since the colonial period for the immigration of huge number of people of different castes, religions and classes, particularly the people of higher caste or Brahmanisation imposed the Sanskritic or Bramanised culture on them, and as a result they had been losing their traditional culture.

In the post-independence period jotdari and zamindari system have been abolished by the government, as a result of it many jotdar families lost their lands and became helpless. They lost their gravity; being poor they have to spend their lives ordinarily. Many successors of the said jotdar family have been going outside the houses and working in different sectors as a labourer.[44] It is true that many Rajbangshis have taken education and become educated and serving in different places of the country positively. But, it is also true that many of the Rajbangshis having no way for their livelihood or source of income they have been working as agricultural labourer, industrial labourer, house servant in the town. Practically, it is the present scenario of the town of North Bengal, particularly of the northern portion of North Bengal that most of the labourers including men and women working on the road, house servants, helper of mason are Rajbanshis.

After partition of India in 1947, Goalpara district of undivided North Bengal was included to Assam though it was shifted to Assam in 1874 which was a part of greater North Bengal, but in 1947 there was a chance to the Rajbanshis to form a separate state for the Rajbangsis of greater North Bengal on the basis of their culture, tradition and language. Unfortunately, there was no strong movement for the demand for their own community. It is relevant to mention here that the Rajbanshis of Assam preferred to remain with Assam. So as a result of division unity of the Rajbangsis got a setback.

Linguistically, Rajbangsis had their separate language, but since the colonial period Bengalisation was started in the

Rajbangsi language, they read and write through Bengali version in their education. In the post-colonial period for the pressure of the Assamese Rajbangsis were bound to accept the Assamese as their medium of language. So, linguistically they lost their own entity.

At the time of partition in 1947 the Rangpur district, the heartland of the Rajbangsis, was also included to then East Pakistan, now in Bangladesh. Economically, socially and culturally Rangpur district was most valuable to the Rajbangsis of greater North Bengal. By losing the district they lost their gravity and heart of the community. Not only that many Rajbangsis left the district means their own country losing rights and property and after coming in this country many of them became helpless.

As a result of these incidents, many discontents and grievances have been accumulated in the mind of Rajbanshi people. They cannot forget that once they had thousand acres of lands, huge number of fishes in the ponds rivers and water-fields (bils), huge number of milk and dahi in the house, huge honey would found in the forest, they had no scarce, they had no tension.[45] Many successors of the jotdar families have become helpless losing their everything, they have been going outside the houses. It can be said that these deprivations and discontents are one of the root causes of the present socio-political tension of North Bengal.

References

1. Basu, Swaraj. Dynamics of a Caste Movement -The Rajbansis of North Bengal, 1910-1947, (Manohar Publishers & Distributers, New Delhi, 2003), p. 62.
2. Sanyal, Charu Chandra. The Rajbansis of North Bengal, (Asiatic Society, Calcutta, 1965).
3. Basu, Swaraj. Dynamics of a Caste Movement, p. 62.
4. *Ibid*, p. 21.
5. *Ibid*, p. 21.
6. Sunder, D.H.E. Survey and Settlement of the Western Duars in the District of Jalpaiguri, 1889-95, (Printed at the Bengal Secretariat Press, 1895), p. 21.
7. Hunter, W.W. A Statistical Account of Bengal, Vol. X, (Concept Publishing Company, Delhi, First Published in 1877), p. 255.

8. *Ibid*, p. 255.
9. Basu Swaraj, Dynamics of a Caste Movement, p. 62.
10. Sutradhar, Kartik Chandra, Hitasadhani Theke Greater Cooch Behar, Ekti Oitihasik Parjalochana, in Uttar Banga, Sahitya-Sanskriti, Edited by Asutosh Barman, (Sangbedan Malda, 1420 B.S), p. 48.
11. Sunder, D.H.E. Survey and Settlement of the Western Dooars, p. 48.
12. Interview with Ramesh Roy, 49 years, S/o late Santeswar Roy, Vill & P.O. Chapani, P.S. Samuktala, Dist-Jalpaiguri.
13. The author has noticed the process of making Sutka, Sidal, Chheka Shak in the house of Rajbanshi people of many villages and the author personally tasted it.
14. Chakroborty, Shitangshu Prosad, Paribartanshil Jibaner Shrote Jalpaigurir Rajbanshi Samaj, Kiratbhumi, Jalpaiguri Zela Sankalan, Protham Khanda, (Jalpaiguri, 1995, Edited by Arabinda Kar), p. 192.
15. Interview with Jagat Singh Barman, 64 years, Takoamari, Rashik Bill, Cooch Behar.
16. Interview with Kaitalu Barman, 65 years,Takoamari, P.O. Rashik Bill, Dist. Cooch Behar.
17. Barman, Upendra Nath, Rajbanshi Khsatriya Jatir itihas (In Bengali), (Jalpaiguri, 1388 B.S).
18. Interview with Bimal Roy, teacher, Gomirapara High High School, Berubari, Jalpaiguri.
19. Sanyal, Charu Chandra, The Rajbansis of North Bengal, pp. 27-32.
20. Basu, Birendra Prosad. Dev Deuler Des, Jalpaiguri, p. 26.
21. Uttarbanga Sambad, 16 Oct, 2013.
22. *Ibid.*
23. Interview with Harihar Adhikary, 65, S/O Murari Mohan Adhikary, Village Bolbari, Maynaguri, Jalpaiguri.
24. *Ibid.*
25. *Ibid.*
26. Interview with Binapani Adhikari, 55, C/o Harihar Adhikari, Domohoni, Bolbarigram, Moynaguri, dated 17.10.13.

66. *Ibid.*

28. *Ibid.*
29. Prodhan, Amar Roy, Jiban Nadir Banke Banke, (Sangbedan Malda, 2012, Edited by Ananda Gopal Ghosh and Kartik Chandra Sutradhar), p. 29.

30. Hunter, W.W. A Statistical Account of Bengal.
31. *Ibid*, p. 163.
32. *Ibid.*
33. Interview with Bimal Roy, op.cit.
34. Sarkar, Provat Ranjan. Bangla O Bangali, 1988, p. 89.
35. Barman, Upendra Nath, Rajbansi Kshatriyo Jatir itihas, p. 42.
36. Sanyal, Charu Chandra. The Rajbansis of North Bengal.
37. Interview with Bimal Roy, op. cit.
38. Sufi, Motahar Hossein. Bangla Sahitye Rangpurer Abadan, (Bangla academy Dhaka), 54.
39. Roy, Subhajyoti. Transformations on the Bengal Frontier, Jalpaiguri 1765-1948 (Routledge Curzon, London, 2002), 57.
40. *Ibid*, p. 58.
41. Chowdhury, H.N. Cooch Behar State and its Land Revenue Settlement, (Cooch Behar State Press, Cooch Behar, 1903), pp. 145-146.
42. *Ibid*, 146.
43. Roy, Subhajyoti. Transformation on the Bengal Frontier, p. 58.
44. Interview with Dhirendra Nath Roy, 68, S/o Late Hrishikanta Roy, Gaburapara, Belakoba, Jalpaiguri.
45. Interview with Prosanta Kumar Singha, 74, S/o Late Nagendra Nath Singha, Sajnapara, P.O. Srirampara, Dist. Jalpaiguri.

4

The Marginalised Potters of Nongpok Sekmai in Manipur

Keisham Ingocha Singh

Introduction

Pottery is one of the oldest human skills or art forms which require a lot of training and hard work to create items of cultural relevance. It is the measure of a country's civilisation and is called the lyric of handicrafts. The antiquity of a place is decided by the pottery unearthed there (Vaishnavi Bala, 2009). Clay is most abundant of all materials and as such the earlier men were found associated with the clay. The development of craftsmanship called pottery was made out of necessity during his course of life. It was some accidental fire, which produced the knowledge that clay hardened on firing and this shape stayed for all time (Gurcharan, 1979:13).

In India, the tradition of pottery making is very ancient with pots for storage of water and grains always in demand. It is believed that Indian pottery began during the Indus Valley Civilisation (Viswanathan, n.d.) and has continued to evolve through the ages. There is proof of pottery making, both handmade and wheel-made, from all over India. Manipur (a state in northeast India) is noted for her rich traditions and culture which find expressions in their various dance forms, music, dress, and other customary practices. In the hoary past man lived in wilderness solely dependent on Mother Nature. He started settled cultivation and domestication of animals when he reached the threshold of civilisation. During this period as it was essential man started making containers for various purposes: to store his food and later for cooking (Brajeshwori, 2002:29). Pottery in Manipur, therefore, is a very old art that has been in existence since time immemorial. The pottery exclusive to Manipur is in a perfect unification with other aspects of the total system, adjusting physical environment, social life and social process for the continuity of social structure (Laishram *et al.*, 1999). Most of the pots are handmade and are of different colours (red, dark red and black). Traditionally, pottery making in Manipur is practised by women without using wheel. In the valley area, the tradition of the development of pottery through the handling of clay is one of the earliest skills known to the *Chakpas*[1] of Manipur. From time immemorial lumps of clay were hand-moulded to form containers, toys and idols. This form of craft is an expression of nature, creativity and values of their way of life. As found today, this craft is restricted to some villages which are inhabited by the Chakpas and women belonging to this community are known for their expertise in making different types of pots meant for ritualistic and ceremonial purposes. Places associated with pottery making in Manipur are Andro, Sekmai, Chairen, Thongjao, Nungbi and Oinam. Nongpok Sekmai village in Thoubal district of Manipur (where the present study was carried out) is strictly associated with making pots of red ochre colour (Lisam, 2011) called *uyan* which is a flaring mouthed globular curry-pot having fish bone pattern and paint of *kuhi*[2] (*Pasania pachyphyla*) solution at the shoulder region.

With the development of science and technology, rapid urbanisation of twentieth century world, a drastic change in the world economy came into existence. As a consequence of globalisation, many ethnic groups are compelled to leave their ancestral occupation to cope with the changed economic structure. People switched over to other economic activities which can provide them a better socio-economic life (Medhi *et al.*, 2012). Owing to the rapid changes taking place in the economic front, Indian artisans and craftsmen are worried that their trades will die out one day. Owing to the reasons cited, pottery in India and everywhere is dying a slow death. In China, the pottery craft has come under risk of disintegrating as the small industry has been faced with low efficiency problems and weak profit margins ("Pottery craft a dying art", 2013). Manipur is no exception as far as decline in the age old tradition of pottery making is concerned. According to Lisam (ibid), "In the past, pottery was in great demand, each family needed them in rituals, festive occasions and also for daytoday domestic use. However with the advent of metal utensils in the nineteenth century, the pottery industry in the state has declined. Unavailability of suitable clay, lack of expert potters, custom of producing pots only during season when there is less rain, the tedious work of firing are some factors causing hindrance to the tradition of pottery making. As the financial returns of the production of Manipuri pottery is quite negligible and unless proper guidance and financial assistance are provided the pottery of Manipur is on the verge of extinction".

Review of literature on status of pottery indicates marginalisation which is a slippery and multi-layered concept. Whole societies can be marginalised at the global level while classes and communities can be marginalised from the dominant social order. Similarly, ethnic groups, families or individuals can be marginalised within localities. To a certain extent, marginalisation is a shifting phenomenon, linked to social status. When a craft dies, artisans and their business die resulting in disappearance of an entire history, a legacy, a tradition and knowledge. Trades become marginal when they cannot enter into the arena of existing market economy thereby making groups engaged in the occupation economically marginalised. Here, economic marginalisation means being economically insignificant. Economically marginalised people are likely to have tenuous involvement in the economy as there is no definite or constant income of their own. Their income may be from different sources depending upon the occupational traits they hold on. It is not unusual for people to combine, or move between, these various ways of getting money in their struggle for survival. The meager amount that they earn out of the occupation is not enough for sustenance. It is because of the market situation where the incoming superior readymade items always attract the customers to choose and buy leaving behind their inferior products. Marginality is an experience affecting millions of people throughout the world. Poverty, dependency, and feelings of shame are everyday aspects of economic dislocation and social marginalisation (Burton & Kagan, in press). Peter Leonard (1984,

p. 180) has tried to sum up social marginality as *'being outside the mainstream of productive activity and / or social reproductive activity'.*

Study area

Nongpok Sekmai is a pottery village in Manipur which is situated at a distance of 35 km. east of Imphal in Thoubal District of Manipur. The village is bounded on the east by Shikhong, on the north and west by Gwarok Maring village and on the south by Ukhongshang and Salungpham. This village enjoys a climate similar to the valley areas of Manipur. According to Census of India (1991:9), the Sikhong-Sekmai area which is an extension of the Eastern Hill system belongs to the Barail Series and Simsang formation (Garo hills). One can reach the village from Imphal via Yairipok or Charangpat. The Sekmai River flows down towards the northwestern side and joins the Thoubal River at Chandrakhong. Sikhong bazar, the most immediate market place at Nongpok Sekmai, is the primary outlet of their products— the earthen pots. Most of their products are transported to the nearby markets by various means. At present Imphal-bound buses and other public conveyances transport earthen pots to the main market in Imphal town. As the village falls under the "notified areas" of the Government of Manipur, it has a local self-government in the form of Sikhong Sekmai Nagar Panchayat which is divided into nine wards and pottery making is confined to only three wards i.e. ward Nos. 2, 3 and 4.

The society consists of seven *yeks*[3] in different proportions" Khuman (71 households), Mangang (49 households), Angom (48 households), Luwang (42 households), Moirang (20 households) and Kha-Nganba (19 households). The presence of all the seven clans of the Meitei (the largest community in Manipur) is a clear indication of the self contained nature of the village. The society being patrilineal and patriarchal, men play important roles in various social activities and engage in major economic pursuits. Marriage within the village has been a regular practice although inter-village marriages are on the rise these days.

Distinctiveness of Nongpok Sekmai, in terms of religious beliefs and practices is discernible by the presence of three local deities (*umang lais*[4]) called Nongpok Ningthou, Ikop Ningthou and Sawang Ningthou. The people of Shikhong areas worship

Nongpok Ningthou while the people of Lilakambong, Makha Leikai and Mayai Leikai (three localities in the settlement area) worship Ikop Ningthou. Sawang Ningthou is worshipped by the people of Awang Leikai.

The village is no more an isolated as the modern means of transportation and communication have reached the village. Movement of people from one place to another place for various purposes is increasing due to the emerging transport facilities. Apart from this, communication keeps them informed about the world's events and trends thus bringing in positive changes in the life of the people of Nongpok Sekmai by enhancing job and education facilities. The ultimate result is the improvement of their socio-economic conditions.

Although traditional pottery making plays an indispensable economic and socio-cultural role within the Nongpok Sekmai society, the potters who are women (both married and unmarried) have lost their earlier importance as makers of pots of royal dignity. In the olden days, pots from this village were used in *Walhoushang* (the royal kitchen) because of which they occupied a social status equal to that of other groups including the Meitei. Traditionally, the potters of Nongpok-Sekmai were skilled *uyan* makers. Life of the people revolved round the pots so much so that all transactions were made in terms of "*pot*"[5] (see Table 4.1) and values were measured depending on the size of the pot. But today the potters are facing difficulty in keeping the tradition

Fig. 1. *Kambi.*

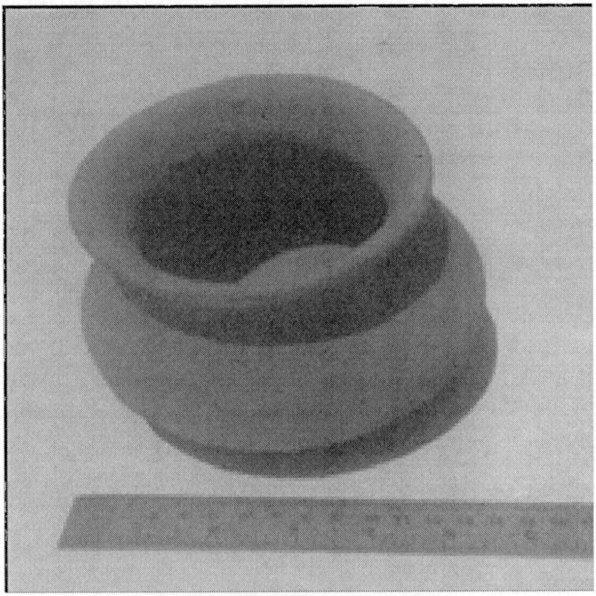

Fig. 2. ***Sangom chaphu.***

Fig. 3. ***Uyan.***

Table 4.1: Unit of measurement in terms of pot

Sl. No.	*Unit*	*Type / Name of pot*	*No. of pot*
1.	1 *Pot*	Small pot (*Shangom chaphu* – pot for milk)	100
2.	1 *Pot*	Medium pot (*Uyan* type – pot for cooking curry)	50
3.	1 *Pot*	Big pot (Water storing pot)	20

alive. Despite its potentialities for self-employment, the number of potters in Nongpok Sekmai has reduced drastically and new types of pottery like *kambi*[6] and *sangom chaphu*[7] have started featuring in the industry indicating a struggle for existence.

Aims of the study

Keeping in view of the observable changes in the pottery making tradition in Nongpok Sekmai, the present study aims

- To give a socio demographic profile of the potters in Nongpok Sekmai.
- To assess the status of pottery and potters in Nongpok Sekmai.
- To find out the reasons or factors responsible for economic marginalisation.

Significance of the Study

Few ethnographic studies of pottery villages in Manipur have been attempted. However no anthropological study addressing marginalisation of potter groups has been undertaken. This study is an attempt to explore the present socioeconomic status of the potters of Nongpok Sekmai from anthropological perspective. Such a study may provide a body of knowledge that promotes logical thinking and generalisation for the sustainable development of marginal trade like pottery in the national context. The finding of this study may be a contributing factor for planning and development strategies and the knowledge gained from this research may contribute while framing economic policies and development for the artisans in the national level. This study may help in conserving the traditional wisdom of the occupation and also in paving the way of improving the tradition in the changing scenario.

Methodology

Primary data were collected directly from the field using four research tools such as in-depth interviews, household survey, observation and focus group discussion. A number of questions for each tool were formulated to achieve the desired objectives of the study. In-depth interviews of every potter in the village were conducted with the help of interview schedules regarding the present occupational shift and the trend of socioeconomic marginalisation. Stratified random technique based on their income has also been applied for assessing detailed information about their social life in relation to pottery occupation. The schedules were pre-tested before administering in the field. The interviewees were given a uniform instruction highlighting the purpose and objectives of conducting the interview.

Both qualitative and quantitative methods have been used data collection. As the present study focuses on the social life of the potters, socio-demographic data which included political life, occupation, language, religion, education, social organisation and pottery were collected through survey. Four focus group interviews were also conducted among the potters. A checklist was used to guide the focus group interview. The focus group interview was employed to assess their group characters and behaviours of self-rejection from the mainstream and the factors that led them to it. Four to six potters attended in each FGI whose names were not recorded though responses during the sessions were tape recorded. Recorded data were sorted and analysed with simple statistical method.

Findings

Pottery making is a traditional occupation which is confined to females. Out of 612 women, only 59 (9.64 per cent) of 21 to 74 years are engaged in pottery. Maximum number of potters (35.60 per cent) is found in the age range 50 to 59 closely followed by women in 60 to 69 years (28.81 per cent). There is distinct decrease in number among the younger and older age groups. 59.32 per cent of them are illiterate, 16.95 per cent read and write, 20.34 per cent read upto tenth class and the rest read upto class XII. Monthly individual income of the potters is very low with 71.19 per cent earning a mere amount of Rs 2677 (Table 4.2).

Table 4.2: Demographic Profile

Indicators	*Classification*		*f.*	*%*
Age	20-29		4	6.78
	30-39		4	6.78
	40-49		10	16.95
	50-59		21	35.60
	60-69		17	28.81
	70+		3	5.08
Literacy	Illiterate		35	59.32
	Read and write		10	16.95
	Under Matric		12	20.35
	Upto- XII		2	3.39
Marital Status	Unmarried		1	1.69
	Married		58	98.30
	Married	Living with husband	40	68.96
		Separated	1	1.72
		Widow	17	29.31
Family Type	Nuclear		24	40.68
	Joint		25	42.37
	Single		1	1.69
	Broken		9	15.25
*Income	= 17,850		0	0.00
	8,925 – 17,849		0	0.00
	5,355 – 8,924		5	8.47
	2,678 – 5,354		12	20.34
	= 2,677		42	71.19
Housing	Traditional		6	10.16
	Slightly Modern		53	89.83
	Modern		0	0.00

* Prasad's income classification revised for 2014 using real-time update tool.

Traditionally, pottery was the primary income generating occupation among women. However, the study recorded 19 occupations other than pottery among women (Table 3.3).

Table 3: Occupational traits of female (612)

Sl. No.	*Occupational Trait*	*f.*	*P. C.*
1.	Farmer	12	1.96
2.	Housewife	191	31.21
3.	Potter	59	9.64
4.	Weaving	35	5.72
5.	Embroidery	12	1.96
6.	Dress designing	1	0.16
7.	Beautician	2	0.33
8.	Social worker	1	0.16
9.	Rice mill owner	2	0.33
10.	Chengkok shubi	2	0.33
11.	Shop keeper	2	0.33
12.	Business	5	0.81
13.	Hotel manageress	3	0.49
14.	Vegetable vendor	3	0.49
15.	House work	2	0.33
16.	Beautician	2	0.33
17.	Teacher	7	1.14
18.	Asha worker	2	0.33
19.	Angalwadi worker	3	0.49
20.	Nurse	1	0.16
21.	Student	181	29.57
22.	Too old to work	15	2.45
23.	Too young to work	62	10.13
24.	Unemployed	7	1.14
	Total	612	99.99

The type of pot manufactured today is no longer restricted to the traditional *uyan*. The most commonly manufactured types of pot are the traditional *uyan, kambi* and *shangom chaphu* using the turn-table method. In most of the households, the traditional *uyan* has been replaced by vessels of metal and other alloys like pressure cooker, sauce pans etc.

Prasad's social classification revised for 2014 using real-time update tool, was used for the socioeconomic status classification for the potters of Nongpok Sekmai. Maximum number of potters (71.19 per cent) is found in the fifth (Lower) social class, which is

Table 4.1: Socio-economic Status of Potters

Sl. No.	*Social Class*	*Classification of per capita income / month (as on January 2015)*	*f.*	*P.C.*
1.	I (Upper Class)	= 17,850	0	0.00
2.	II (Upper Middle Class)	8,925 – 17,849	0	0.00
3.	III (Lower Middle Class)	5,355 – 8,924	5	8.47
4.	IV (Upper Lower Class)	2,678 – 5,354	12	20.34
5.	V (Lower)	= 2,677	42	71.19
		Total	**59**	**100.00**

followed by social class IV (Upper Lower Class) (20.34 per cent). The remaining 8.47 per cent only can attain III (Lower Middle Class) social status (Table 4.4).

The society though endogamous traditionally is slowly becoming exogamous. Out of the total 58 married women, 16 are from different adjoining villages like Ingourok, Hijam Khunou, Ukhongsang, Chandrakhong, Pitra, Charangpat, Icham Khunou, Keirembikhok, Shikhong and Kakmayai. These villages are situated within a radius of 2-5 kilometers from the village. Some women are from still farther places like Wangjing, Lamding, Thouba and Tentha (Thoubal district) and Kwakeithel and Kanto (Imphal west district) (Table 4.5).

Table 4.5: Native Village of married women

Sl. No	*District*	*Name of village*
1.	Thoubal district	Ingourok, Hijam Khunou, Ukhongsang, Chandrakhong, Pitra, Charangpat, Icham Khunou, Keirembikhok, Shikhong, Kakmayai, Wangjing, Lamding, Thouba and Tentha
2.	Imphal West	Kwakeithel and Kanto

It is also observed from the finding that there are skilled and unskilled potters in the village. Out of 59 potters, 69.49 per cent are skilled potters and the remaining 30.50 per cent are unskilled potters (Table 4.6).

Table 4.6: Frequency distribution of Skilled and Unskilled Potters

Sl. No.	*Occupational Trait*	*f.*	*P. C.*
1.	Skilled	41	69.49
2.	Unskilled	18	30.50

Kamphang situated at the foothill of Gwarok hill on the western side of the village is the place from where raw material is procured. But today some potters collect clay from another site at Ingourok and pots are manufactured by hand and beater technique. Pot making starts by preparing dough of clay. This is done by kneading clay and *nungjreng* (coarse sand) in the proportion of 3:1. The prepared dough is then rolled on a wooden plank using both hands to make a solid cylinder. Then the rod is flattened into a thin slab by pressing the paste on the plank. Curving followed by joining the two shorter ends, it is turned into a tube. One of the open ends of the tube is also closed either by squeesing or adding another round cake of the clay paste. The neck and rim are made with a piece of wet coarse cloth and by the joint digital movement. Shaping of the body of the pot is done with a wooden beater. The pot is kept either on the *Lepsum,* a wooden prop or knees of the potters. The potter taps with the wooden beater on the outer surface and force of the beater is restricted from the inner wall with a biconvex or oval shaped stone held by the other hand. The pot is then dried in the shady area for about 3-5 hrs. There is a second and final shaping. Then the pots are again dried in the shady areas for about five to seven days. Firing is done in open air with straw.

The village is well connected with Imphal and other neighbouring villages. Imphal bound public vehicles ply from

Table 4.7: Modern Communication gadgets possessed by potters/families of potters

Sl. No.	*Item*		*f.*	*P. C.*
1.	Mobile phone	Have	51	86.44
		Have not	8	13.55
	Total		59	99.99
2.	T. V. Set	Have	29	49.15
		Have not	30	50.84
	Total		59	99.99
3.	Radio	Have	46	77.96
		Have not	13	22.03
	Total		59	99.99
4.	DTH	Have	5	8.47
		Have not	54	91.52
	Total		59	99.99

early morning till late evening after every 15 minutes from Shikhong bazaar, the main market in the village. Numerous auto rickshaws are also serving as means of communication with other villages and smaller townships like Yairipok bazaar and Thoubal bazaar. Means of communication is good as the village has been exposed to modernity and globalisation. Out of 59 potters, 86.44 per cent own mobile phones (either by the potters or one of the members of the family) and the remaining 13.55 per cent do not have. Regarding about the T. V. set, 49.15 per cent of the potters family have T. V. set in their family and the remaining 50.84 per cent of family do not have. Nearly one by fifth of the families have radio with 77.96 per cent and only 22.03 per cent do not. Only 8.47 per cent have acquired DTH pay channels among the potters family (Table 4.7).

Discussion

The above findings suggest the traditional *uyan* manufacturing is no more a sustainable livelihood system in Nongpok Sekmai. Decreased demand of products, low socioeconomic status, decreased number of women with traditional knowledge, inadequate raw material, preference of modern occupation, traditional technology and improved means of communication are identified as the factors behind their socioeconomic marginalisation.

(i) Decreased demand of products

Fast decline in the demand for the traditional *uyan* both within and without the village has put the potters in a difficult situation. The introduction of products of modern technologies such as ceramics, plastic and metallic utensils which are more durable, attractive and cost effective is affecting economic status of the potters. "Many families now prefer to buy aluminum utensils rather than earthen pots" says one of the participants in a FGI (FGI-2: 17/10/14: Mayai Leikai/N.S.). The tradition is greatly challenged by the inevitable replacement and under this circumstance potters have lost and are still losing their traditional rural markets and their position within the community. In an attempt to save the traditional knowledge from extinction and also to provide income to the illiterate and poorly educated potters, other types of pots like platter, decorative items, piggy bank and flower pot are manufactured.

(ii) Low socio-economic status

Socio-economic status (SES) is an economic and sociological combined total measure of a person's work experience and of an individual's or family's economic and social position in relation to others, based on income, education and occupation. When analysing a family's SES, the household income, earners' education and occupation are examined, as well as combined income, versus with an individual, when their own attributes are assessed (NCES, 2008). Literacy in the village compared to the earlier generation has improved. Improvement in literacy is a good social change. However, the present day potters being low in educational level as compared to the younger generation have limited scope to earn a respectable income from better paid jobs, governmental or non-governmental. Regarding about this situation one participant stated, "I have no other option except pot making because I'm illiterate and also old" (FGI-3: 20/10/14: Awang Leikai/N.S.). As the level of literacy increases, the younger generations become more inclined to the salaried jobs leaving behind the traditional occupation. "The literate younger have wider range of other occupational traits leaving behind the traditional occupation" said one of the participants in a FGI (FGI-3: 21/10/14: Awang Leikai/N.S.). Another woman participant lamented, "My children have not followed into this profession and I will not continue much longer as I am becoming old" (FGI-3: 21/10/14: Awang Leikai/N.S.). Only individuals who cannot enter into the arena of the modern world glue into the traditional occupation. "We are poor. We have no other option to earn money as I am illiterate and old" (FGI-3: 20/10/14: Awang Leikai/N.S.), said one participant. Since pot making is a traditionally inherited knowledge which requires no educational qualification, the potters did not give much importance to education when pottery existed as a flourishing trade. Today they are unable to earn enough through pot making and yet unable to switch occupation.

As most of the potters have very low income and no or low educational qualification, their socio-economic status is low. "I can't carry on. There is no money in this anymore. Many of us are leaving the jobs. At least we can make better money elsewhere. And the government has not helped at all." (FGI-4: 22/10/14: Awang Leikai/N.S.), said one of the participant in a

FGI. Because of this status, they are not able to maintain a respectable living standard and therefore voluntarily marginalise themselves from the main stream. They avoid company of better placed families and individuals as the difference becomes distinct especially at the time of making contributions for ceremonial, religious and social gatherings. They live with a low profile and become insignificant.

(iii) Decreased number of women with traditional knowledge

Women are in general keepers of cultural traditions and knowledge. They build strong communities through supporting religious functions, producing handicrafts, using natural medicines, wearing indigenous traditional dress and performing indigenous songs and dances. Roles of women in maintaining intangible heritage are of particular significance, and encompass what may be described as fundamental domains and expressions of cultural heritage, which are very often central to maintaining cultural identity. In Nongpok Sekmai, potters are women. Women born and brought up in the village are familiar with the traditional knowledge and hence can carry forward the tradition. "I have been born and brought up from this village. As far as I remember, almost all the families in this village had been engaged in this occupation. But now only a few of us retain this occupation" (FGI-3: 20/10/14: Awang Leikai/N.S.). Today, partners from outside the group are slowly making entry into the village. This has resulted in a gradual decrease in the number of women with knowledge of the traditional occupation. These women try their hands at other occupations to supplement the family income and some are engaged in pot making as unskilled artisans. Others have opted for small scale business like vegetable vendor, dress designing, beautician, teacher, asha[8] worker, anganwadi[9] worker and nurse. Regarding about the decrease number of individual participanting into the occupation, one participant commented, "My children have not followed into this profession and I will not continue much longer as I am old" (FGI-3: 21/10/14: Awang Leikai/ N.S.). "The younger generation does not want to joint this occupation because it is tedious job, less profit and dirty" (FGI-3: 21/10/14: Awang Leikai/N.S.). The decline in the number of skilled potters greatly affects the quality and quantity of goods.

Further there is no scope to train the younger generation as most of them do not find the occupation lucrative, hence young unmarried women have more or less stopped participation in the traditional occupation. "The younger generation does not want to joint this occupation because it is tedious job, less profit and dirty" (FGI-3: 21/10/14: Awang Leikai/N.S.).

(iv) Inadequate raw material

Production is impossible without raw materials. Kamphang was the place from where good clay was procured for making *uyan*. Due to continuous digging, today this site can no longer supply sufficient raw material leading to retardation in the rate of manufacturing. As an alternative means, clay from another site known as Ingourok is used. But the quality of clay is not suitable for *uyan* making. People look for quality in a product and the sub-standard quality of *uyan* made of clay from Ingourok has failed to convince buyers as quality cannot be compromised.

(v) Traditional technology

Pottery in Nongpok Sekmai is produced solely using traditional technology. One potter said, "We still follow the traditional method of making pots" (FGI-1: 14/10/14: Makha Leikai/N.S.). Owing to use of outdated technology, production is possible only during season when there is less rain. The seasonal mode of production does not guarantee regular income throughout the year. Such a condition makes survival difficult.

(v) Improved means of communication

In the past, the village remained remote with limited means of communication with the outside world. Improved means of communication brings remote populations/groups close to other groups. Women in the village have started seeing a life better than what they had been seeing. Exposure to better opportunities and better living standards has invariably marginalised the traditional trade as more and more women have become aware of better occupational opportunities.

Conclusion

The potters of Nongpok Sekmai are struggling for survival in an era of globalisation where culturally important items are fast losing significance. It is only because of demands that markets survive. In a village like Nongpok Sekmai where change in economic sector is rapidly taking place, gradual decline of a less profitable trade such as pottery comes as no surprise. Though the tradition has not become extinct, possibilities of extinction cannot be undermined as unavailability of suitable clay, lack of expert potters, customs of producing only with simple technology and only during favourable season, low financial return, better job avenues etc have emerged as factors for economic marginalisation of potters. The study has also revealed the helplessness of potters who are caught between tradition and modernity, who are trying their best to produce and sell at markets where the goods are no longer in demand, who are trying to use their skill in designing items which may attract buyers.

Recommendations

Traditions need to be preserved. But when survival becomes difficult, people tend to compromise. Occupational shift becomes the only solution and when such a shift takes place, age old traditions die. Death of a tradition marks the disappearance of a knowledge which had been transmitted and carried forward through generations. If such compromises continue, the cultural identity is at risk. There is every need to preserve traditional knowledge in general and the pottery making knowledge of Nongpok Sekmai in particular. Some suggestions which may hopefully check complete marginalisation and eventually extinction of pottery making in Nongpok Sekmai are:

- Government intervention to promote the trade by giving training to artisans to improve quality, quantity and design of their products to be competitive in local or national market.
- Workshops on saving time, resource and capital will enhance the trade.
- Diverse groups of community members should be motivated to make combined effort to preserve the knowledge of cultural pride.
- Enhancing the quality of machineries and organising proper training to develop the creativity and skill will surely help in preserving the tradition.
- Employment opportunities to the new generation and ultimately uplifting the socio-economic condition of the potters will attract participation in the trade.

- Government supported loan facilities will save the potters from desperate situations and thereby stop them from shifting occupation.

References

Burton, Mark, and Carole Kagan. "Marginalisation." In *Community Psychology: In pursuit of wellness and liberation,* edited by Isaac Prilleltensky and Geoff Nelson, in press. www.compsky.org.uk.

China Daily. "Pottery craft a dying art." August 7, 2013. http://www.chinadaily.com.cn/life/2013-08/07/content_16877838.htm (accessed February 20, 2015).

Hodson, Callan T. *The Meitheis - A Study of the Tribe of the BrahmaputraValley.* India: Obscure Press pub., 2006.

Laishram, Imoba, Thiyam Rabikanta, and Chirom Rajketan. *Pottery in Manipur.* Imphal: Mutua Museum, 1999.

Leonard, Peter. *Personality and Ideology.* London: Macmillan, 1984.

Lisam, Khomdon Singh. *Encyclopaedia of Manipur* 3. New Delhi: Kalpaz Publication, 2011.

Maibam, Brojeshwori Devi. *History of Pottery Technology in Manipur: A Historical Study,* Unp.Ph.D. Thesis. Canchipur: Manipur University, 2002.

Medhi, Bishmita, Bijay Singh Mipun, and Sailajananda Saikia. "Changing Trend of Occupation among the Brass Artisan Moria Community of Brahmaputra Valley, with special Reference to Kamrup District." *IOSR Journal of Humanities and Social Science (JHSS)* 5 (2012), no. 5: 26-30. www.iosrjournals.org.

Director of Census Operations, Manipur. *Census of India 1991,* series 9. Manipur, 1996.

Moirangthem, Kirti. "Archeological study of the Chakpa." In *Manipur, Past and Present: The Heritage and Ordeals of a Civilisation* 4, edited by Naorem S. Singh, 425. New Delhi: Mittal Publishers, 2005.

Sharma, Rahul. "Revision of Prasad's social classification and provision of an online tool for real-time updating." *South Asian J Cancer* 2 (2013), no. 3:157.

Singh, Gurcharan. *Pottery in India.* N. Delhi: Vikas Publishing House, 1971.

U.S. Department of Education. *National Center for Educational Statistics,* 2008. http://nces.ed.gov/programs/coe/glossary/s.asp

Vaishnavi Bala. "Pottery: The lost Indian art." *Merinews,* November 4, 2009. http://www.merinews.com/article/pottery-the-lost-indian-art/15787518.shtml&cp (accessed February 20, 2015).

Viswanathan, Priya. "Tied to the Past Traditional Professions of India." www.dollsofindia.com (accessed January 30, 2015).

End Notes

1. Naorem, Sanajaoba, *Manipur, Past and Present: The Heritage and Ordeals of a Civilisation* 4. (New Delhi: Mittal Pub., 2005), p. 425.
2. Laishram Imo et. al., *Pottery in Manipur* (Imphal: Mutua Museum Pub., 1999), p. 30.
3. Thomas C. Hodson, *The Meitheis - A Study of the Tribe of the BrahmaputraValley* (India: Obscure Press pub., 2006), p. 85.
4. Lisham Khomdon, *Encyclopedia of Manipur 3* (New Delhi: Gyan Publishing House, 2011), p. 338.
5. *Pot* is a unit of measurement applied by local potters to indicate a bagful of pots.
6. *Kambi* – earthen plate used in ritual and social ceremonies by the Meiteis.
7. *Sangom chapu* – earthen pot for storing milk.
8. Accredited Social Health Activist (ASHA) one of the key components of the National Rural Health Mission is to provide every village in the country with a trained female community health activist ASHA.
9. Anganwadi Worker, a lady selected from the local community, is a community based frontline honorary worker of the ICDS Programme. She is also an agent of social change, mobilising community support for better care of young children, girls and women.

II

Ethnic Identity and Marginality

5

Assam as a Settler State: Contextualising Identity and Social Conflicts within a Colonial – Settler Colonial Paradigm

Sanjib Goswami

Introduction

The news of a major communal riot between indigenous Bodo people and Bengali Muslims migrants in Assam was reported in the BBC on 23rd July 2012 with a headline: "Thousands flee rioting in Indian state of Assam".[1] Within a few days, further media reports indicated that the rioting had led to nearly a hundred people being declared dead.[2]

As the violence spread to other districts, the state remained tense and the army was called in to control the rioting with shoot-at-sight orders. Several media reports also reported that nearly half a million people had become homeless or were displaced in these riots. A report on the riot by Subir Bhowmik of the BBC mentioned that the riots were ignited by infiltration of outsiders into the Bodo areas. This, he said, led to ethnic tension between the state's indigenous population and Bengali Muslim immigrants from Bangladesh.[3] Changing demography, loss of land and livelihood and the intensified competition for political power has been adding a deadly potency to the migration issue in Assam. The question, he went on to say, revolved around who has a right to stay in Assam.

Assam has witnessed several violent incidents in the past. In the Bodoland Territorial Area District (BTAD) itself, there were four major disturbances between 1993 and 1998 that had resulted in the death of over 300 persons and displacement of nearly half a million people.[4] Likewise, there were several other communal riots when the Assamese people clashed with either the Bengali Hindu or the Bengali Muslim migrants. In 1983, the Nellie massacre is another example of immigrant – indigenous clashes in Assam where nearly 1,383 people were initially killed in just a matter of few hours.[5] Media reports suggest that over 20,000 people have died in different violent incidents over the last few decades in the state.[6]

Earlier, there had also been several indigenous movements in Assam, especially when the Naga, Mizo and Khasis communities struggled for statehood and clashed with the Assamese community. During 1960-61 and later in 1972, Assam also witnessed the language riots between the Assamese community and Bengali Hindus when several lives were lost. In the recent past, there has also been reports of violence between indigenous communities themselves, most notable being the Karbi – Dimasa clashes of 2005-06; the Rabha – Garo clashes of 2011; the Bodo – Adivasi clashes of 2014 and the clashes between different factions of the Bodo and Karbi communities. During all these conflicts and strife, the state also witnessed the growth of militancy as a corollary to the other movements that were going on.

Militancy in Assam started since independence. The first of the militant group was the National Socialist Council of Nagaland (NSCN) that struggled for an independent Nagaland. Later, the militancy problem became acute and endemic with the Assam Agitation, when the United Liberation Front of Assam (ULFA) was established in 1979 and wanted Assam to secede from India. Further, separatist groups also began to form along ethnic lines. For example, the National Democratic Front of Bodoland (NDFB) and the Bodo Liberation Tigers (BLT), both demanded more autonomy to the Bodo community while organisations such as the Dima Halam Daogah (DHD) and Karbi Liberation Peoples Tigers (KLPT) struggled for the Dimasa and Karbi communities respectively. As violence thus became intense since 1980, Assam was declared a disturbed area and was brought under the

Assam Disturbed Areas Act 1955. The Armed Forces Special Powers Act was made applicable in 1980 which gave special powers to the army to operate in a civilian setting to control violence. With the increasing socio-political polarisations in the region since 1947, as many as 32 militant / extremist organisations were operating in Assam by the turn of the century.[7] It is thus seen that Assam presents a complex picture of inter as well as intra community conflicts laced with militancy. I therefore argue that by framing Assam in a settler colonial context we can have a better historically grounded and inclusive analysis of the conflict situation in the state. But before I elaborate on the settler colonial framework, I present briefly some of existing scholarship and approaches that analyses and interprets these conflicts.

Interpreting Conflicts in Assam

Scholarship on the conflicts and migration issues in Assam predominantly consists of journalistic write-ups, scholarly writings by researchers, or reports of the government. Some of the prominent scholars whose writings on contemporary Assam assume importance include Amalendu Guha[8], Hiren Gohain[9], Sanjib Baruah[10], Yasmin Saikia[11] and Sanjay Hazarika[12] Sanjoy Hazarika, amongst others.

One approach on analysing these conflicts is to posit it within colonialism and argue that it was the colonial state that created fissures in society that has led to the conflicts. In his book *Planter's Raj to Swaraj: Freedom Struggle and Electoral Politics in Assam 1826 – 1947,* Amalendu Guha states that it was the colonial state that provided the initial stimuli for the growth of community consciousness among the Assamese by first encouraging immigration into Assam from neighbouring Bengal and then by imposing Bengali as the official language of the province. The need to induct outsiders into Assam, such as tea labourers and Muslim agriculturist, apparently owing to the acute manpower shortage in Assam magnified the problems in post-colonial period. Guha identifies the rise of Assamese identity consciousness as a result primarily of economic reasons in relation to the presence of immigrants.[13] Likewise, Hiren Gohain in his book *Assam: A Burning Question* also attributes the beginning of community consciousness in Assam to colonial decisions that generated among the Assamese a fear that they would be eventually marginalised in their own homeland.[14] Like Gohain, many other authors also prioritised the colonially influenced Bengali chauvinism of the migrant Bengali Hindus as the key factor that antagonised the Assamese and created a cleavage between Assamese and the migrants. Apurba Baruah, for example, blames the elite of the Bengali society as imposing the Bengali language on Assam and blames this as the reason for the growth of anti-Bengali sentiments among the local people.[15]

A second approach contextualised the conflicts in the Assamese micro nationalism that was generated by the Assamese language. In *India Against Itself: Assam and the Politics of Nationality*, Sanjib Baruah suggests how language continued to occupy centre stage in Assam's social struggle that gave rise to the Assamese micro nationalism. He opines that the violence is due to the binary used in colonial interpretations that has led the indigenous ethnic groups, including the ethnic Assamese that they may become a minority in the state.[16] Yasmin Saikia in her book *Fragmented Memories: Struggling to be Tai Ahom* also deals with a fascinating problem of language in Assam.[17] She writes that even though there has been migration and settlement in the pre-colonial period, the Ahoms and other migrants of that period adopted the Assamese language building up a 'we' or plural society. But in the post-colonial period this plural society had become fractured as the indigenous people saw the Assamese and other migrants as dominating their traditional social, cultural and political space.[18]

Changing demography, either due to colonial policies or post-colonial politics, is also another approach that is forwarded to understand the violence. As the issue of illegal migration from Bangladesh occupies a large scholarly debate in the context of violence in Assam, Samaddar writes that this debate is crucially a demography issue.[19] His argument is that the problem of immigration is not merely about nationality, identity, and numbers but has to be seen in the constructed history of the borderlands in the colonial past. Seeing Assam as being constantly exposed to hostile neighbours and Muslim migrations, writers such as Hazarika sees this Assamese – immigrant conflicts more as a concern of a broader human security that encompasses political, cultural and environmental issues.[20]

Other contemporary scholars analyses the violence by arguing that the lack of development and internal colonial policies of the union government generates these conflicts. Sanjib Baruah, in his book *Durable Disorders: Understanding the Politics of Northeast India*, points out how lack of connectivity to the region is one of the major causes of the chronic violence and insurgency. Myron Weiner, who analysed the violence in Assam from an economic viewpoint, also mentions of large number of immigrants whose presence in the state has shaken the foundation of Assamese social structure. This, he says, created solidarity among the Assamese but generated cleavages between the Assamese and the indigenous tribals. Thus, he refers to a 'unique triangular relation' in societal relationships in Assam which was unique to the state and not seen elsewhere in India.[21] Other writers such as B. G. Verghese, Gulshan Sachdeva, H. N. Das and Jayanta Madhav also view development as the only panacea to conflict. Likewise, writings on ethnicity and identity-based conflicts by such scholars as Apurba Baruah, Manorama Sharma, Udayon Mishra and Tilottama Mishra also broadly reflect how the skewed and backward nature of economic and political development in the region has differentiated the region from the rest of India.

India's northeast has thus been viewed largely through the prism of identity, conflict and migration literature. Reviewing the scholarly discourse on the topic of social conflicts in Assam, it appears that traditionally these have been conceptualised within a framework of either contested space or ethnic identities within a host of binary relationships such as colonisers – colonised; internal coloniser – internally colonised; native – non-native or local – immigrant. But as I have mentioned above, the conflicts in Assam are complex and are not inter-community but intra community as well and as such a strictly binary interpretation is unable to explain the complexities. In addition, the triangular formation of social relationships in Assam, as mentioned by Weiner, Baruah and several other scholars, presents another deep-seated underpinning to analyse the violence holistically. As such, economic theories of class conflicts or scholarship on the cultural clashes, which are primarily based on a binary unequal relationship, are inadequate to explain the contemporary Assam situation.

Creation of Triangulation and Ossification of Identities

The uniqueness of Assam's social relationship is its triangular social relationship. While Saikia mentioned of a 'we' (plural) community in the pre-colonial period, community identity in Assam became ossified in the colonial and post-colonial period. This ossification was the result of colonial practices, such as the indirect rule system, whereby colonial agents divided the people first through a 'line system' and then by a policy of disparate legal systems such as customary law for some and general law for others. At the same time, different family laws for the major religious communities and the haphazard etching of caste, community and tribe in the census created further differentiation of identities. In due course, the Government of India Acts of 1915, 1919 and 1935 legally recognised the hills areas as 'backward' and excluded them politically from the purview of the new provincial legislature and the High Court. Jafa analyses the effect of the Act of 1935 in Assam by stating that due to these Acts, the North Eastern hill tribes were effectively excluded from the administration of India from 1873 onwards. This gave the colonial agents exclusive access to these areas, restricted inter-mixing and allowed the administrators to reconstruct the tribal traditions and create a separate ethno-national identity. The 1935 Act permanently reinforced these demarcations in society in a more artful manner.[22]

As the Constitution of India drew heavily from the provisions of the Government of India Act 1935, the colonial paradigm of ossified relationships thus continued into the post-colonial period. This continuation of the colonial paradigm in official policy discourse, further amplified the distinction between subjects governed by customary law and subjects governed by general law in Assam and led to distinctness in social relations between the Assamese people and the ethnically defined indigenous groups. At the same time, the issue of migration to Assam got highlight in successive colonial census of 1911, 1921 and 1931 census in the state when pointed references were made to the invasion of land hungry migrants, mostly Muslim.[23] This created a third group identity in Assam. Thus, colonialism in Assam moved from its traditional role of administration / exploitation and a civilising mission of elites to one of constructing and managing identities between populations of the state.

In the post-1979 period, the issue of migration became further intensified. As the Assam Movement articulated widespread concern of the presence of illegal immigrants and took advantage of popular resentment, the Chief Election Commissioner of India, S.L. Shakdher, reinforced the already existing hostile perception towards immigrants by concluding that the large increase of population of 34.98 per cent in Assam in 1971 over the 1961 figures was due to influx of a very large number of persons from neighbouring countries.[24]

While Baruah refers to the considerable opposition to immigration, at the same time he shows how several vocal spokesperson of the Assamese community, such as Ambikagiri Roychoudhury, were willing to co-opt as Assamese, all those who agreed to accept the Assamese culture. The Assam Sanrakshini Sabha, i.e., the Assam Preservation Society founded by the Roychoudhury, for example, had a policy of welcoming as members immigrants who chose to identify with Assamese culture, accepted Assamese as their language and declared themselves members of the Assamese nationality. This insistence on Assamese language as the sole identity marker of the Assamese people however led to alienating the tribal communities that were earlier acknowledged as integral to the Assamese community.

As the indigenous people thus searched for their own identities and political space within the framework of the Indian state, the Bordoloi committee decided to continue with the colonial paradigm of exclusionary administration and formulated the Sixth Schedule of the Indian Constitution. While the 1947 partition had divided the people into two clear religious groups, the lack of a homogenising nationalism continued to create further divisions between the Assamese, the tribals and the migrants. It had therefore become evident that by the middle of the twentieth century, the three societal formations of the colonial period had become ossified in their political and socio-cultural identities in Assam and were unable to think beyond themselves. Post-independence, all these fissures resulted in the region as a whole to lag far behind the rest of the country in most of the important parameters of social cohesion and growth.

In contemporary Assam, the three groups identities created by colonial agents (i.e. Assamese, indigenous / tribals and migrants) therefore act in opposition to each other. This has given rise to new forms of identity politics and violence. Identity politics is the diverse experience of different individuals and the understanding of oppression and / or the possibility of a shared alternative. In general, notions of identity is either a case of anthropological study or one in which individuals may have several different although related identities to choose from when manoeuvring in a complex and dynamic social environment. In that sense, all individuals have multiple role-based identities and these identities exists either in harmony with each other or in opposition to our other roles. Stryker suggests that people become members of a particular group because of a common identity and shared belief system that makes collective action possible. Smith *et al* argues that high group affiliation through repeated activities within a group can lead to ossification of identities into an "us" versus "them" attitude.[25]

Scholars agree that the history of Assamese identity formation and its transformation is a colonial construction where the pre-colonial 'we' society, mentioned by Yasmin Saikia, has become ossified. In the post-colonial period, this ossification of group identities has led to reverse assimilation as many groups or classes of people such as the Nagas, the Mizos, the Garos, the Bodos, the Karbis and the Misings asserted themselves separately in the political sphere of the state and moved away from the Assamese community. In the process, it has brought into sharp focus the widening parameters of the Assamese nationality, chiefly as a result of real or perceived demographic changes. The political history of Assam therefore presents a picture of assimilation and conflict of the various tribes and migrant communities with the Assamese community.

The census figures have over the years showed the Assamese people to be an ethnic minority. In 1911, the Assamese language speakers were a mere 21.69 per cent of the total population in Assam, which had grown to 60.89 per cent in 1971. This increase was not due to rise in Assamese speakers but simply due to change in the territory of the state and how some groups of immigrants preferred to identify themselves as Assamese.[26] But in subsequent years, when the immigrants stopped identifying themselves as Assamese, the Assamese language speakers started to decline from 57.81 per cent in 1991 to 48.80 per cent in 2001.[27] Yet, even though it is not a majority community, the Assamese held the political domination in the state and no tribal or minority migrant has been able to become the Chief Minister of Assam in the post-independence period.[28]

Commenting on this domination of the Assamese in the state, Gosselink states:

> When Assam was established as a full-fledged state in the Indian Union in 1947, the Assamese realised that they had significantly more power under the new Indian Constitution than ever before under the British. Possessing independent power for the first time in 120 years, the majority Assamese were blind and indifferent to the claims of the Bengali minority groups and the tribal communities for a share in the fruits of independence.63 Instead of trying to integrate the minority tribal groups within Assamese society, the Assamese endeavoured to acculturate them by imposing the Assamese language upon them.[29]

Gosselink further states that tight political embrace of the Assamese community led the minority hill tribes of Assam to mobilise in the late 1950s for greater autonomy. Fearing that the Assamese linguistic hegemony and expansion would eventually lead to the elimination of their own cultural identity, the tribal groups increased their agitation for the creation of new political authorities within Assam wherein they could practice self-determination of language and culture. This gave birth to several tribal autonomous councils such as the Bodo, the Karbi, the Dimasa, the Mising, the Tiwa, the Sonowal-Kacharis and the Rabha-Hajong autonomous councils.

The political and cultural hegemony of the Assamese community has thus encouraged the growth of communal feelings and inter-community hatred which has prevented the emergence of a multi-ethnic Assam composed of varied religious and linguistic groups. The more desperate the movement to deport illegal immigrants or to restrict minority rights, the more it has encouraged the formation of an opposition coalition that challenges the domination of the Assamese community. Thus, the ethnic conflict in Assam is no longer an Assamese majority versus minority struggle for dominance, but has become a minorities versus minorities struggle for rights.[30]

Settler State as an Alternative Starting Point

As I discuss the different approaches and framework to understanding violence in Assam, I have found all the scholarly work useful to my research on the issue. However, what these discourses do not explicitly address is an approach to the triangular social relations and the effects of ossification of identities in Assam. I have therefore offered settler colonial studies as an alternative framework. This encourages a greater analytical frame across time and space. In view of the above discussion, I therefore turn to an exposition of settler colonial studies towards understanding the violence in Assam where I liken the Assamese to settlers.

The concept of a settler state requires that it be differentiated from a colonial state. Settler, in a settler colonial context, is different from the English dictionary meaning of the word that means 'a person who settles in an area', and refers to those migrants / colonisers / conquerors who come to stay carrying their sovereignty and a political agenda. More importantly, Elkins & Pederson say that while colonialism is generally understood to mean a "relationship of domination" by which an invading foreign minority governs an indigenous majority according to the dictates of a distant metropolis, settler colonies try to weaken or get rid of that metropolitan control and also of the indigenous population as quickly as possible.[31] They further mention that when the indigenous people finally disappear, settler colonies could develop into what D.K. Fieldhouse refers to as "pure" settlement colonies. Osterhammel calls this situation as "colonies with colonialism".[32] Raymond Evans, quoting Lemkins, mentions of settler colonies as those where there is "destruction of the national pattern of the oppressed group and then the imposition of the pattern of the oppressor either upon people left territorially fixed or upon territory cleared of its inhabitants to allow for colonisation of the area by the oppressors own nationals in order to destroy or cripple the subjugated people in their development".[33] He uses the term "indigenocide" to describe the three way onslaught on the lives, land and culture of the indigenous people. Rather than simply resource extraction and exploitation, the dominant settler group in a settler state seeks to erase the indigenous either through assimilation, indigenocide (cultural or otherwise), and/or appropriation of land and resources.

Veracini brings out the important difference in social formations in the colonial and settler states. He argues that settler states establish inherently triangular relations between settler – indigenous – exogenous Others.[34] He compares the narrative of classic colonialism and settler colonialism to the difference between a circle and a line, where colonialism takes a circular form, which consists of an outward movement, followed by interaction with colonised 'others' and a final return to an original location. In contrast, he says that the narrative generally associated with settler colonial enterprises resembles a line where the traveller moves forward and do not envision a return home. Finally, settler colonists transform and establish a political order in their new home.[35]

And so, while colonialism reinforces the distinction between colony and metropole, settler colonies erase it with the settlers trying to establish themselves as the indigenous. Thus, unlike colonialism which can be decolonised, it is difficult to decolonise settler colonialism and leads Patrick Wolfe to say that in a settler state, "invasion is a structure and not an event".[36]

The brief scholarship of a setter state above thus demonstrates that such states are founded by groups who assume a super-ordinate position vis-à-vis native inhabitants. To constitute a settler state, the settlers must therefore necessarily remain politically dominant over indigenous and migrant communities, who may present a threat to the settlers' supremacy. In this sense, settler rule is a form of political domination. At the same time, settler states have shown more resilience to decolonisation because they represent a socio-political hegemony of a dominant group that is prepared to resist any change including indigenous resistance. As we have seen in Assam where the colonial paradigm still persists, transformation of these states, after decolonisation, is generally more difficult and complicated. While conventional colonial states are superimposed on civil society and organised around economic and geopolitical objectives such as exploitation, land appropriation, building military control and / or monopolising trade, settler states are not superimposed but are rooted in it. As such, in Assam, the colonial metropolitan has been turned inside out into a new form of political domination, which can be described as 'replacing a white sahib with a brown one'.[37]

The above exposition of a settler state demonstrates three main features. First, it aims to achieve autonomy from a central authority (or metropole) in the exercise of political authority. This gives the settlers greater room to manoeuvre in moulding economic, social, and political structures as per their choice. The second feature of stable settler rule is to consolidate control over the indigenous and migrant population. This often results in a successfully restricting political mobilisation and ensuring economic dependence of the indigenous and migrants, sometimes through the use of overt or covert physical repression. Thirdly, a settler state aims to establish settler supremacy by developing settlers' class solidarity in the state's cohesion. As internal conflicts within the state and the dominant community along class, ethnic, political, or cultural lines may result in cracks in the settler regime, often ideological glue such as use of language, creating fear of outsiders and/or material incentives help promote settler solidarity.[38]

It is my argument that in Assam, the ethnic Assamese, such as the Ahoms and caste Hindu Assamese, through their linear movement to Assam, their hegemony on the politics and the Ahom king's nationalisation of land (and subsequent *paik* system) depict settler characteristics under settler colonial studies.[39]

Later, when the colonially constructed identities set the Assamese, the immigrants and the indigenes apart from each other, the better political manipulation and educational awareness of the Assamese helped them assert and maintain their hold on an autonomous political authority and discourse. In post-colonial Assam, just like settlers trying to break away from the metropole, the Assamese too developed a discourse that highlighted internal colonialism of the union government as its political ideology in the state. This sought to project mainland social practises as decadent. Then through several socio-political movements (such as the language movement, the anti-foreigner movement, and the refinery movement) the Assamese community sought to position themselves separately from the mainland people. These movements, which started during the colonial period, laid stress on the Assamese language and framed the Assamese as a distinct politico-linguistic community.

A deeper probe into the literature of Assam also reflect that just like classical settler societies, the Assamese too have used different methods at different times to exert their socio-political domination in the state. These included, amongst others, such initiatives as containment (separation and segregation of migrants and indigenes who live in different locales / suburbs in Assam); erasure (cultural assimilation by use of Assamese language or Hinduisation process); intimidation (strikes, hidden violence, threats in the political life); removal (expulsion, deportation); restriction (in property purchase, jobs for migrants); exclusion (attempts at legal and social exclusion using son-of-the-soil concept).

These initiatives have helped the Assamese to consolidate their position as they have often attempted to remove the indigenous and migrant peoples from the economic resources (land) or from the political formations (government). As such, both dispossession and attempts to establish legitimacy by the Assamese went hand in hand through the use of political, cultural, and economic hegemony. For example, while such dispossession in Assam has been through land and / or political alienation, Clause 6 of the Assam Accord which contemplates "constitutional, legal, cultural safeguards for the Assamese people" is seen by some of the tribal groups as an attempt to establish legitimacy. This has helped to consolidate and unify the Assamese as a necessary step towards establishing a hegemonic political authority. In the end, the political dispensation of the Assamese exhibited two settler contradictory features: on the one hand they built up a hegemonic autonomous socio-political authority and on the other they still desired the resources and support from a central pool as a way of dispossessing indigenous and migrant people.

Conclusion

While colonial agents in Assam cited administrative convenience as the primary reason for dividing the people, they demonstrated a paternalistic attitude towards the tribals while at the same time an antagonistic attitude towards the migrants. As discussed above, this kept the social division alive, not only in the colonial period but also in the post-colonial period. The problem in Assam, I argue, is that colonial history framed post-colonial existence and turned the indigenous people, the Assamese and the migrants into prisoners of the very history, census and law that constructed them. Thus, the quest for justice has turned into a permanent preoccupation of domination, rebellion, strikes and violence. The continuation of the colonial paradigm can also be said to have resulted in incomplete decolonisation in Assam. Since settler formations show resilience to decolonisation, one implication of framing Assam as a settler state is also to advance decolonisation as a necessary goal in the quest to achieve social cohesion and justice. Indeed, the elaboration of the settler framework might be closely paralleled to the development of de-colonial projects for equitable justice that aim to achieve social inclusion. This should therefore lead to strategies and solutions that adhere to modernist concepts of democracy, progress and peace and abort the inequalities that colonialism has created.

The effective date when decolonisation took place in India was on 15th August 1947. On that day, the British colonisers left and India gained independence. But during the period 1826 to 1947, the period when colonialism was the dominant regime in Assam, the colonial changes in administration and identity left behind impacts that resonate in post-colonial Assam. This has created challenges to social cohesion. As the process of imagining India as a single unit emerged in the late nineteenth century and led to decolonisation, this imagination therefore did not occur in the same pace in Assam. Framing Assam as a settler state may help in a new imagination of effective decolonisation and interrogation on how to address these power-laden distinctions that not only affect traditional settler societies but also shape other democratic societies such as Assam.

As the inability to demonstrate fluidity in identity gave rise to several disjunctions in social relations, scholars suggest various solutions to address the Assam situation. These include decentralisation of power; a conscious attempt to improve the educational and economic level for all and a sustained effort to reintroduce and deepen secular socio-political relations. However, as I discussed, the paths of Assam's economic and social development do not conform to the binary of class or caste relationships as found in the rest of India and these measures have not been successful. There is a dynamic yet violent interconnection between immigration, the marginalisation of native peoples and the domination of the Assamese settlers and these interconnections can be better understood if framed differently.

Since analysis of the conflicts and its reductions should lead to a socially cohesive state, I shall briefly touch upon the issue of social cohesion here. Tangible definitions of social cohesion often overlap. When defined in terms of social cohesion, a society is said to be socially cohesive where people feel empowered and has a sense of belonging and a shared vision for well-being. Social cohesion in this context should be understood as promoting a sustainable inclusive and democratic society. It must hold societies together and provides access to the people to fully participate in the political, socio-economic and cultural aspects of society. It therefore necessarily means that the exclusion of some groups of people (either by domination or by homelands), who have been either traditionally or situationally marginalised (like indigenes or migrants), or where there is political hegemony of a dominant group, works against this democratic process and goal of social cohesion. As I discussed, when viewed from the centre, the stress on an Assamese identity based on a common Assamese language may well be seen as 'unification' or 'assimilation', yet when observed from the periphery, the same process can be interpreted as 'cultural invasion' and 'linguistic elimination' of non-dominant and marginalised indigenous and migrant communities and leads to conflicts. In conclusion, I would like to suggest that by framing Assam as a setter state using settler colonial studies, we would be able to better understand how colonialism and settler colonialism intersect and how the ossified triangular identity formations have developed and continue to underpin social relations and conflicts in the state.

References

1. *BBC News Asia*, "Thousands flee rioting in Indian state of Assam," July 23, 2012, http://www.bbc.co.uk/news/world-asia-18952933 [accessed: 12.8.2012].
2. *The Economist,* "A Neglected Crisis," August 25, 2012, p. 23.
3. Subir Bhaumik, "What lies behind Assam violence?" *BBC News India*, July, 26, 2012, http://www.bbc.co.uk/news/world-asia-india-18993905 [accessed: 12.8.2012].
4. Subir Bhaumik, "Internal Displacement in North East India: Challenges Ahead," in *The Fleeing People of South Asia: Selections*

from Refugee Watch, ed., Sibaji P. Basu (New Delhi: Anthem Press, 2008), pp. 254-255.

5. Figures of death of Nellie massacre varies from 1200 to 3000. See Donald L. Horowitz, *The Deadly Ethnic Riots*, (Berkley: University of California Press, 2001), pp. 228-229.; Manirul Hussain, "The North East Today: Displacing Identities, Displaced Identities," in *The Fleeing People of South Asia: Selections from Refugee Watch*, ed., Sibaji P. Basu, (New Delhi: AnthemPress, 2008), p. 261.
6. This data has been computed from various sources. The Institute of Conflict Management (ICM), New Delhi mention 7679 people killed in extremist violence during the period 1992-2012. In addition, the Assam Movement (1979-85) saw the death of nearly 5000 persons, of which 852 were Assamese Hindus. Deaths had also occurred in the Assamese – Bengali language riots of the 1960s and 1970s and the tribal – non-tribal clashes. For details please see the ICM website at: www.satp.org.
7. For details, see the website of the Institute of Conflict Management, New Delhi at www.satp.org.
8. Amalendu Guha, *Planter Raj to Swaraj : Freedom Struggle and Electoral Politics in Assam 1826–1947*, (New Delhi: Indian Council of Historical Research, 1977).
9. Hiren Gohain, *Assam: A Burning Question*, (Guwahati: Spectrum, 1985).
10. Sanjib Baruah, *India Against Itself : Assam and the Politics of Nationality*, (New Delhi: Oxford University Press, 1999); Sanjib Baruah, *Durable Disorders: Understanding the Politics of Northeast India*, (New Delhi: Oxford University Press, 2005); Sanjib Baruah, "From Memories of the Past to a Vision for the Future: Resolving the Crisis of Citizenship in Northeast India", in *Contested Space and Identity in the Indian Northeast*, (New Delhi: Academy of Third World Studies, 2008); Sanjib Baruah, "Ethnic Conflict as State - Society Struggle: The Poetics and Politics of Assamese Micro-Nationalism," *Modern Asian Studies*, 28, no. 3, (1994).
11. Yasmin Saikia, *Fragmented Memories: Struggling to be Tai Ahom*, (New York: Duke Publication, 2004); Yasmin Saikia, *"The Tai Ahom Connection,"* Seminar paper in *Gateway to the East: A symposium on Northeast India and Look East Policy*, New Delhi, (2005), http://www.india- seminar.com/2005/550.htm [accessed: 15.02.2012].

12. Sanjoy Hazarika, *Strangers in the Mist: Tales of War and Peace from India's Northeast*, (New Delhi: Penguin Books, 1994) ; Sanjoy Hazarika, *Rites of passage: border crossings, imagined homelands, India's East and Bangladesh,* (New Delhi: Penguin Books India Pvt. Ltd., 2000).
13. Guha, *Planter Raj to Swaraj : Freedom Struggle and Electoral Politics in Assam 1826–1947.*
14. Gohain, *Assam: A Burning Question.*
15. Apurba Kumar Baruah, *Social Tensions in Assam Middle Class Politics, (*Guwahati: Purbanchal, 1991).
16. Baruah, *India Against Itself : Assam and the Politics of Nationality*, 183 ; Baruah, *Durable Disorders: Understanding ThePolitics of Northeast India*, p. 165.
17. Saikia, *Fragmented Memories: Struggling to be Tai Ahom.*
18. Historians do not have an accurate detail of where the Ahoms came from. From South China to Thailand, their origin is cited differently by different scholars.
19. Ranabbir Samaddar, *The Marginal Nation – Transborder Migration from Bangladesh to West Bengal. (*New Delhi: Sage Publications, 2003).
20. Sanjoy Hazarika, *Strangers in the Mist: Tales of War and Peace from India's Northeast.*
21. Myron Weiner, *Sons of the Soil: Migration and Ethnic Conflict in India*, (Princeton: Princeton University Press, 1978), p. 82.
22. Vijendra S. Jafa, "Administrative Policies and Ethnic Disintegration Engineering Conflict in India's NorthEast" (2001) http://www.satp.org/satporgtp/publication/faultlines/volume2/Fault2-JafaF.htm [Accessed: 7 June 2013].
23. Srinivas K. Sinha, *Report on Illegal Migration into Assam*, (Guwahati: Governor of Assam, 1998), Ch II.
24. *Ibid,* Ch III.
25. Joanne R. Smith, Deborah J.Terry and Micheal A. Hogg, "Social identity and the attitude-behaviour relationship: Effects of anonymity and accountability," *European Journal of Social Psychology,* 37, no. 2 (2007): pp. 239-257.
26. Baruah, *India Against Itself : Assam and the Politics of Nationality*, p. 52.
27. Sushanta Talukdar, "Less than 50 per cent Assamese speakers in Assam," *The Hindu*, January 9, 2008, http://www.thehindu.com/todays-paper/tp-national/less-than-50-per-cent-assamese-speakers-in-assam/article1175679.ece [accessed on: 13.03.2015].

28. Except for seven months when Anowara Taimur (6th December.1980 to 30th June 1981) was Chief Minister, but she was an Assamese Muslim and not an immigrant Muslim.
29. Robert G. Gosselink, "Minority Rights and Ethnic Conflict in Assam, India" *Boston College Third World Law Journal,* 14, Issue 1, Article 5, (1994): p. 91.
30. *Ibid*, p. 103.
31. Caroline Elkin and Susan Pedersen, eds., *Settler Colonialism in the Twentieth Century,* (New York: Routledge, 2005), p. 2.
32. *Ibid*, p. 2.
33. Raymond Evans, ""Crime Without a Name": Colonialism and the case for "ingenocide"," in *Empire, Colony, Genocide: conquest, occupation and subaltern resistance in world history*, ed., A. Dirk Moses, (New York, Berghahan Books, 2008) p. 142.
34. Lorenzo Veracini, "On Settlerness", *borderlands ejournal*, 10, no. 1, (2011): pp. 1-3.
35. Lorenzo Veracini, "Telling the End of the Settler Colonial History," in *Studies in Settler Colonialism: Politics, Identity, and Culture*, eds., Fiona Bateman and Lionel Pilkington, (New York: Palgrave Macmillan, 2011), pp. 204-218.
36. Patrick Wolfe, "Settler colonialism and the elimination of the native", *Journal of Genocide Research,* 8, no. 4, (2006): pp. 387–409.
37. Himani Bannerji, Shahrzad Mojab and Judith Whitehead, eds., *Of Property and Propriety: The Role of Gender and Class in Imperialism and Nationalism*, (Toronto: University of Toronto Press Inc, 2001), p. 23.
38. Ronald J. Weitzer, *Transforming Settler States: Communal Conflict and Internal Security in Northern Ireland and Zimbabwe*, (Berkeley: University of California Press, 1990), pp. 26-28.
39. For a detailed reading of the Ahom period, see Heramba K. Barpujari, ed., *The Comprehensive History of Assam*, (Guwahati: Assam Publication Board, 2007), Vol. 1 – 5.

6

An Anatomy of Ethnic Conflict and the Mass Media in Assam

Uttam Kr Pegu

Introduction

North-East India exhibits heterogeneity at its extreme with high level of ethnic, cultural and linguistic diversity not found in any other region. This diversity is reflected in the patterns of conflict which are varied in their nature with each state having a distinct set of location-specific concerns and grievances. By virtue of its location Assam is characterised by socio-political instability and economic backwardness. While the flow of immigrants, rising socio-economic aspirations and lack of infrastructure has retarded the process of development and integration, lack of consistency and firmness in dealing with the immigrants has added to insecurity amongst the local communities as influx of immigrants' poses economic, social and cultural threats. This has resulted in a continued violence in the state which poses a threat to adversaries resulting in conflict.

This study examines media coverage of ethnic conflict in Assam and the increasing debate on the ethics of reporting conflict and the constructive role media could play during conflict and post-conflict scenario. If the media plays a role in escalating conflict, it seems logical to examine how it could contribute towards mitigating conflict and restore peace in the region. In other words, if the media could support forces that lead to conflict, it also has the power to support the forces of peace.

The study explores how individual journalists and the media collectively address the ethical complexities of covering conflict. Ethical issues relating to fundamental techniques of news reportage on conflict and the wide range of professional responsibilities of journalists which are grounded in economics and politics have been taken into consideration. Furthermore, it seeks to contribute to the theoretical refinement and practical realisation of conflict conscious journalism as a tool for use by media practitioners in conflict-affected areas.

As the study is premised on understanding the ethnic conflict in Assam, it is worth examining the reasons for ethnic conflicts. While it is believed that the root causes of the problem in the North-East are ethnic resurgence and social and cultural insecurity, failure to implement the Assam Accord of 1985 and the conflicting stand on illegal migrants (Determination by Tribunals) Act, 1983 which has further complicated the issue and made the situation even more volatile. The unabated trans-border migration has altered the demographic profile of Tripura; it has also threatened to change that of Assam and other North-Eastern states. Democratic governance has resulted in only expansion of government and less of governance. It seems that the extension of Sixth Schedule has not helped the state in any way.

Ethnic groups in Assam began voicing their aspirations for self-determination that ranged from the demand for autonomy within the Indian Union to complete secession after Independence. Nagaland, Meghalaya and Mizoram were carved out of Assam in 1963, 1972, and 1987 respectively. This has set the trend for territorial demands based on tribal, ethnic and linguistic identity since the 1980s. Sixth Schedule of the Constitution, which granted special protection and privileges to the tribal people of the region, covered the Naga tribes and the tribal population of Meghalaya, Mizoram and Tripura. It aimed at safeguarding the interests of the tribal people and their cultures and customs. Ironically, the Bodos who lived in the plains of Assam was not included within its ambit initially.

In 1979, the AASU and the All Assam Gana Sangram Parishad (AAGSP) launched the anti-foreigners agitation against Bangladeshi immigrants, popularly known as the Assam Movement. It enjoyed unprecedented mass support from all the constituent ethnic groups and ended with the signing of the historic Assam Accord in 1985. The constituent ethnic groups of the Assam Movement were not happy with the aftermath of the Assam Accord as many found that some of the clauses of the Accord were not as favourable as they would have liked it to be. This resulted in the launch of the ABSU movement under the leadership of Upendranath Brahma who was very instrumental during the Assam Movement. The movement vehemently asserted for self-determination of the Bodo people.

Brahma could mobilise and gather support of the Bodo people and in 1987 he decided to launch a revolution which aimed at attaining Bodoland by 1990 through a 50-50 vision of Assam. The demands were for a Bodoland within the Indian Union and not within Assam. The Bodo nationalism in Assam, thus, emerged as a retaliation against the dominant discourse of the greater Assamese nationalism. The series of agitations against the Indian state and the Assamese nation epitomises their demand. Somehow in the popular belief of the Bodos, their existence itself was against a variety of odds ranging from that of neglect, exploitation, alienation and discrimination for several decades. Resultantly, the necessity and demand for a separate state of Bodoland grew louder by them. Only such a move would address the social errors and would meet the economic and socio-cultural aspirations of the Bodo people. Moreover, they also felt that within the greater Assamese culture, they have no chance of preserving their own cultural heritage.

Bodo leaders vehemently opposed Clause 6 of the Assam Accord, which promised safeguards to protect the cultural identity of the "Assamese People". This led to the fear that it would give legitimacy to the imposition of the Assamese language and culture on the Bodo people and other tribal communities of Assam. The Bodos, along with other tribal communities, resented the campaign of assimilation as they felt that such a clause would only jeopardise cultural diversities in an atmosphere dominated by the Assamese culture. This resulted in the Bodo-Assamese clash in the late 1980s. Their initial demand for autonomy turned into a demand for a separate state which eventually was spearheaded by the Bodo Security Force later renamed as the National Democratic Front of Bodoland. The struggle for Bodoland needs to be seen as a resistance against the greater

Assamese nationalism and the urge to preserve its culture, which is so intricately linked to their identity. The successive waves of violence in the Bodo-dominated areas were a reflection of such an aspiration for a separate statehood which is free from the clutches of deprivation and exploitation.

Methodology and Research Design

This study is primarily based on content analysis of media texts. While attempting to critically examine media representation of the ethnic clash between the Bodos and Muslims in July 2012, a total of 100 news items which include hard news, feature articles, editorials, and opinions pieces published between July to December 2012 were selected from the Assam Tribune. Moreover, it was necessary to examine the Assam Movement (1979-85), Assam Accord (1985) and BTAD Accord (2003).

It is important to examine these because it would provide deeper understanding on the ethnic conflicts in Assam particularly the Bodoland movement. The state has witnessed a series of violence in 1993, 2008, 2012 and the 2014 ethnic clash between the Bodos and the Adivasis in the BTAD-dominated areas. The content analysis yielded some descriptive and some inferential data that gives a detailed picture of the nature of coverage on ethnic conflicts in Assam.

Analysis and Discussion

Ethnic assertion in Assam is the story of a struggle against all odds - be it mis-governance or that of sheer neglect. Subsequently, the aspiration for a distinct identity among the ethnic groups resulted in a number of movements demanding autonomy. This is because of a flawed Assam Accord, 1985 which has alienated the groups that had identified themselves with a common Assamese identity (Roy 1995, pp. 41-43). Gradually the non-Assamese groups developed a desire to be separate and hence have come up with a struggle for a separate identity. Why did that happen? Its answer rests in the two-way politicisation of the ethnicity elements and state role along with the element of deprivation and domination.

While the media in North-east particularly in Assam concentrates mainly on the disquieting stories of unrest and insurgence, its predominance on violence and a narrow reading of the implications of ethnic violence are responsible for a substantial misunderstanding of the region. The region has always been in the limelight for all the wrong reasons. It has rarely portrayed the regions equally long history of peace, social collaboration, political reconciliation and democratic participation. Media portrayal on ethnic conflicts is flawed on many aspects particularly due to its inability to focus on the rationality of such demands and its insensitivity to the implications of ethnic identity struggles in the region.

In this aspect a discussion on ethnic struggles in the public sphere becomes all the more important if we are engage the public in a meaningful understanding of such issues. Public sphere is a concept created in the eighteenth century and further developed by Jürgen Habermas, who stated that the public sphere was characterised by its critical nature in contraposition to the representative nature of the feudal system (Boeder, P., 2005). This critical nature is endangered by the power of the mass media that transforms most of the society in a passive public, the objectives of a consumer's culture. According to Habermas, the public sphere can best be described as a network of communicating information and points of view which is reproduced through communicative action. The principles of the public sphere according to him involves an open discussion of all issues of general concern, where issues relevant to the public good could be subject to informed debate and examination. According to Hauser, it is a discursive place where people can interchange their opinions to create a common judgment (Hauser, G., 1988).

The academia and the media projects North-east as a mosaic of ethnic conflicts and violence and in this sense much of what goes on in the region is learned through the media. Needless to reiterate how people from other parts of the country view the region. Bill Bernback says, "All of us who professionally use the mass media are the shapers of the society. We can vulgarise that society. We can brutalise it. Or we can help lift it onto a higher level". MacNair (1999) observes that the media provides a platform for public political discourse and expression of dissent, give publicity to governmental and political institutions, and serves as channel for the advocacy of political viewpoints. Over the last decade, the rapid change in the media particularly in the news content and format has brought every issue under public scrutiny, thereby facilitating participatory democracy like never before. Much of this change has been spectacular for the evolution both of democracy and the public sphere.

Conflict communication has always been one of the biggest challenge for media practitioners as it needs to be dealt with greater sensitivity and conscientiousness. It has been seen to be believed not just in Assam but elsewhere. The mass media sensationalise such issues in order to earn more television ratings or viewership (never mind how you do it). This is epitomised in the ethnic conflicts that the state of Assam has witnessed for instance the conflict between the Bodos and the illegal migrant (2012) which seems to have been under-reported and not presented with full spectrum of facts, thus it was misleading those it is supposed to inform or educate. The state of Assam continued to reel under communal violence affecting not just the Bodos and the Muslims particularly in the BTAD areas and somehow in the popular imagination of the national and the social media it was projected as a conflict between the Hindus and the Muslims which was far from reality.

It is argued that a purposeful and impact bearing information dissemination can only emerge after a proper understanding of the political, historical and cultural contours. How many media organisations communicate ethnic conflicts in a manner it is supposed to do? It only feasts on violence and the pangs of the effected people. The more it is sensationalised, the higher the chances of its viewership or circulation figures. In such a scenario, it is necessary to examine the gaps in the dissemination of information. Media coverage of ethnic conflicts is mystified in a manner which is supposedly baffling. It is seen that the quantum of media coverage on such issues are not sufficient to keep the people meaningfully informed. The media professionals need to realise the complexity and interconnectedness of the web of issues into which ethnic conflicts are interwoven, especially if they want to engage in a meaningful communication with the public.

The media seem to be indifferent on the inconsistencies and contradictions that are contained in the Acts pertaining to citizenship. Such indifference has only fueled the situation as is evident in Assam 2012. One among the galaxy of such social errors is the Illegal Migrants (Determination by Tribunal) Act of 1983 and the Assam Accord of 1985 which according to D N Bezbarua is flawed on many aspects, while we may have our reservations on his pontification. He asserts that: "The greatest disservice done by the Assam Accord is by considering 25th March 1971 as the cut-off-date for the migrants which is against the Government of India Act 1935 or one who migrated after the 19th July 1948 and was registered as a citizen of India on an application made by the migrants for that purpose before the commencement of the Indian Constitution". (*The Assam Tribune*, 16th January 2013).

Moreover, the failure to implement the infamous Clause 6 of the Assam Accord (reasons best known to the politicians) and the conflicting stand on determining the illegal-migrants in the state has further made the situation even more volatile. There are apprehensions that political negligence has only opened the floodgates of unabated trans-border migration particularly from Bangladesh. How does this matter to anyone even if it has threatened to alter the demographic profile of Tripura and Assam? Other North-eastern states seem to be following suit. There is no denying the fact that the governance particularly in the region has resulted only in expansion of government with less of governance. It seems that the Sixth Schedule has only made the political waters in North-East murkier. How have the ethnic communities of the region benefitted from the lofty ideals of the Sixth Schedule? The purpose of fostering development through such an enterprise perhaps has been defeated on all fronts.

The arbitrary choice of 15th March 1971 as the cut-off-date for migrants from former East Pakistan in the Assam Accord is a clear violation of Article 6 of the Indian Constitution. The cut-off-date for migrants from former Pakistan as stipulated in Assam Accord and the constitutional validity of Section 6A of the Citizenship Act 1955 has been challenged in the Supreme Court by the Assam Sanmilata Mahasanga, the National Democratic Front of Bodoland (Progressive) and the Indigenous Tribal Peoples' Federation. It also contends that Section 6A of the Citizenship Act violates Articles 6, 14, 29(i), 235 and 355 of the Constitution. There are stiff oppositions on the cut-off-date spearheaded by the AAMSU and such a yardstick may not be the right way of determining a foreigner.

The series of controversies and debates on identifying foreigners have been going on for decades and would perhaps continue to go on as the checks and balances and regulatory measures in the country in this endeavour seems to be ineffective. Absence of a well-defined policy has encouraged the flow of illegal migrants in the region. The Assembly Elections in the state of Assam has been scheduled in 2016 and the issue that has been racked up is quite untimely. The cut off dates for detection of foreigners would only make the process of identification of citizens through the National Register of Citizens more ambiguous. What should be the cut-off year then? To quote Col (Retd) Manoranjan Goswami: "It has come to general perception now that National Register of Citizens is the panacea to solve the problem of illegal migrants staying in Assam. AASU feels updating of 1951 to 1971 voter list as reference to be the basis for detection". (*Assam Tribune*, 16th January 2013). Will this solve the problem?

The reasons for ethnic violence that Assam witnesses frequently are primarily because of the divisive policies of the central government. As we continue to debate on the loopholes contained in the faulty government models, we need to re-assess why it has miserably failed to meet the aspirations and development needs of the people. The media which is supposed to be a harbinger of information also has to be blamed for being mute spectators and for flaring up conflicts by misreporting or by not reporting them at all. In the 2012 Bodo versus the illegal migrant case, majority of Indians would not have understood what was going on in the state of Assam. Surprisingly many of the foreign media such as the BBC World and the Euro News covered the issue quite openly as they probably had no stake in suppressing the truth.

The ethnic violence that erupted in Assam in 2012 is much more complex than what the think tanks and the media would make us believe. As the reporting unfolded the real tragedy through the terrified faces of the many thousands in the relief camps, it is apparent that this was no one-sided riot if one looks at it very closely. The Bodos, Bengali Hindus, Adivasis and the Muslims have all suffered as a consequence. If one were to carefully follow media coverage on the conflict then it would seem that only one community has suffered. The fact remains that both the Bodos and the Muslims have equally suffered, but somehow in the popular imagination of the media and the people, there was only one aggressor.

The possible role and the impact of media in conflict-ridden societies need to be introspected. Conflict sells better than co-operation, but then how do we tell the Journalists to ensure balanced reporting with a view to preventing the escalation of conflicts. It frequently goes beyond control in situations where information is scarce. Offering a variety of information that contains a range of facts, perspectives and opinions would perhaps be a de-escalating measure. The way in which journalists report on conflict can drastically affect the audiences' perception of the situation and thus may further deteriorate the situation. Furthermore, there is a very fine line between one's objectivity and viewing events with a certain attitude towards conciliation. News gathering, to be sure, is a highly imperfect art. The news media has a greater responsibility to play than it normally does during conflict.

While we are made to believe that no journalist can be completely objective but then they can help bridge the information gap between the opposing sides. The Bodos and the Muslims in the state have a long history of animosity which has further been aggravated by the formation of the BTC in 2003. No one denies that there are illegal migrants in the state to which even the Supreme Court admits. But then is it proper to brand a particular religious community as illegal migrants? It is an irony to note that 'illegal immigrant' is today a euphemism in Assam which has its own political manifestations. We should not ignore the historical fact that labourers from East Bengal had migrated to the state at the beginning of the twentieth century. The census decadal growth figures seem to be evasive on the dramatic rise in Muslim population. There is no denying the fact that the porous borders has made Assam vulnerable to an influx of illegal migrants from across the fence. However, in the absence of a proper statistical detail would it not be inappropriate to presume that Assam has been 'swamped' by Bangladeshi Muslims?

Conclusion

Media has a major role to play in mitigating conflict by disseminating knowledge to the public with the widest coverage. Conflicts and perceived sense of denial or deprivation have a mutually sustaining relationship, as conflicts add to deprivation, which in turn fuel conflict. Effect of both constrains economic development and well-being of people which becomes a source of deprivation and alienation. Moreover, conflict prevails where information is scarce and in this aspect the media has an important role to play in mitigating conflict.

Media that are sensitive towards promoting tolerant and diverse viewpoints can be both informative which in turn could mitigate conflict to certain extent. There has to be diversity in terms of reporters of different race, religion and culture in order to counter-balance prejudices. The diversity is an important measure of the media's role in conflict. The media can lead society by example, or can increase divisions in society. The ability to impart and share information in real time, both globally and locally via multiple communication channels has expanded the media's role in precipitating, ameliorating, and communicating ethnic conflict. Media should encompass the factors responsible for escalation of conflicts. We cannot talk of peace and a political solution and still persist with the policy of inclusivity and as the saying goes "There is no way to Peace. Peace is the way".

References

Baruah, A. K. (2004), *'Identity Crisis in North East India and its consequences'*, in Thomas Vattathara and Elizabeth George (Ed) *Peace Initiatives-A North East India Perspective*, Guwahati: Don Bosco Publications, pp. 17-27.

Anastasio, P.A., Rose, K., and Chapman, J. (2005), "The divisive coverage effect: How media may cleave differences of opinion between social groups", *Communication Research.* 32(2):171-192.

Bhattacharyya, Arpita (2012), *"Understanding the Historical Conflicts behind Today's Violence in Assam"*, Available at www.americanprogress.org/wp-content/uploads/2012/08/Bhattacharyyaassam.pdf. Accessed on December 20, 2014.

Benedict, Anderson (1991), *Imagined Communities: Reflections on the origin and spread on Nationalism*, London: Verso.

Basumatary, Dulen (2012), "Assam Movement and its Impact on Tribals", *International Indexed and Referred Research Journal,* IV (45), pp. 35-36.

Baruah, Sanjib (1999), *India against itself: Assam and the Politics of Nationality,* University of Pennsylvania Press, Pennsylvania.

Borah, Pankaj (2012), "Cultural reconstruction and ethnic Movements in north-east India: an analysis on the Bodo Movement", *International Journal of Social Science Tomorrow*, 1 (6), pp. 1-4.

Bhaumik, Subir (2009), *Troubled Periphery: Crisis of India's North-East.* Los Angeles: Sage Publications.

Barbora, Sanjay (2005), *"Autonomy or Death: assessing ethnic autonomy arrangements in Assam, Northeast India"*, [www.nesrc.org] URL: www.nesrc.org/NESRC/Sanjay/autonomyCrG.doc. Accessed on January 14, 2015.

Bora, Shakuntala (2006), *'Ethnic Struggles in Assam: An Observation'* in Prasenjit Biswas and C. Joshua Thomas (Ed) Peace in India's North-East Meaning, Metaphor and Method, Essays of Concern and Commitment, New Delhi: Regency Publications, pp. 459-468.

Chaube, S.K. (1999), *Hill Politics in Northeast India.* Hyderabad: Orient Longman.

Das, H.N. (2004), *'Ethnicity and Insurgency in the North-Eastern Region of India'*, in Thomas Vattathara and Elizabeth George (Ed). Op. cit. pp. 66-83.

Datta, Brijendranath (1990), *"Ethnicity, Nationalism and Sub-Nationalism, with Special Reference to North-East India".* In D. Pakem (Ed). *Nationality, Ethnicity and Cultural Identity in North-East India.* New Delhi, Omsons Publications, pp. 36-44.

Goswami, Namrata (2012), *"Violence in the Bodo Areas: Deciphering the Causes"* (India: Institute for Defense Studies and Analyses.

Lakshmi, Rama (2012), *"India blocks more than 250 Web sites for inciting hate, panic,"* The Washington Post, August, available at http://www.washingtonpost.com

Mochahari, Monjib (2008), *"Bodoland: The Paradise Unexplored," Assam Times,* available at http://www.assamtimes.org/blog/2087.html.

Misra, Udayon (2012), "Bodoland: The Burden of history", *Economic and Political Weekly,* XLVII (37), pp. 36-42.

Pegu, Uttam (2014), Media Coverage on Ethnic Conflict in North-East India: An Analysis on the Issues and Challenges in Conflict Communication in *Global Journal of Finance and Management.* Vol. 6, No. 1, pp. 89-92.

Ronen, Dov.1986, *'Ethnicity, Politics and Development: An Introduction'*, in Dennis L. Thompson and D. Ronen (Ed), Ethnicity, Politics and Development, Boulder: Lynne Rienner Publishers, pp. 1-9.

Subba, T.B. (1991), *Ethnicity, State and Development: A case study of Gorkhaland Movement in Darjeeling,* New Delhi: Vikas Publishing House.

7

Tribal Movement as 'Nationalism': An Analysis of the Jharkhand Movement

Ankur Goswami

Introduction

The aim of this paper is to discuss the tribal movements in India through the lens of Nationalism. The main focus of the study will be the Jharkhand Movement, which was based on tribal identity and dates back to the 1857 rebellions. The paper looks at the movement, through the concepts and theories of Nationalism, as developed by Ernest Gellner, Benedict Anderson, T.K. Oommen, G. Aloysius and Anthony Smith.

Tribal movements of central India have been generally analysed through the identity politics based on regionalism paradigm. Unlike the movements of Kashmir, Punjab or Assam which are categorised as national or sub-national movements striving to form a separate political community, the tribal movements of central India have supposedly shown no such orientation and even an analysis from this perspective is absent.

The basis of Jharkhand movement lied in the shared cultural and collective memory of the various tribal communities and their collective action during the colonial period as expressed in the *Santhal Hool* or the *Brisa Munda* movement. It will be argued that, there did exist, a sense of common identity among the various tribal groups and they did constitute a nation. Thus, the paper tries to understand, whether that the Jharkhand movement can be called a nationalist movement, striving for a separate political community, which was reflected in its initial demand of political autonomy.

The paper focuses upon the debate, on tribal population in pre-and post-independence period; of them, constituting a separate culture distinct from Hinduism or as propounded by G S Ghurye, of tribals being 'Backward Hindus' and being a part of broader spectrum of Hindu culture.

Resistance to Autonomy

The origin of the Jharkhand movement lies in the post-colonial period, this movement continued till end of the twentieth century, culminating with the formation of the Jharkhand state under the union of India. Aloysius says that the present movement for a separate state is in many ways a continuation and extension of their heroic tradition of struggle against the British imperialism and local feudalism[1] ; making it imperative for us to understand the pre-independence forms of the movement.

The tribal had a simple life and pattern of economic activities. They heavily depended upon land and forest over which they had the traditional rights, called *khuntkatti or bhuinhari.* Things began to change after *Munda* and *Oraon* tribal communities jointly selected a common leader or '*Raja*'. He was given voluntary contribution in kind and a few days of labour every year by the people. People from outside the region were brought into the area by the *Raja* for military and religious purpose. The *Raja* made land grants to the Brahmins who played a major role in legitimising his role. This outsider influence contributed to the disintegration of tribal communities by incorporating them in the social division of labour, represented by the caste system. The *Raja* later on granted the 'outsiders' his customary rights inland. In course of time these people became landlords or zamindars.[2]

However, the first real entry of the British into this region took place in 1772 when the *Maharaja* (the then princely ruler of the region) called them for help in a revenue matter. The British system bore harshly on the indigenous population. They turned land into private property through Permanent Settlement Act 1793. Uniform administrative machinery was also introduced.

Commercialisation of forest, mining activities and industrialisation brought the British to the most exposed areas.[3] The new system demanded proofs for land ownership, but the tribal had no title deeds to their land and so could not prove their ownership in the British court. The court language was Hindi which the tribal did not speak. The court officials did not know the languages of the tribal. The latter had no word for such a term as *rent* in their languages.[4] Also they had a specific cultural system with an altogether different world outlook. An important feature in this cultural configuration is their conception of the man-tree and man-animal relationship.[5] The indigenous people with a sensitivity born out of isolation and with a relatively intact mechanism of social control, revolted.[6]

The first resistance was put by Kurmis and the Santhals supported by other communities. They killed the agents of the East India Company and robbed the 'Bengali and Hindu' who had come as purchasers of land.[7] Starting with individual tribes, these outbursts often spread to other groups becoming general configuration. Some of the examples are; The great *Kol* Insurrection (1831-1832), the *Santhal* Rebellion (1855), the *Birsa Munda* Revolt (1895-1900) and *Tana Bhagat* Movement (1914-1920).[8]

The formal beginning of the Jharkhand movement can be traced backed to the *Adivasi Mahasabha* formed in the year 1939, through the merger of organisations concerned with different aspects of tribal upliftment, like the Roman Catholic Cooperative Society, Chhotanagpur Charitable Association or the Chhotanagpur Improvement Society.[9] These organisations were primarily associated with the missionaries; both Catholic and Lutherans working in the tribal area. Owing to the exposure given to them by the Christian missionaries, a sense of new political awareness developed among the tribal people in the national context. During 1930s and 1940s the tribal population of the eastern states of colonial India continuously protested against the colonial administration and demanding control over land and forest, and against the arbitrary power of the *thekedars*, forest guards etc.[10]Although, these movements were suppressed by the colonial government, the demand for Jharkhand was identified by the Adivasis of different followings. The tribal who were converted to Christianity and had benefited from the social services of missionaries (primarily education) played an important role in the formation and articulation of the movement. The Jharkhand movement started with the demand of an autonomous state exclusively for the tribal population of the Chhotanagpur plateau comprising the tribal populated areas of what were then the states of Bihar, Madhya Pradesh, Orissa and West Bengal. Due to the presence of this Christian component the movement of Jharkhand was identified by the RSS and the Congress government in Madhya Pradesh as a Christian inspired separatist movement, similar to the Muslim demand of Pakistan.[11]

The history and trajectory of the Jharkhand movement in its various aspects i.e. identity, ethnicity etc. has been summed up by G. Aloysius, according to whom, the earlier phase of the movement had been marked by a 'rejection of the *sahib* and *diku* ways of life...at least among the masses'. Subsequently, it retreated 'from being a struggle of tribal masses to preserve, strengthen and assert their distinct ethnic culture, identity, values, history and independence... into a movement for the "development", of the tribal much along the same path as their non-tribal neighbours'. According to Alam, the latter part of the above is caused by the failure of the State to make indigenous people partners in development.[12] Today, the most important political discussions within the movement centre on the theme of development.[13]

Today, the State has acquired a status equivalent to the predatory colonial agents, as the past epoch's land alienation and loss of community identity get linked. In the popular consciousness there are elements of continuity with the past perceptions of alien authority and State behaviour.

Aloysius further says that once again the tribal dissatisfaction has gathered momentum; however, its expression could not be any more in the same old form of 'tribal' revolt, it now became a movement for a separate State.[14]

Locating Jharkhand Movement

As according to Christophe Jaffrelot, Nationalism is an ideology which promotes one's own identity against others. Nationalism is the construction in response to cultural domination by other culture. The series of revolts- due to the reasons stated before-resulted in acceptance by the British of the distinct culture, life style and economic system (Nationality in modern parlance).[15] Nationalism is primarily an ideology which is a negative one, by which I mean it, rises in response to the 'other'. It is against this 'other', nationalism constitutes and defines itself. The Indian nationalism is a classic example of this, as it rose in response to the cultural, social and economic domination of the British.

Ernest Gellner defines Nationalism as the congruence of culture and power. It is the congruence between the two that constitutes nationalism. The consciousness of the imperative for such congruence between culture and power is the ideology; the attempts to bring about this congruence, the movement; the actual congruence, the nation.[16] If we examine the Jharkhand movement in its earlier phase in the light of above definition of nationalism, we can draw a hypothesis that the Jharkhand movement can called tribal nationalism, as the movement was against the cultural domination of both the British and native caste Hindus, and aspired to form a separate political community. We will examine this hypothesis in more detail below.

Gellner's theory is primarily a modernist theory of Nationalism. In the modern phenomenon of nation, a particular form of congruence between culture and power as transition and social change is being indicated.[17] The modern consciousness of the imperative for a fusion between culture and power, and the conscious concerted attempts to bring this about, that is, nationalism both as an ideology and a movement, has two referential points, one external and the other internal. The external reference is to other cultures, nations and nation states, which are perceived as obstacles in the way of one's own nationalism. This obstacle need not always be actual control by another culture as under imperialism, but could be a graded one. Under this aspect nationalism seeks to liberate one's own culture from the determinative influences and interferences of other culture. While this consciousness and concern was not entirely absent in ancient times, it came to be established among the community of nation-states only in modern times.[18] As it has been well established, the Adivasis as a community did face incidents of both cultural and economic imperialism during the colonial period and their resistance against it was reflected in various tribal revolts. As mentioned above the Jharkhand movement and earlier tribal revolts were directed against the 'external' factors of Hindu cultural system and colonial power structure. The concern for preserving their own culture and tradition was one of the main issues of the movement in Jharkhand since ancient period.[19]

The industrial development and its auxiliary developments in the form of education mainly brought through the Christian missionaries helped into the development of political consciousness among the tribal population. The presence of pre-modern tribal "nation" consciousness can be traced back to the various uprisings, but its modernist articulation in relation to political power was formulated in the colonial period. The demand for a separate administrative unit in Chhotanagpur was first placed before the Simon Commission in 1928 by the Chhotanagpur Unnati Samaj, led by Bishop Van Hoeck and Juel Lakra.[20] Further, the mobilisation of the nation's masses in nationalism takes place not merely on the basis of a certain primordial affinity in culture in ancient times, but on the basis of a commonality of political purpose and destiny as the emergence of a socio-political community. Earlier the identity of tribal people of Jharkhand was tied to the local community or *jat*, such as *Munda* and *Santhal*. A unified adivasi identity began to be strongly articulated with the founding of the *Adivasi Mahasabha*. The mass of men and women who were hitherto excluded from the arena of public power through ascriptive hierarchical structures of privileges/ liabilities in society and dynastic rule in polity, now emerge politically in nationalism to constitute the new politico-civil society of equal rights and liabilities. Such is the specific form of congruence between culture and power in modern nationalism.[21] That means, though the shift is towards a regional identity, the emphasis on a cultural or ethnic dimension has remained, which has been reflected in the concept of 'nationality' to describe their identity. This aspect of nationalism is very much evident in the demand and causes of the Jharkhand movement, which had a well-articulated demand of formation of an autonomous tribal state. The Jharkhand Coordination Committee declared in 1987 that-

The Jharkhand question is in essence a nationality question... The foundation of the claim of this political-geographic region is its cultural unity, geophysical uniformity and structural similarity of economic life.[22]

The ethno-symbolic theory of Nation and Nationalism developed by Smith is quite helpful in the explanation of the above-mentioned hypothesis. According to this perspective, modern nationalism's origin lies in the pre-modern forms of collective cultural identity such as those embodied in ethnies. Smith explores the origins of nations and national identity and finds them in ethnic identity as a pre-modern form of collective cultural identity. Smith defines 'ethnies' as, "Named human populations with shared ancestry myths, histories and cultures, having an association with a specific territory, and a sense of solidarity".[23] In his view, "Collective cultural identity refers not to a uniformity of elements over generations but to a sense of continuity on the part of successive generations of a given cultural unit of population, to shared memories of earlier events and periods in the history of that unit and to notions entertained by each generation about the collective destiny of that unit and its culture".[24] The ethno-symbolic approach throws light on the 'nationalism' character of the Jharkhand movement. The participating tribals in the movement, do constitute 'ethnies', as described by Smith in his theory, as they had a well-developed notion of cultural homogeneity and separateness from others, of their past and territorialisation of their respective communities. Led by the Oxford-educated *Munda Jaipal Singh*, the Adivasi Mahasabha's aim was to unite tribals against exploitation by 'outsiders' rather than to join the struggle against colonial rule.[25] The rhetoric of Mahasabha leaders emphasised tribal language and culture and their long occupation of the region as grounds for demanding political autonomy.[26]

The Jharkhand Party, presented a memorandum which was for the formation for a separate statehood, for good and efficient administration of the backward region belonging to ethnic groups.[27] For Smith the need for a homeland, a national space of one's own is a central tenet of nationalism. Only on a homeland can ethnic members come to feel their political fraternity and social cohesion.[28] Indeed, nationalism is always about a possession of land, it is through such retention that nation building starts. This makes ethnic members to think of their community as a territorial unit with special economic problems and peculiar resources, rather than simply as a culture of routine folkways.

For Oommen, when a collectivity develops the feeling that it does not belong and/or is treated as outsider, it becomes *ethnified.*[29] Such transformations represent instances of 'ethnification', which is defined as a 'process' through which the link between the territory and the culture is attenuated. This results in a denial to full-fledge participation in economy and polity to immigrant collectivity. So, it can be said that it is the ethnification, which results in the disagreement of the original collectivity.[30] Giving this 'ethnic' idea, the dimension of territory, is what I mean as Nationalism. Tribal of Jharkhand has opposed any kind of State involvement, as it feels exploited in the hands of the bourgeoise, which the modern day State involvement has created.

The participants of the Jharkhand movement did constitute a nation as they had a set of common understandings and aspirations, sentiments and ideas, which bind the population together in their homeland. Smith defines Nation, as a human group conscious of forming a community, sharing a common culture, attached to a clearly demarcated territory, having a common past and a common project for the future and claiming the right to rule itself.[31] This is the political aspect of any nationalism movement, which quite successfully captures the nature of the Jharkhand movement; its constituents and demands.

There is another concept developed by Smith which proves quite useful in the analysis of Jharkhand movement from a nationalism paradigm. The concept of 'Nation without State', - which is defined by the lack of its own State by a nation and thereby an impossibility to act as a political institution on the international scene. 'Nations without states' can be used to refer to those territorial communities who are conscious of their own identity and desire for self-determination included within the boundaries of one or more states, with which, by and large, they do not identify. In Nations without States, the feeling of identity is generally based on their own common culture and history (which often goes back to a time prior to the foundation of the nation state or, to employ Smith's theory, to its ethnic roots), the attachment to a particular territory and an explicit desire for self-determination. Again, this concept is quite useful in understanding the Jharkhand movement in its totality. The tribal population of the Chhotanagpur plateau who constituted the Jharkhand movement, was a 'Nation without State', and aspired to form a separate political community of their own on the basis of cultural differences reflected in their 'ethnie'.

Benedict Anderson in his seminal work *Imagined Communities* proposed that nations are imagined communities. He proposed that, nation is constructed from popular processes through which residents share nationality in common: It is *imagined* because the members of even the smallest nation will never know most of their fellow members, meet them, or even hear of them, yet in the minds of each lives the image of their communion.[32] This understanding both shapes and is shaped by political and cultural institutions as people 'imagine' they share general beliefs, attitudes and recognise a collective national populace as having similar opinions and sentiments to their own. It is imagined as a *community*, because, regardless of the actual inequality and exploitation that may prevail in each, the nation is always conceived as a deep, horizontal comradeship.[33] Ultimately it is this fraternity that makes it possible, over the past two centuries, for so many millions of people, not so much as to kill, as willing to die for such limited imaginings. Though this concept of nation as imagined communities, is a modernist theory and relies primarily on the role of print capitalism, but if we extend the definition of imagined communities and the basis of it to past, then clearly we can say that the participants of the Jharkhand movement, imagined a community, which constituted of their brethren and they had a clear idea of this imagined community as they were well aware of the 'other' culture against whom they defined themselves. Their idea of nation, if analysed from this perspective was a self-definition which was constructed against the 'other' nation represented by *'dikus'* and *'sahebs'*. They distinguished themselves by their endurance, heroism and sacrifice while fighting an unequal battle against the mighty imperial power.[34]

Today the people are against major irrigation projects or industries, as it is opening the area to *dikus* and thus to exploitation and terror. This is the source of unification cutting across ethnic identities.Thus, the identity of *Jharkhandis* is counterpoised against that of the *dikus*, providing psychological basis for the national dimensions in the growing self-awareness.[35]

Why not seen as 'Nationalism'

Before we go on to discuss, why the Jharkhand movement has not been seen as a 'Nationalist movement' we must discuss the term 'tribe' and the community it supposedly represents, as the very definition of the term 'tribe' lies at the heart of this argument. According to Xaxa, the British colonial government used the term 'tribe' to describe a certain category of people in India in their census, whom they found to be different from the dominant section of Indian society.[36] This differentiation was grounded primarily on the religious aspect. Tribes were identified and described as those who practiced animism. Indeed this singular definition of tribes does not captures the differences occurring across the lengths and breadth of the country and hence the tribes includes within them a wide range of groups and communities different in language, technology, geographical locations, ecological settings, level of development.[37] The whole concept of tribe, based on religious difference from the Hindus has been a point of debate, both between academicians and administrators and thus the question of whether the Jharkhand movement or any other tribal movements of central India falls under the category of nationalist or regionalist movement is based on the discourse of the tribal identity and its relationship to Hinduism.

For Xaxa, Language and region have been the driving force behind the re-organisation of the society and polity in India.[38] Also, religion and caste are the factors that are present in societies, which may be different from one another on the basis of region and language. Therefore, it is against this commonality (of religion) that the tribes have been posited and constructed by socio-anthropologists. Thus, to the colonial administrators and ethnographers tribes came to be constituted as people who practiced animism or tribal religion, and placed them outside historical textual religion. Tribes came to be conceptualised in terms of the contrasts with the universal/general features of the Indian society, than the particular features they embodied. But for the common people it was not the common features that mattered, but region and language (often referred to as ethnicity). Therefore, tribes in regional context were posited against dominant regional community; happening to be distinct linguistic and cultural community. Thus, the tribes were not conceptualised as the ones being outside the Indian social structure; the difference was seen as that of 'type' and not of 'kind'.

Ghurye's conception of tribe as 'backward Hindus' set the tone of future line of thinking, which is aggressively articulated by the *Sangh parivar*, and has become the dominant pattern of thinking regarding tribes. He regarded the tribals as 'imperfectly integrated classes of Hindu society or backward Hindus, rather than aborigines.[39] By bringing religion at the forefront of the conception of what constitutes tribes, the ideologues of this position and the *Sangh parivar* show marked continuity with the colonial tradition. And yet there is a departure in a certain respect from that tradition. In colonial literature, tribes were no doubt characterised by their distinctive religion but they were also seen in conjunction with other dimensions especially their isolation from the larger society. The latter view entailed that they were a society unto themselves and hence constituted a different society vis-à-vis the larger society. What is new as far as the advocates of *Hindutva* are concerned is that they have begun to conceive tribes solely in terms of religion. Yet, even here the proponents of *Hindutva* represent a position, which is different from the colonial point of view.

The colonial tradition classified tribes as animists, a pointer that they belonged to a religious tradition other than that of the major religions of India. The advocates of *Hindutva*, however, conveniently overlook this fact and categorise them as Hindus.[40]

The State says that they do not constitute a nation as they do not share a common language, therefore they cannot claim any right to self-determination.[41] Hence, if the movement is not for self-determination then it must be secessionist. But what is crucial here, is the growth of sense of community; an inversion of the sense of loss. This particular cultural configuration compensates for the absence of a common language.[42]

Conclusion

We tried to co-relate the various definitions of what constitutes nation and nationalism, of various eminent theorists on the topics with the intrinsic features of the Jharkhand movement. The study of Jharkhand movement through the lens of nationalism required us to locate the mass base and its nature as well as that of the movement from its origin to culmination. The analysis of Jharkhand movement through the conceptual paradigm clearly shows that the Jharkhand movement which was very much explicit in its demand and had tribal as its mass base indeed was 'nationalist' movement. The argument which is wish to propose is that the tribal movements of central India and particularly the Jharkhand movement are not categorised as national movements because of the dominant discourse of tribal identity in India from the religious aspect. This dominant discourse views the tribal of India as constituting a part of the wider Hindu religious system and sharing a common ethnicity and ancestry.

References

1. G. Alosyius, "Ideologies and Hegemony in Jharkhand Movement" in *The Jharkhand Movement,* ed. Ram Dayal Munda and S. Bosu Mullik (Copenhagen: International Work Group for Indigenous Affairs, 2003), p. 207.
2. Bipul Kumar, "Ethnic demand and the Jharkhand movement," *Rajagiri Journal of Social Development* 1, no. 2 (2010): 02.
3. S. Bosu Mullik, 2003, "Jharkhand Movement: A historical Analysis" in *The Jharkhand Movement,* ed. Ram Dayal Munda and S. Bosu Mullik (Copenhagen: International Work Group for Indigenous Affairs, 2003), p. 254.
4. Kumar, "Ethnic demand and the Jharkhand movement," *Rajagiri Journal of Social Development,* 02.
5. Javed Alam, "The Category of Non-historic Nations and Tribal" in *The Jharkhand Movement,* ed. Ram Dayal Munda and S. Bosu Mullik (Copenhagen: International Work Group for Indigenous Affairs, 2003), p. 197
6. Mullick, "Jharkhand movement", p. 255.
7. *Ibid*, p. 256
8. Alam, "The Category of Non-historic Nations and Tribal Identity", p. 195.
9. Albert Horo, "Jharkhand Movement", *International Journal of Humanities and Social Science Invention*, 2319-7714.(2013):04.
10. Nandini Sundar, "Adavasi vs. Vanvasi: The Politics of Conversion in Central India", in *Proselytisation in India- The Process of Hinduisation in Tribal Societies,* ed. S, Yemuna and K, Dharmendra (New Delhi: Aakar Books, 2009), p. 120.
11. *Ibid.*

12. Alam, "The Category of Non-historic Nations and Tribal Identity", p. 198.
13. Alosyius, "Ideologies and Hegemony in Jharkhand Movement", p. 209.
14. *Ibid.*, p. 207.
15. *Ibid.*, p. 210.
16. G. Aloysius, *Nationalism without a Nation in India* (New Delhi: Oxford University Press, 1997), p. 14.
17. *Ibid.*
18. *Ibid.*, p. 15.
19. Albert Horo, "Jharkhand Movement", p. 04.
20. Arunabha Ghosh, "Ideology and Politics of Jharkhand Movement an Overview", *Economic and Political Weekly* 28, no. 35, (1993): p. 1788.
21. Aloysius, *Nationalism without a Nation in India,* p. 15.
22. Carol Upadhyaya, In a paper presented at 'The Conference of Indian Sociological Society', December 1996.
23. Anthony D. Smith, The Ethnic Origins of Nation (New York: Blackwell, 1986), p. 153.
24. Montserrat Guibernau, "Anthony D. Smith on nations and national identity: a critical assessment", *Nations and Nationalism*, Vol. 10, no. 1/2, (2004): p. 125.
25. Susana Devalle, *Discourses of Ethnicity; Culture and Protest in Jharkhand* (New Delhi: Sage Publications, 1992), p. 139.
26. Jyoti Sen, "Tribal identity: A case study from Chhotanagpur" in *Self Images, Identity and Nationality,* ed. Chaterji, P.C. (Simla: Indian Institute of Advanced Study, 1989), p. 149.
27. Albert Horo, "Jharkhand Movement", p. 05.
28. Smith, *The Ethnic Origins of Nation*, p. 163.
29. T.K. Oommen, *Citizenship, Nationality and Ethnicity: Reconciling Competing Identities* (Cambridge: Blackwell Publishers, 1997), p. 45.
30. *Ibid.*, p. 13.
31. Smith, *The Ethnic Origins of Nation*, p. 153.
32. Benedict Anderson, *Imagined Communities: Reflections on the Origin and Spread of Nationalism* (New York: Verso, 1991), p. 6.
33. *Ibid.*, 07.
34. Ghosh, "Ideology and Politics of Jharkhand Movement an Overview", *Economic and Political Weekly,* p. 1788.

35. Alam, "The Category of Non-historic Nations and Tribal Identity", p. 199.
36. Virginius Xaxa, "Tribes, Conversion and the *Sangh Parivar*" in *Proselytisation in India- The Process of Hinduisation in Tribal Societies,* ed. S. Yemuna and K. Dharmendra (New Delhi: Aakar Books, 2009), p. 20.
37. *Ibid.*, p. 21.
38. Virginius XaXa, "Politics of Language, Religion and Identity: Tribes in India", *Economic and Political Weekly*, Vol. 40, No. 13 (Mar. 26 - Apr. 1, 2005): p. 1363.
39. G.S. Ghurye, *The Scheduled Tribes* (Bombay: Popular Book depot.,1959), p. 171.
40. XaXa, "Politics of Language, Religion and Identity: Tribes in India", *Economic and Political Weekly*, p. 1365.
41. Santosh Rana, "Jharkhand Movement" in*The Jharkhand Movement,* ed. Ram Dayal Munda and S. Bosu Mullik (Copenhagen: International Work Group for Indigenous Affairs, 2003), p. 111.
42. Alam, "The Category of Non-historic Nations and Tribal Identity", p. 197.

8

Historicising Tribal Identity in India

Vulli Dhanaraju and R.K. Bijeta

I

Tribal identity mainly focus on ethnic identity. This means that ethnic homogeneity, along with other factors, characterises a tribe. Tribe represents a historical continuity and exclusiveness. Groups which had been living together without losing or diluting their specific characteristics were formed into tribe. The formation of the tribal identity, as indeed that of tribes, was a product of territorial, economic, ecological and technological isolation. In other words, human groups of a similar ethnicity which remained isolated than the rest of the world through geography, or the use of a specific primitive technology or through economic specificity were formed into a tribe and came to acquire a tribal identity.

Defining the concept of tribe in such a manner in India is still continuing due to the fact that very few studies have developed this issue, rather most of the scholastic studies on tribal themes are associated with tribal welfare. In this respect, Andre Beteille concludes that anthropologists in India both before and after independence have been concerned more with the practical problems of definition.[1] Thus, many scholars have also referred to tribe as a type of society representing stage in social evolution, signifying a set of characteristic features and specific mode of social organisation.[2] They have explained four major sequential stages of evolution from 'band' to tribe to 'chiefdom' to the state.[3] Later on, some of them have denied of the existence of any difference between tribe and chiefdoms, band and tribes, who however, do not reveal a meaningful direction.[4]

The logic of defining 'tribe' is easily understood if it is linked to the debates of Constituent Assembly where Jaipal Singh a member favoured the use of the term 'Adivasi' instead of 'Scheduled Tribe'. This was rejected on the ground as argued by Dr B.R. Ambedkar, Chairman of the Drafting Committee of the Constitution that the word Adivasi is really a general term, which has no specific *legal de jure* connotations. He argued that the term 'Scheduled Tribe' has a fixed meaning because it enumerates the tribes.[5]

Another dimension of the term tribe is that in spite of various definitions and designations given to it, during last two decades, anthropologists and others have come across of a new term, that is 'indigenous people' which also conceptually challenges the earlier meaning of the term for tribe. The term 'indigenous people' to a large extent are similar to that of the term 'native' used during the colonial period. Since the distinctions of physical, racial traits and religion do not show many differences as compared to the non-tribal population the question of habitat, language and dialect have been regarded as the basis of tribal identity.

However, defining of tribe is very difficult task, precisely because they have had no written records either held or written by them. Whatever writings are available, they are written by 'others', with different interests and compulsions. These are mostly divorced from the objective and subjective conditions of the tribal people.

II
Tribal Identity in Ancient India

Identity formation must be perceived as a dynamic process that can be dealt with historical changes. There have been extensive research on the tribal identities in colonial period but very few studies have done on the pre-colonial period. Neeladri Bhattacharya has criticised them for the little interest shown by them on the pre-colonial tribal situation; he stated that, "the social lives and practices of forest dwellers and peasants, shifting cultivators and pastoralists, were crucially affected by the way they were seen by state and society, as well as the self-conceptions of their own practice. Research on the theme, limited as it is, has tended to focus on the colonial period, and arguments about dramatic changes in state attitudes have often been made on the basis of implicit unexplored assumptions about pre-colonial societies".[6] This makes it imperative to at least take a quick look at the pre-colonial dominant constructions of the tribes. As K.S. Singh[7] believe that though the colonialists claimed that all references to the tribes in pre-colonial India were contemptuous, it was not so. This is his quotation from *Kiratarjunetyanr,* "the Kirata King is a master of martial arts. Do not disregard him as a mountain dweller". But rather than proving the point of Singh this unfortunate quotation proves the opposite point that mountain dwellers were generally looked down upon, but the *'Kirata'* king was an exception.

Unlike Singh, Romila Thapar[8] does not find it necessary to see the dominant culture's perception monolithically i.e. either as positive or negative. In her work, she examines the image of the barbarian in ancient India. She thinks the image draws its genesis from "the curious situation of the arrival of the Indo-Aryan-speaking nomadic pastoralists in northern India who came into contact with the indigenous population (possibly the remnants of the urban civilisation of the Indus) and regarded them as barbarian". She adds that the distinction that was made with the indigenous population was a linguistic one (between the Sanskrit speakers and the non-Sanskrit speakers) and to a lesser degree, a racial one.[9]

The word that was used to describe the 'other' in Sanskrit was *mleccha.* This word did not always refer to the tribes. Its usage varied according to the circumstance and times. But we have to follow the trajectory of this word to find out what the attitudes towards the tribes were by the Aryans.

The Indian Anthropologists have been influenced by the colonial administrators, ethnographers in the writing of tribal history as H.H. Risely[10] has proposed the theory of Aryan invasion. It has been reflected in the writings of Indian traditional anthropologists and historians. The usual way of writing ancient Indian history of tribals in the words of Bhowmic: "At first, the

Aryan invaders through the North-West Frontier of India penetrated the mainland. The early settlers who resisted them were either completely annihilated or, in compelling circumstance, some of them merged with them. The rest were pushed back into the interior jungles, to the dales and the forest side inhospitable regions of our country, where somehow they were able to preserve their own culture and traditions". However, it has been vehemently criticised by the recent scholars. Jaganath Pathy[11] has stated in his work as it implicitly assumes that the proper history of tribal India had begun only with the Aryan invasion; firstly, prior to Aryan invasion, there was hardly anything substantive in the indigenous societies worthy of anthropological investigation. Secondly, the invaders forcibly absorbed a part of the tribal India while the other part was pushed into the interior, which remained, more or less isolated with their pristine culture and tradition.

Thapar has rejected the theory of Aryan invasion by stating that: "the historians therefore cannot but the theory that a large number of Aryans conquered northern India, enslaving the existing population and thereby established their language and culture, both entirely alien to the indigenous tradition. It has to be conceded that, if there was a conquest, it was limited to parts of the extreme north. It is more likely that groups of Aryan speaking people migrated into northern India, and settled and mixed up with the indigenous population. This culture that resulted evolved from this interaction". Pathy[12] has stated that the theory of Aryan invasion is still deplorable for several reasons: Firstly, it has been generally found that the capacity of hunters and gathers to fight is relatively much stronger than that of the pastoralists (Aryans). Hence one tends to be skeptical about how the Aryans conquered the hunters and gatherers. It may be mentioned that iron which could have given a better offensive capability was used only around 800 B.C., after 700 years of Aryan immigration. Secondly, if the Aryans were in need of fertile lands in river banks, the primitive inhabitants had no use of such land; which normally must have been covered by dense jungles. The common habitations of the hunters and gathers have been uplands all over the world, except where such land is unavailable in the vicinity. This is precisely because their struggle against nature and their appropriation of subsistence is easier in thinner forests of the hills than those of the fertile plains. Kosambi[13] rightly said: "primitive man would live in thinner marginal jungle, not in territory now bearing the deeper, cultivated soil; that is, the best localities for the food gatherers were approximately where they are found today".

Aloka Parasher Sen[14] has used the word to denote tribals as forest dwellers and understand how the state perceived the forest dwellers and sought to subordinate and assimilate them. Geography and the perceived existence of the hostile tribes defined the frontiers of the empire and both had to be mastered for the expansion and integration of the state. Though the Mauryan Empire was supposed to be the first centralised government in the subcontinent, Parasher Sen argues that the unconquered territories in the fringes of the empire determined the structure of the centre too. The attitude of the centre towards these fringes varied from fear to attempts at appropriation. In a quote from Kautilya, Parasher Sen proves that the jungle tribes were equated with wild animals, all of who were considered unnecessary in an ideal *janapada,* or settlement. The earlier Brahminical view was to avoid contact with the forest dwellers (known as *mleccha, atavikas).* But, Kautilya advices direct contact with them and to use them against the enemy as spies. This was supposed to keep them from looting and plundering.

By the time of the Mauryan Empire, a distinction seems to have emerged about various tribes amongst the dominant culture. Thus, Kautilya mentions *aranyacaras* and *atavikas.* The *atavikas* have connotations of a 'wild and savage tribe well entrenched in the jungle fastness who were ostensibly a nuisance to the State'.[15] The *aranyacarus* were on the other hand, tribes who were entering into some kind of negotiations with the centralised State. They were seen to be lower than the people *inhabiting janapadas* but tamed unlike the *atavikas.*

Another level of the pre-colonial construction of the tribe also betrayed some grudging respect to the jungle tribes. Thus, the *atavikas* were seen to be 'well-organised and brave, practically autonomous and fond of looting and killing'.[16] Yet, Romilla Thapar believes that *mlecchas* were also incorporated in practice into the social, political and religious systems and were the progenitors of many of the essentials of Indian culture.[17]

Once the distinction with the language was made, the territorial distinction was also made with *Arya-varta* where the correct rituals were performed, or as Parasher Sen points out, as the area where the *Dhbarmasastras* prevailed.[18] This definitely places the areas other than *Arya-varta* at a disadvantage. She also thinks that the establishment of the *Varnashrama* society also went hand in hand with these developments. Thapar says that by the second half of the first millennium B.C. that saw the extensive urbanisation of the Ganges valley, the city dwellers were made to look down upon the forest and hill dwellers who were the tribes. The names of tribes mentioned during this period include Sabara, Pulinda, Mutiba and Kirata.[19] By now it included groups ranked as mixed castes, technologically backward tribes and communities along the frontiers as well as people speaking a different tongue. Later foreigners like *Yavanas* and even Arabs were included among the *mlecchas.* More than what the barbarian did, her/his exclusion was based on certain notions of ritual purity.

Even the Jains and Buddhists had pejorative terms to describe the tribes. Parasher Sen proves that it was the social organisation of these societies that were supposed to place them at a barbaric level from the societies of the *janapadas.* Jain monks and nuns were warned to avoid the areas of 'unlearned and barbaric people'.[20]

As mentioned, it was the social organisation of those societies that is pointed out to be the reason for their barbaric nature. The social organisation not based on *varnashrama dharma* was seen to be outside civilisation. This is particularly interesting because Buddhism is seen to be a religion that came to be as a questioning of the *varna* social structure.

R.S. Sharma has also discussed about the status of tribals in ancient India. It was the time when the Aryans and, at a later stages' the high caste Hindus made all efforts to have their hegemony over the tribals. He applies historical materialistic approach to the understanding of history. Explaining his approach to social formation which took place in ancient India he puts down his basic postulate."[21] According to the hypothetical position taken by Sharma, he considers tribals of ancient India as representing class society. Class to him is a "group of people as either owns the means of production or is deprived of these.

In the initial stages of social development dispossession from the fruits of production becomes a prelude to class formation."[22] He rejects the anthropological proposition on the strength of historical evidence available to him that the tribal society centres on kinship organisation. He argued that the axis of the tribal life revolved on mode of production. There used to be tribal chief among them to whom the tribesmen submitted whatever they procured in the forests. At his level, the chief redistributed whatever food collections he got. It was an exchange system.

Whatever literature shows that the tribals did not constitute the core of the society. They always remained encapsulated within the environs of hills and forests though there are no accounts of their collective ethnicity, it is stated that they practiced a pastoral life characterised by animism. Social formation in the shape of a well defined ethnic identity and a state was also absent. They were, by and large, a classless and stateless society.

III
Tribal Identity in Medieval India

The identity of the tribals in medieval India is also controversial subject as scholars perceived the tribal from the state formation perspective while others vehemently rejected this notion. There is little information available about the tribal status during medieval period.

Suranjit K Saha's[23] article attempts the processes through which the early states emerged from within the mountain and forest regions of east-central India over a long period from A.D. 450 to A.D. 1320. It finds that the classical Hindu states to the north, particularly the Gupta empire, did indeed provide the principal ideological role model for the rise of those local and regional states, but that the latter were in the main home grown political structures built by autochthonous leaders from below to upwards. These highland states also appear to have played a crucial historical role in the gradual fusion of the lineage based local societies into a subcontinent wide pan-Indian society. He argues that an adequate understanding of the current tribal situation in the micro region, and indeed in the rise of India, would require an understanding of the spatiality differentiated process of political and material development rooted deep in its history. At the core of that understanding must recognise that

India's so-called mainstream society is built out of progressive coalescence intertwining of locally evolved processes and structures that India has been built from below to above.

Describing the process of state formation among the tribals of northern India during the medieval period, K. S. Singh observes,[24] "Following the eclipse of the Gupta Empire the wide eastern tract extending from the Himalayan foothills to the Vindhya Mountains (Kaimer range) witnessed the emergence of the rural foci of political power, led by autochthonous chieftains. Such communities as Doms, Bhars and Cheros in south Bihar, Kharwas in the Sone-Damodar Valley, Gonds and Rakshels on the Chhattisgarh region and the Bhumij on the jungle mahals of Bengal filled the vacuum in the country in the medieval period. The doms founded kingdoms at the Himalayan foothills, in the thirteenth century one of their princes ruled at Ayodhya. The Bhars occupied a large area extending from Bundelkhand and Sagar to the eastern districts and in Uttar Pradesh and Bihar as far as Bhagalpur and Tirhut".

While discussing the process of state-formation among the tribals, Singh provides a broad based data in support of his argument.[25] The process can be observed at its peak during the thirteenth century, during the period the aboriginals, especially mongoloid Ahoms, established their states in Upper Assam. The Chutiyas and Kacharis had their kingdoms sometimes before thirteenth century.[26] The Khasi kings had established relationship with about 15 neighbouring states in the plateau.[27] The Gonds, a powerful group of tribal's now mostly found in Madhya Pradesh, Odisha, and Andhra Pradesh formed states in parts of Central India.[28] Similarly during this period the Nagbansis and the Cheros established their principalities in the Shahbad and Palamau regions of Bihar.[29]

In western India, the erstwhile princely state of Banswara and Dungarpur were founded by Bhil rulers. The popular legends Banswara associates with the killing of a Bhil chieftain Bansia, and Kushalgarh with that the Kushala Bhil. It is believed that their head lie buried in the foundations of the palace gates. The image that arises from such legends is one of the establishments of kingdom by the Rajput chiefs in the area heavily inhabited by the tribals.[30]

What is important is that the diverse tribals of the northern and western India which were loose collectivities characterised by varying ethnicity, having the least mark of social differentiation, got to the intensive process of state formation. The tribal chieftains' dominion over the neighbour regions in northern India could not continue for a longer period. It was because of the fact that the non-tribal Hindu elements constituted a majority and the tribal ethnicity was not acceptable to them. In course of time the Rajputs in Bihar, Madhya Pradesh and Rajasthan, established their ascendancy over the tribal hegemony and drove them to forests and hills. It was a watershed in the history of the tribals in India. A new process of ethnic-transformation began. The tribals on one hand took to the acceptance of Rajput ethnic attributes and on the other, accepted Rajput political subjugation.

For northern Indian states, the diverse tribal groups came in direct contact with the local rulers who were in most of the cases Rajputs. Despite the heterogeneous tribal groups found in medieval India, there was no dispute to hold Gond, Santhal, and the Bhil as the numerically dominant collectivities of the country. The basic categories of the knowledge, namely, theory, method, and data, about these groups relate to the social conditioning constituted by the then historical forces. The tribal ethnicity in terms of its primordial dispositions, isolation, images, character attributes-therefore, bears the imprint of the relationship between the tribal groups on one hand and the Rajputs on the other.

One of the main factors that were an impact on both tribal identity and subsistence was the military conflict between ruling class that shows in both the Maratha and Mughal periods. The chieftain societies of different tribes like the Gonds or the Khakkars also participated in these conflicts. At the same time the tribals who were peasants or gatherers in the forests were forced to support their own chieftains and therefore formed bands in forests and formed important part of the chieftains' mercenary army. In this context it is important to remember that the term 'tribes' has been used very loosely for communities which were existed in a lineage society. In keeping with this definition many communities that were later described as peasants by the British were termed tribes by the accounts of the medieval period.

Chetan Singh's[31] early article on the role of tribal chieftains in Mughal administration clearly identified warrior and ruling classes of indigenous kingdoms as superior tribal linkages. Amongst these were the Jats, the Kakkhars, Baluchis and Afghans in this vein, the chief feature of their society not only being their blood and kinship line of descent but also their pastoral and non-sedentary occupational characteristics.

In a later article K.S. Singh is however more categorical about the mention of hunters and gatherers as primitive people. For example, he writes of their references in *Akbarnama* where tribal people were described as "men who go naked living in the wilds, and subsist by their bows and arrows and the game they kill". He also argues that the medieval texts show that in case of tribals like the Gonds "that people of India despise them and regard them outside the pale of their realm and religion". Such an identification of tribals as outside the realm of the sedentary cultivation was contingent upon the development of a system of land administration which was an important characteristic of the Mughal in sixteenth and seventeenth centuries.

The Maratha rulers did not recognise the tribal chiefs as the local kingdom instead they had always conflicts with them. O Malley[32] said that in 1804, a Maratha governor killed about 7000 Bhils and another in 1806 'boasted that he put 15000 to death in 15 months'. Before that the British perceptions of tribes were conditioned by their own contingencies. For example, the Anglo-Maratha conflicts of the eighteenth century led to descriptions that described the Gond chieftains as the "lords of the rugged hills" and their subjects as people who were prone to anarchic behaviour and "habitual depredations". Some of these depredations were described as "ravages of lawless tribes" who assisted the errant and "chaotic rulers".

Sumit Guha's[33] latest works shows that early British accounts in the region of Khandesh and Central India argues that the complex interrelationships between pre-colonial regimes of natural resource management, environmental changes and tribal subsistence in the Maratha period. The resultant identity of people as tribals is then governed by the multiple contexts of survival within which these people used to live. Larger patterns of resource use and the impact of other forces on them also determined the political economy of such identities and survival systems. In the analysis of state's perspective of land it has been pointed out that even in pre-British period 'the rulers, like the Marathas, saw the forest as an obstacle: tree cover multiplies the danger from robbers, rebels and tigers'. Jungle clearance has been equated in terms of fresh revenue possibilities though it had been an arduous and difficult task.

Nandini Sinha's[34] work shows that for the region of Mewar similar themes have been explored. She asserts that forested and hill regions were integrated into wider imperial systems of South Asia. Moreover the panorama of economic activities in any sub-region was far more diverse than is often realised. There were no clear-cut stages or phases like hunter-gatherer, herder, settled cultivators and artisan and city dweller.

The accounts of Gonds, Santhals, and Bhils given by Haimendorf, James Tod and others for the medieval period show that the tribal groups enjoyed a lot of freedom, occupied entire tracts, and lived as the "Lords of Pass" the masters of valleys, forts, and villages and passes.

Pathy[35] has summarised the nature of the state formation among the tribals. He said that interesting warfare amongst the chiefs might have given military victory to some them, who eventually established kingdoms. The subjects however neither completely belonged to single state. For instance, the kingdom of Bhils never covered all the Bhils, whereas they contained Varlis, Minas and also non-tribals in their territory. The stability of these states depended primarily on economic prosperity, and next on the military strength. No wonder therefore the early kingdoms disintegrated within a century or even within decades, and the later kingdoms pursued the policy of reclamation and extension of cultivation, development and adoption of new technology, and of extensive irrigation. In other words, their stability depended on the amount of surplus they could generate from agriculture.

The medieval 'official' argues that the tribal uprisings for the restoration of their original home state were nothing short of a rebellion. The social conditioning constituted by the history created a situation for the tribals that they had to accept the non-tribal hegemony. The Rajputs, for instance, rulers took all opportunities to suppress the tribals. On a broader perspective, the tribals of northern India, especially Bihar, central and western India had hardly begun the process of state formation.

Along with these kingdoms, there were numerous small tribal chiefdoms, spread all over the country. Several of these relied heavily on shifting cultivation. The chiefs either received a small tribute from the village or lineage headmen, in return for protection or took share in the produce. In either case, it does not appear to have constituted a serious burden for the producers. The aristocracy minority interfered little in the conditions of production and often exploited less their own people than the neighbouring tribes. There was of course extra economic coercion, but the obligations were so diffused that it could make regulated reproduction, without ever being challenged. Simultaneously, the conquest of weaker tribes or clans yielded not only wealth but also slaves for the production process. Cutting across tribal boundaries, slavery was, in one or other form, almost universal in most of the chiefdoms. The chiefs also derived substantial wealth from the transit trade through their territory.

IV
Colonialism and Tribals

Tribal history in India is largely a product of colonial ethnography. Though the early sources for information about the tribals were the accounts of travellers, administrators and Christian missionaries, a systematic study of these people in India begins with the establishment of the Asiatic Society of Bengal. Anthropological studies in India until independence were confined to the study of tribes and were geared largely to the need of colonial administration, with its years of experience in governing the 'nature' and some administrators realised fairly well the importance of anthropology in all works relating to the people under their charge.

Colonial administrators produced a good amount of writings on the tribals, perhaps their writings formed one of the discursive realms in constituting the people living on the margins as 'tribe'. These writings include ethnographic notes, monographs, administrative reports, census, missionary reports and other informative reports. This is primarily meant to produce knowledge about these people, so as to enable colonial governance effective. In this sense anthropology can be said to have developed as part of the colonial administrative system. In order to implement imperialist and colonial policies in the countries they conquered and brought under their rule the compilation of knowledge about these people was necessary. Therefore, certain anthropologists turned to be the apologists of the colonial regimes. In the beginning it was mainly the biological studies of the tribal people and also was concerned with the origin, evolution and diversity of these people. It was concerned only with a limited and restricted study and never moved beyond the study of humans. Such studies lacked the understanding and interpretation in historical perspective, but only provided data for administrative purposes.

The necessity of making census in Indian States during British era was not simply aiming at the census of population; rather it was more of documentation of the natural resources of the localities. This became useful as a wealth for making capital, which was rightly understood by British rulers. The first census report by Baine during 1891, the then Commissioner for Census of India included all tribal groups as ' Forest Tribes', and kept the same under the sub-heading of 'Agricultural and Pastoral Castes'. Their number was estimated at 16 million, who were again classified as 'Animists' or 'people following tribal religion' in the census report of 1911 by Gait; as 'Hill and Forest Tribes' in the Census Report of 1911 by Hutton. These people by that time were numbering two million and later on came to be known as ' Backward Tribes' in the Government of India Act 1935, and as ' Tribes' in the Census Report of 1941 accounting for a total population of 2.47 crores. Similarly, over the time the term 'tribe' in Indian context, by and large, is synonymously used as *Adivasi* (original settlers), *Girijan* (Hill dwellers), *Vanyajapt* (Forest caste), *Adimjati* (Primitive caste), *Janajati* (Folk Communities) and *Anusuchit Janajati* (Scheduled Tribe). Identification of the tribal groups through various factious names not only brought many common masses into its fold, but also imposed various new names, which the tribal people even do not know.

Sumit Guha[36] assumes that rather than taking these communities as actually being primitive, we have to see them as having been "primitivised" in modernity. In his book he observes that "The role that the modern regime of the forests played in isolating one segment of the population within the newly drawn boundaries of the forest is highlighted in order to make the point that the resulting primitivisation of these peoples is a recent consequence of the breakdown of their political system. It is argued that by concentrating solely on the truncated remnant of the old hierarchy, observers overlooked the living apex of the new one, succumbed to the notion of the simple, primitive and egalitarian forest tribe, and hence failed to see the simplified, primitivised, silvicultural proletariat that it was being hammered into becoming".

Nandini Sundar's book, *Subalterns and Sovereigns: An Anthropological History of Bastar, 1854-1996*, is an implicit critique on the categories of anthropology and history proceeds made initially by colonial officials, between the tribes and castes of India. Colonial officials believed that the tribes—usually communities that lived in or around forested and hilly areas—were the original inhabitants of India, and had been driven into the forests by the incursions of later communities. The tribes, by this account, were autochthonous and largely isolated groups, dependent on modes of subsistence that were primitive in comparison to the castes. They practiced animist religion distinct from that of the castes. This book persuasively shows how even Bastar, often treated as a paradigmatic example of tribal India, resists fitting into the tribe-caste distinction. This supposedly isolated tribal area is extremely diverse linguistically and culturally; it has seen considerable in-migration over the centuries. The political and religious practices prevalent in the region were far from being outside by any "mainstream" of Indian history.

James C. Scott[37] has developed new argument in understanding of primitiveness among the tribals. He argues that the 'hill Peoples' backwardness is a political choice.

Conventional narratives treat these people as backward, barbarous, primitive vestiges of a pre-civilised era. Scott argues this narrative is wrong and instead insists that "hill peoples" are, and have always been 'barbarians' by design. Hill peoples sought to position themselves outside the scope of state power. To avoid the state 'hill peoples' practice both state evasion and state prevention, which involve the adoption of a distinct set of economic, political, social and cultural practices. State evading characteristics are traits 'that make it difficult for a state to capture or incorporate a group or appropriate its material production'. State preventing traits are 'those that make it unlikely that a group will develop internally durable, hierarchical, state-like structures'.

Ajai Skaria[38] has understood the problems of marginal issues in the context of politics of construction of ideas such as jangali, tribal, primitive. He questions the notion whereby tribals were equated with 'wild' and 'primitive' and settled agriculture (under the patronage of state) with civilisation. He also discussed the interdependence between state and tribal policies where revenue rights and authority were shared in a complex web of relationship. There has now been an attempt to question the notion of a uniform British policy all across India and recent researches have pointed out that there was a serious divergence of views on policies related with the forest, land and agriculture.

Thus, the colonial rule's implication in India is one of the vast historical phenomena in Indian history. The colonial rule marked a significant point especially in the tribes of different regions where they were lived under economical as well as cultural deprivation. In order to fully exploit the economic and cultural resources of the country, the British rulers introduced various institutional structures and policies in tribal belts in India. Singh argues that the entry of the colonialism into the tribal regions of India through various philanthropic strategies of the communal tribal mode of production and attributed judicial nature of the regions by way of adopting survey and hence, the emergence of the private right on land.[39] The very entrance of the colonial state into these areas was resisted violently by the tribals of the respective regions.

It has often been assumed that tribal people and their societies lived in insulated and secluded enclaves before the advent of the British in India. This means that their economies and culture was relatively untouched by outside markets and therefore were relatively closed; egalitarian and prosperous communities. These economies were free of exploitation because they had no private property and need rather than the profit motive necessitated their relationships of exchange. In one sense the tribal economy was characterised as being quite the opposite of peasant agriculture under the colonial rule where the peasants held individual titles to land, depended mostly on settled cultivation for their livelihoods and also sold a good part of their produce in the commercial market. But the historical evidence from many of the areas show that such a notion of the tribal economy in the anthropological writings of the 1930s was steeped in ecological romanticism.

The restrictions imposed on tribal people by the British administration through their law enforcement, had endangered the 'freedom of the natives', and forced them to question the imposition of new types of authority. Due to the imposed British policies, a segment of the new native ruling authority emerged, which exploited tribal people in various forms. Their challenges had taken the shape of insurrections witnessed in all the tribal belts of the country from time to time. In every part of India the impact of British rule led to new social formations among the tribal people. Ownership of tribal communities was now replaced by the *de jure* ownership of the state, which ultimately led to the exploitation of the forest resources with total disregard for the needs of the tribal economy. The commercialisation of forest had another aspect, that is, the natural missed forest which provided the tribes with the raw materials for their household implements and bamboo for baskets, and such items of food as mangoes, tamarind, jack fruits, and edible berries, were now being replaced by plantations of teak, eucalyptus and various coniferous etc., all lucrative commercial crops.

Further the new land tenure system deprived the tribal population of their communal rights over forests and lands forcing those two given up many vital activities which were customary rights and essential for day-to-day living. They were brought under a new bourgeois legal, property and administrative setup which uprooted them from their own patterns of justice based on a different set of norms and values. Further, British policies encouraged an influx of zamindars, their representatives, forest contractors, traders, moneylenders, administrators, and educationists (predominantly missionaries) into the tribal areas. These sections of people exploited the tribals with the political and judicial backing of the colonial government. Vast sections of tribal people were transformed into landless labourers and bonded serfs who were economically and socially dependent on the various categories of people described above. This had a devastating effect on every aspect of tribal life. This was an all India process operating unevenly.

In this context there were broadly three processes of colonial expansion that had impact on the tribal people. The first was the process of reclamation of lands for cultivation that led to severe land alienation among the tribal people. The second major factor influencing the patterns of tribal livelihood was the complete ban on shifting cultivation in government forests. The third major process affecting tribal economies was the penetration of industrial capitalism in forested areas. Here the focus was not only on felling of timber but more importantly on the non-timber forest produce which formed an important supplementary part of tribal income. The rise in the world demand for minor forest produce led to the influx of European capital into forested areas and changed the very nature of production relations.

The forest policy and management of forests has been a subject of considerable debate and conflict since the establishment of British rule in India. The imperial needs dictated the British interest in the Indian forest resources, which resulted in the establishment of control over forest resources. The colonial system of forest management was continued even after 1947 with little modifications, emphasising revenue generational and commercial exploitation while its policing orientation excluded tribals who had the most longstanding claim on forest resources. The tribals especially were confronted with colonial forest management that continuously eroded their life-styles and simultaneously the assertion of state monopoly over natural resources deprived them of an important means of subsistence.[40]

Ramchandra Guha[41] has developed the new argument in understanding of natural resources which countered the Marxist frameworks of social formation. He argues that Marxian framework of mode of production does not take into account the exploitation of natural resources. He has focused on 'modes of resource use' to point out how human beings either used natural resources rationally or exploited them on an unlimited scale. He argued there emerged 'ecosystem people', 'omnivores' and 'carnivores' and focused on colonial forestry to point out its role in dislocating 'ecosystem people'. His work definitely helps in understanding the changes in the socio-economic position of tribals. Geeti Sen [42] argues that the forest policies formulated under the British rule still exercise deep impact on the contemporary forest policies in India. She claims that "the forest laws enacted by the British colonial rule are still in force and with the government claiming the jungles as its property to be exploited even at the cost of extensive marginalisation of *Adivasis*.

Ajay Skaria[43] examines the forest policies in the Dange tribal region of the Western India. He argues that how the Dange tribal society underwent transformation due to the colonial state intervention through forest policies. He argues that penetration of the colonial state apparatus, especially the forest department, deprived the Dange hill tribes by evolving a plan based intermediaries' exploitation and at the same time, transformed their identity. Kavitha[44] pointed also out the strategies adopted by the Forest Department, not only to control tribes but also use them as cheap labour in forest conservation activities in different parts of the Madras Presidency. She argues that the pattern of modernity, initiated by the colonial forest policies, negatively affected the forest dependent tribes in South India. Velayatham Saravan[45] argues that the commercialisation of the forest resources, initiated by the British deprived the forest based tribal economy by denying the customary access to forest resources. He maintains that the British forest policies created favourable atmosphere for the plain-based intermediaries for exploitation in tribal areas.

The establishment of British rule brought about a revolution in the nature and extent of the contact of the plains people with the tribals. The spread of the non-indigenous moneylender is indeed a peculiar feature of Indian economic history in the nineteenth century whose connection with the British occupation and the British Judicial system cannot be disputed. With the transition to money economy and the establishment of novel concepts regarding land rights and judicial procedure, the more enterprising moneylenders who did not belong to the same society came in large numbers. And along with him in the Agency areas, there was naturally found migrating classes who were keen to sense these opportunities and intended to exploit them.[46]

Further, the colonial economic policies during the nineteenth century destroyed the occupations of a number of tribals. The salt policy of the government dictated by considerations of revenue was instrumental in destroying the trade of koravas, yerukulas, banjaras etc. The governments' forest policy prevented free grasing of the cattle owned by these groups (cattle was crucial in transporting the merchandise) and prevented them from collecting forest produce which they bartered for salt.[47]

Around the last quarter of the nineteenth century, the increasing rate of crime against property induced the administration to adopt the concept of hereditary criminal, responsible for the large number of crimes in the countryside. The trading communities who were for a brief period classified as 'wandering tribes' were now put into this new category, which was a precursor to them being classified later as criminal tribes.[48] In 1871, Criminal Tribes Act was restricted in its application and extended only to certain provinces in north India. For instance, the trading communities of Madras presidency, the yerukulas, koravas, banjaras and lambadies were declared criminal tribes in 1913 under the Criminal Tribes Act of 1911.[49]

The intervention of the British in the name of checking incursions can be seen as deliberate and determined attempts to establish control over forests. At the same time the government never warned the Mansabdar/Muttadars[50] against activities such as annexation of *muttas* and leasing the villages to non-tribals and imposition of additional taxes in the case of Andhra Agency areas. This enabled traders from the plains to exploit the tribals under the cover of judicial and official machinery. This intrusion posed a grave danger to the self-sustaining subsistence lives of the tribals. The tribals, caught between different exploiters, finally resorted to Rampa rebellion in 1879. The government appointed Sullivian to enquire into the causes for the Rampa rebellion and sought suggestive remedies.

There was also much resentment against the lower level forest officials, who acted as a new kind of police force. They demanded gifts and services during their tours and threatened to lodge cases of violation of forest laws unless the people paid them money.[51] During the late nineteenth century this resentment fed in to several major uprisings against the British by forest dwellers.

It is not as if the tribal people of the country were mute spectators to colonial interventions. The earliest tribal revolts can be traced to mid nineteenth century with the Kol rebellion. Thereafter the *zamindari* areas of Chhotanagpur faced several other rebellions prominent amongst which was Birsa Munda's rebellion against the *dikus* or outsiders in the region. In response to this movement the British were forced to enact the Chhotanagpur Tenancy Act in 1885.[52] Several princely states also saw tribal movements in response to adverse changes in land and forest management. Prominent amongst these was the Maria rebellion in Bastar in 1876 and 1910 which was meant to be against police repression and forest laws. Here too, the slogan was 'Bastar for Bastaris' against outsiders.[53] David Arnold[54] worked on the tribal resistance to the colonial state intrusion in the Rampa and Gudem areas of the Andhra agency area. He shows how the restrictions imposed by the forest departments on shifting cultivation and minor forest products resulted in series of tribal revolts. He argues that the socio-economic conditions of certain tribes like the *Koyas* and *Konda Reddis* were disrupted by the commercialisation of forest and their subsistence economy was replaced by money and commercially oriented economy. Consequently, the Andhra region witnessed a series of tribal revolts against the colonial state's forest policies. In all these cases there was a perception that the Rajas had begun to deprive the tribal people of their customary rights especially after the advent of the British. It is because of this that tribal elites led the revolts against the Rajas.

The Impact of the British rule over the tribal lands and forestry can be viewed as a conflict between two opposing forces. For the British it is a struggle for power and maintenance of the statuesque and for the tribes it is a struggle for their very survival. The impact is studied from two perspectives; the British and the Tribal. For the British it is viewed as development in terms of conservation of forest resources and exploitation of forest wealth for infrastructural development such as railways, shipyards, and roads and buildings. In the process they encouraged outsiders from the plains to inhabit in the tribal villages for promoting settled agriculture. The tribals were discouraged from carrying out shifting cultivation. For them the British rule is of displacement and loss of livelihood.

V

Independent India also adopted this integrationist approach towards tribals. Assimilation is the loss of ethnic attributes of minorities as a result of interaction and its absorption into the dominant group would lead to 'antagonism, tension and increasing alienation of each from the other.'[55] Integration can be seen in the political, economic and administrative integration within a framework of cultural plurality where minorities can join the majorities without losing their linguistic, religious and cultural identity.

Thus, Tribals are now the main sufferers in the 'welfare' politics. The development projects often involve displacement of the tribes. Forceful acquisition of their land for construction of dams, for mining operations, industries, national parks etc have forced them to leave their traditional way of life. They end up becoming unskilled labour and migrate to urban areas for work. Nearly 50-60 million people have been displaced by development projects in India as a whole and tribals constitute at least 40 per cent of them. Cash payment does not really compensate the tribals for the difficulties they experience in their lifestyle and ethos. It's also difficult to rehabilitate them as they cannot be resettled in other tribal areas. Land is traditionally divided among the tribes and one tribe cannot enter the area of another tribe. In the case of the Andaman, as we will see further, the tribes have become a mere tourist attraction. So 'Development' might be taking place but most of the time, at the cost of their way of survival.

References

1. Andre Beteille, 'Anthropology and Some Indian Problems', *Institute of Social Research and Applied Anthropology*, Calcutta, 1972, p. 188.
2. E.R. Service, *Primitive Social Organisation*, Random House Inc, New York, 1962; M.H. Fried, *On the Concept of Tribe and Tribal Society*, Transactions of the New York Academy of Sciences, Serious-II, No. 4, pp. 527-540.
3. *Ibid.*
4. M. Godelier, *Perspectives in Marxist Anthropology*, Cambridge University Press, London, 1977, pp. 76-87.

5. N.K. Behura and Nilakantha Panigrahi (ed), *Tribals and the Indian Constitution*, Rawat Publication, Jaipur, 2006, pp. 6-7.
6. Neeladri Bhattacharya, 'Introduction', *Studies in History,* 14. 2, 1999, pp. 165-171.
7. K.S. Singh, *Tribal Society in India: An Anthropo-Historical Perspective*, Manohar, New Delhi, 1985.
8. Romilla Thapar, *Ancient Indian Social History: Some Interpretations*, Orient Blackswan, Delhi, 1978, pp. 152-193.
9. *Ibid*, p. 152.
10. H.H. Risely, *The People of India*, Thacker Spink & Co, Calcutta and Simla, 1908.
11. Jaganath Pathy, *Tribal Peasantry Dynamics of Development*, Inter-India Publications, New Delhi, 1984, p. 46.
12. *Ibid*, pp. 47-48.
13. Kosambi, *An Introduction to the Study of Indian History*, Popular Prakashan, Bombay, 1975.
14. Aloka Parasher Sen, 'Of Tribes, Hunters and Barbarians: Forest Dwellers in the Mauryan Period', *Studies in History*, 14, 2,1998.
15. *Ibid*, p. 179.
16. Kautilya quoted in Aloka Parasher Sen, 1998, p.179.
17. Romilla Thapar, op.cit., 1978, p.181.
18. Aloka Parasher Sen, op.cit., 1998, pp.173-191.
19. *Ibid*, p.159.
20. *Ibid*, p.177.
21. R.S. Sharma, *Material Culture and Social Formation in Ancient India*, MacMillan India Limited, Delhi, 1983, p. XVI.
22. *Ibid*.
23. Suranjit K Saha, "Early State Formation in Tribal Areas of East Central India", *Economic & Political Weekly,* Vol. 31, No. 13 (March 30, 1996), pp. 824-834.
24. K.S. Singh, 'A Study in State Formation among Tribal Communities', in R. S. Sharma (Ed), *Indian Society: Historical Probings*, People's Publishing House, New Delhi, 1984, p. 318.
25. *Ibid*.
26. Amalendu Guha, 'Ahom Migration: Its Impact on Rice Economy of Medieval Assam, *Artha Vignana*, 2 (9), 1967.
27. Bani Prasanna Misra, 'Agraraian Relations in a Khasi State', Economic and Political Weekly, XIV,1979, pp. 888-892.
28. C.Von Furer Haimendorf , *The Gonds of Andhra Pradesh*, Vikas, New Delhi, 1979.

29. R.D. Holder, "An Abstract of the Annals of the Nagbasi Raj Family of Chhotanagapur", *Man in India*, Vol. II, 1928.
30. Brijraj Chouhan, *Towns in the Tribal Setting*, National Publishing House, Delhi, 1970, p. 27.
31. Sumit Guha, *Environment and Ethnicity*, Cambridge University Press, Cambridge, 1999.
32. Cited in Jaganath Pathy, op.cit.,1984.
33. Sumit Guha, 'Claims on the Commons: Political Power and Natural Resources in Pre-Colonial India', *The Indian Economic and Social History Review,* 39, 2 and 3, 2002, pp. 181-196.
34. Nandini Sinha, *State Formations in Rajasthan: Mewar during the Seventh- Fifteenth Centuries*, Manohar, Delhi, 2002.
35. Jaganath Pathy, op.cit., 1984, pp. 53-54.
36. Sumit Guha, *Environment and Ethnicity in India: 1200-199,* Cambridge University Press, Cambridge, 1999, p. 8.
37. James C Scott, *The Art of Not being Governed: An Anarchist History of Upland South East Asia*, Yale University Press, New Haven & London, 2011.
38. Ajai Skaria, 'Being Jangali: The Politics of Wilderness', *Studies in History*, Vol. 14, No. 2 1998, pp. 193-215. Also see Ajai Skaria, *Hybrid Histories: Forests Frontiers and Wildness*, Delhi, 1998.
39. K.S. Singh, op.cit.,1985, p.12.
40. Ranjith Guha, *Elementary Aspects of Peasant Insurgency in Colonial India*, Duke University Press Books, Delhi, 1983.
41. Ramchandra Guha and Madhav Gadgil, *The Unquiet Woods: Ecological Change and Peasant Resistance in the Himalaya*, Oxford University Press, New Delhi, 1992.
42. Geeti Sen (ed), *Indigenous Vision: People of India Attitudes Environment*, Sage Publications, New Delhi, 1992.
43. Ajay Skaria, 'Timber Conservancy, Desiccationist and Scientific Forestry: The Dangs, 1840-1920', in Grove, V. Damodaran and S. Sangwan (ed), *Nature and Orient*, Oxford University Press, New Delhi, 1999.
44. Kavitha Philip, *Civilising Natures: Race, Resources and Modernity in Colonial South India*, Orient Longman, New Delhi, 2002.
45. Velayutham Saravanan, 'Commercialisation of Forests, Environmental Negligence and Alienation of Tribal Rights in the Madras Presidency, 1792-1882', *Indian Economic & Social History Review,* Vol. 35, No. 2, 1998, pp. 125-146.

46. G.S. Ghurye, *The Aboriginals- "So-called"- and their Future*, Gokhle Institute of Politics and Economic, Pune, 1943, p. 49.
47. Report on the Administration of the Madras Presidency during the year 1889-1890, Government Press, Madras, 1890, p. 27.
48. Meena Radha Krishna 'The Criminal Tribes Act in Madras Presidency: Implications for Itinerant Trading Communities', *Indian Economic Social History Review*, Vol. 26, No. 3 July-September, 1989, p. 275.
49. *Ibid*, p. 269.
50. Mutta refers to a group of villages. The head of the Mutta is called a Muttadar. The Raja of Jeypore is believed to have appointed these tribal headmen to collect the revenues and pay to him annually thorough Zamindar.
51. Richard Tucker, 'Forest Management and Imperial Politics: Thana District, Bombay, 1823-1887', *Indian Economic and Social Historical Review*, 1980, p. 290.
52. K.S. Singh, op.cit., 1985.
53. Nandini Sundar, *Subalterns and Sovereigns: An Anthropological History of Bastar (1854-1996)*, Oxford University Press, Delhi, 1997.
54. David Arnold, 'Rebellious Hillman: The Gudem-Rampa Raisings, 1893-1924', in Ranjit Guha (Ed), *Subaltern Studies: Writings on South Asian History*, Vol. I, Oxford University Press, New Delhi, 1982, pp. 88-142.
55. V.Venkata Rao, *A Century of Tribal Politics in North-East India,1874-1974*, S. Chand, New Delhi, 1976, 546.

III

Gender and Marginality

9

Status and Identity of Tea Garden Women: A Case Study of Tamulbari Tea Estate in Dibrugarh

Sunanda Sahu

Introduction

Men and women are like two wings of a bird which only in unison can take a lofty flight. Therefore, both the wings have to be developed equally for progressive development of a society. In a patriarchal society like India the scenario is not the same because the role of male is considered more important than the female. Tracing back to history it is found that the status of women is changing. In the present scenario though the participation of women in different occupational and professional sector has increased, still they need to cope up their day to day situations in an unconditional ways. These gender inequalities give importance to the study of identity and status of women. Women play an important role in the upliftment of society.

Status is primarily a position in a social structure which involves rights, duties and reciprocal expectations of behaviour. An individual carries his social position around in his head, so to speak, and puts it into action when the appropriate occasion arises. Not only does he carry it in his head but others also carry it in theirs, because social positions are matters of reciprocal expectation and must be publicly and commonly conceived by everyone in the group. An individual who has a purely private conception of his status is insane and socially useless (Davis, 2007).

Each person occupies many different statuses. We sometimes speak of the status or the social position of a given individual, meaning the sum total of his specific statuses and roles especially in so far as they bear upon his general social standing (*ibid*). From an anthropological view point, status is primarily a position in a social structure involving rights, duties and reciprocal expectations of behaviour, none of which depends the personal characteristics of the status occupant (Kaniampady, 2003). A status as distinct from the individual, who may occupy it, is simply a collection of rights and duties. Since these rights and duties can find expression only through the medium of individuals, it is extremely hard for us to maintain a distinction in our thinking between status and the people who hold them and exercise the rights and duties which constitute them (Davis, 2007).

In the society at the time of interacting situation the identity of each person becomes very important. For example, a husband expects social response from his wife, but not every man has the right to expect such a response from her. A person therefore enters a social situation within an identity already established. His identity refers to his position, or status, within the social structure applicable to the given situation, and establishes his rights and obligations with reference to others holding positions within the same structure. His position and consequently his identity in the particular situation result from all the other positions he holds in other major social structures, especially in other structures most closely related to the one he is acting in at the moment (*ibid*).

Objective of Study

The present study tries to make an attempt to get a brief idea about the status and identity of Tea Garden women. Majority of the women in Tea Garden are engaged in Tea Plantation works. They are considered as most potential labour force of the Tea Industry. It is proposed to carry out a study to understand the status and identity of tea garden women. The main objective of study is to get a glimpse of the status of tea garden women in its socio-cultural, economic and political aspect:

Methodology

The study is empirical based on field study. However, the help of secondary sources were also undertaken. For the purpose of study Tamulbari Tea Estate (Line no: - 3) of Dibrugarh district is selected. It consists of 107 households. This line is mixture of different ethnic groups comprising of Orang, Tanti, Mal, Mura etc. In this line of the Tea Estate, all the communities are Hindus and only one household practise Christianity. This line is a heterogeneous one but for small sample size all are taken in one category as Tea Garden labourers.

Tea Labourers in Assam

Tea is one of the oldest industries in India and today it enjoys the status of one of the best organised industries in India and today it enjoys the status of one of the best organised industries in the country. More than a million workers in India are directly employed in the tea plantations and manufacturing industries (Kaniampady, 2003).

The tea labourers, in Assam are composed of various tribes and castes and belong to multi-linguistic and multi-cultural heritages which display a kaleidoscopic pattern of ethnic mosaic. It is also relevant to note that despite the heterogeneous composition of the population, they always exhibit an apparent unity and integrity among themselves. This kind of manifestation is, of course, one of the most often noticed feature of Indian society that is *Unity and Diversity* (*ibid*).

Tea Plantations and Women Workers

Tea is one of the few industries which mainly depend upon woman labourers to work in the tea beds. Surveys show that the entire North East has as much as 60 per cent women workers and in the case of Assam alone 45 per cent women are employed in the tea plantations. The probable factors that contribute towards having such a large number of women workers in the plantations are: (a) the plantation work is only a special kind of agricultural work and is, therefore, familiar to Indian women, the vast majority of whom live in rural areas; (b) facilities have given to male workers to settle in, or in the vicinity of the plantations and to have their wives and families with them; (c) under the old system, labour contract was based on the principle of utilisation of the able bodied persons of the family of a labourer and fixing the wage rates accordingly; and (d) many women had to seek employment in order to balance the family budget. Although the contract system has been abolished, the wage system and need for supplementary earnings still remain (ed. Kaniampady, 2003).

Status of Women and Social Life

Social life is the basis of human society. It grows out of constant patterning of social interactions and relationships that take place within some institutionalised groupings among human beings (ed. Kaniampady, 2003). It is the characteristics of society which is a network of relationship based on social interactions and is a complex form of individuals in which both are interdependent on each other. Without individuals we cannot imagine a society (Jha, 1994). In order to get a clear picture of social life it becomes very much necessary to give importance to the study of family and marriage. They are considered as the bases of social life. It may be emphasised that the family is considered to be the most important element in the social life, as it forms the first sphere in which individual combine. It is the fundamental social institution that fulfils the various needs of a human being in his life.

Family Life

Family is a primary social group, universally recognised to be basis of all human endeavour and activities. The concept of family has been found to exist since time immemorial and at all the levels of culture (Jha, 1994). Family is the initial platform for socialisation and enculturation, therefore an overall idea of the family life involving the members of the two sexes is expected to reflect on the position of a woman in the family in particular and the society in general. Here, an attempt is made to have some idea about the preference given to a particular sex at the time of birth, socialisation process in the childhood of a girl baby, consent of marriage, husband-wife relationship, widowhood, intra – family relationship etc.

Preferences towards the sex of the child at the time of birth

The attitude of the members of a family towards the sex of a child is considered to be moulded by the overall position of the particular sex in the society and the stereotypic attitude towards the gender. It may also be considered to be reflective of the same. Thus, it is very often found that a boy and a girl child are differently welcomed in a good number of societies. During the present study an attempt was made to know the sex preference of a prospective baby in a family. A total of 50 respondents (25 couples) were interviewed for this purpose. The responses have been presented in Table no: -1which are as follows:-

Table 9.1: Distribution of the Respondents according to their preference of Children

Sl No.	*Preferences*	*Male*	*Female*	*Total*
1.	Boy child	22	21	43
2.	Girl child	02	01	03
3.	Both	01	03	04
4.	**Total**	**25**	**25**	**50**

It is seen from the Table 9.1 that a very small number of people prefer to have a girl child. The respondent those are preferring a boy child are more or less majority in number. A boy is preferred mainly because he is considered to be an economic asset of the family as well as one who continues the father's lineage in the next generation. Few respondents who prefer to have a girl child because of the prospects of better domestic assistance.

Socialisation process and the girl child

The paradox of a human society is that it has a unity and continuity of its own and yet exists solely in the minds and actions of its members which can be resolved only by understanding how the newborn individual is moulded into a social being. Without this process of moulding, which we call socialisation, the society could not perpetuate itself beyond a single generation and culture could not exist. Nor could the individual become person; for without the ever repeated renewal of culture within him there could be no human mentality, no human personality

(Davis, 2007). The nature of socialisation is obviously of such a character as to be greatly affected by the kind of persons who do it (*ibid*).

The equalitarian element in socialisation is perhaps a bit difficult considering age, sex and rank in a particular society. As a corollary of this weakness towards the particular sex of the child, it has been observed that during socialisation process there is a tendency to give more importance to boy child than a female child. An attempt was made to have a quantitative idea of the frequency of importance given towards the sex of the children at the time of socialisation process by randomly selecting 25 couples consisting of 50 respondents in Table 9.2 which are as follows:-

Table 9.2: Distribution of the Respondents according to their importance given to particular sex of a child during the Socialisation process.

Sl. No.	*Importance given to*	*Male*	*Female*	*Total*
1.	Boy child	21	23	44
2.	Girl child	01	01	02
3.	Both	03	01	04
4.	**Total**	**25**	**25**	**50**

Marriage Life

Marriage may be defined as a publicly recognised and culturally sanctioned union between a male and female. Marriage serves as a means for getting together to satisfy sex needs and to start the reproductive process. It is through reproduction, human species is replicated and society is perpetuated. It helps in the division of labour, and helps in creation and perpetuation of a family (Jha, 1994).

Family appears as a result of marriage and it continues through marriage. It is therefore, a very important institution without which the society could never be sustained. Marriage may be defined as a union between a man and a woman such that children born to the woman are recognised as legitimate offspring of both the parents (ed. Kaniampady, 2003). Marriage brings a transition in one's life especially in case of girl where she has to change her residence, assume new role and expectations. After marriage there is a radical change in her status and identity in comparison to the boys.

Due to scarcity of income marriage among the people under study is not considered as a prerequisite for the formation of a family. They live together and perform all the duties and after saving money the marriage rituals are performed by throwing a feast for the entire village. From the investigation it is found that most of the marriages are due to mutual consent and elopement. It also found that young girls and boys get married at a very small age.

To get a glimpse of identity of the women, randomly fifty married women were interviewed by a query that marriage brings changes in their identity or not. Eighty per cent of the respondents were of the opinion that their individual identity vanishes gradually and now their identity is associated with their husband only. The transition is observed in the terminology of their address where they are not called by their name but they are called as wife of so and so. In the older age they are recognised as the mother of their respective children especially sons. They were of the view that as time passes their linkage with the family of orientation becomes very weak and they totally gets involved in the family of procreation by sacrificing their individual identity. *They are of the opinion that it is not that they are unhappy with it but sometimes this questions arise in their mind that do we have any individual identity?* Such type of identity crisis is not observed among their male counterparts.

Among the people under study the husband-wife relationship is very open and cordial. Here majority of the women under investigation are engaged as a worker in the Tea garden like their husband but they are always expected to be loyal and obedient towards their respective in-law families and their husbands. Both husband and wife share equal responsibilities in the maintenance of the family income but division of labour related to household work are more or less totally based on woman. Apart from this she is expected to perform various roles as a daughter-in-law, mother, wife etc.

Widowhood and Remarriage

From the study five widows were found but only one of them got remarried. After investigation it is found that those who have children do not prefer remarriage. According to them in the present society if they will get good match then they can get married because in their society remarriage is socially permitted after the death of their husband. During the course of inquiry it is found that there is one female whose husband got separated and carried away their five old son with him at Arunachal Pradesh. He got married but he do not allow her first wife to be in contact with him and nor with her son. She is facing lots of problem and longing to meet her child. People are forcing her to get remarried. She is so much dissatisfied from her first marriage that she doesn't want to get married. *She raised a question that a female has no right to live without marriage?* Thus, from the above it can be said that females when they are daughter they are treated as others property and after marriage they are recognised through their husband and their family.

The investigation shows that in almost all the households, barring few of them, no married or unmarried woman has been found to head a family. So here the patriarchal norms supersedes where male are considered as the head of the family. Normally after the death of the husband, widow takes up the responsibility but if the in-laws are alive they are considered as the head of the family.

Status of Woman and Economic Life

Economic life is considered very important for the sustenance and movement of a society. It is directly associated with the means of living. It is an important constituent of the community life and plays a deciding role in the formation of the cultural and social structure of the societies. As a matter of fact, the economic life of the people helps us to understand an important feature of their culture. It also deals with the distribution of goods and services in societies and attempts to explain who gets what and why? (Phadke, 2008). It envisages economic activities of people in his social and cultural framework.

Since the area of study is concentrated around the Tea Labourer community where both male and female are equally involved in the Tea plantation work therefore it gives a very good platform to ascertain the status of woman when both the gender are working together. Women work full time in tea plantation, in addition to doing all the household chores including child rearing. Although women's superior dexterity in plucking tea leaves is considered as asset by tea garden managements, they are paid lower wages than men. They have no effective voice in labour unions, which are dominated by men.

In tea plantation there are basically two types of activities like the activities connected with growing and collection of tea leaves and processing of tea leaves. Womenfolk are mostly engaged in the first type of activities. Though both male and female are engaged in earning for the family but always males are kept in higher position than the females. They have a absolute right on their expenditure of the income but most of the females have to take prior permission from their respective husbands on expenditure otherwise it might create conflict in the family. To strengthen the data opinion of 30 working women were taken and it is represented in Table 9.3 which are as follows:

Table 9.3: Distribution of Respondents according to their Freedom of Expenditure on their own income

Sl No.	*Preferences in expenditure*	*Response of the Females*	*Total*
1.	Prior permission undertaken from the husband	21	21
2.	No prior permission undertaken from the husband	03	03
3.	Prior permission undertaken only in some major expenditure.	06	06
4.	**Total**	**30**	**30**

Thus, from the above table it is clear that majority of female do not enjoy absolute right on the expenditure of their own income which is not so in case of their male counterparts. Apart from this most of working woman are overburdened with the dual nature of work.

Dual Burden of Work and Working Woman

Among the Tea Plantation Labourer where both the gender equally participates in the plantation activities, working women are burdened with dual nature of work. They have to concentrate in plantation work as well as in household work also. Cooking for the family without access to basic amenities such as electricity, gas or running water is an arduous task for women. Collecting water from rivers and firewood from forests are primarily women's job. But in case of males they have to concentrate only in plantation work. Apart from this it is only the sole responsibility of the women in the upbringing of the children. Therefore, in case of working women, she has to perform domestic and reproductive responsibilities along with earning for the family.

In performing the dual nature of work and trying to give a balanced approach in all types of work, there is a maximum chance for the occurrence of conflicting situation among the members of the family. A woman tries to satisfy all the people who come across her in the sphere of work, in doing so she sacrifices her wills and expectations. Here an attempt is made to get an opinion regarding the extent of burden experienced by them in performing their works. For this purpose 50 working women are selected randomly and are represented in Table 9.4 which is as follows:

Table 9.4: Distribution of Respondent according to their opinion regarding the extent of burden experienced by them in performing their works

Sl no.	*Opinion Regarding the extent of Burden*	*Female*	*Total*
1.	Over burdened	33	33
2.	Less burdened	12	12
3.	No burden at all	05	05
4.	Total	50	50

Thus, from the above table it is clear that majority of the females feels over burdened in performing their work where as some of them feels less burdened or no burden at all because they think that a female is born to perform the domestic and reproductive work. Now due to the economic backwardness they have to do the outside work but household work is solely females department. From the childhood onward they are trained in this manner.

Political Life and the Status of Woman

The political life is one of the important institutions. It is an important aspect of social control in the society. It is concern with the distribution of power, authority, association and maintenance of law and order in the society. Political life of an individual is an important affair as it is one of the basic social institutions. Political life is mostly associated with powers. It becomes very much necessary on our part to discuss their political performance from the domestic level or family because power distribution actually starts from the family. In this regard from the general scenario it is observed that more male members are observed in the political participation. In our society family is the primary unit and decision-making is one of the important factors in political participation. Therefore, family is a place where we get the knowledge of every aspect of life through the socialisation process so indirectly distribution of power in the family and decision-making capacity becomes very much important to know about the political life as a whole. Political associations are of various types starting from grassroots level to the topmost level i.e. to say from the family level to the mainstream level. Exercising of power starts from the family level. Therefore, it is one of the important factors to assess the status in one's life. Since family is considered as an atom of the society, therefore it becomes the most important place to study the distribution of power. Each and every family contributes towards the mainstream politics.

Among the families under study it is found that power is distributed according to age and sex. The eldest male member is recognised as the head of the family. In the absence of eldest male member, the eldest female becomes the head but there is less impact in the level of authority as compared to their male counterparts. Coming across one family in the line, where a female i.e. an elderly woman is the head of the family but all the decisions are taken by his son. The woman is of the opinion that she cannot take the decisions individually. She is of the opinion that his son is more in contact with the outside world and he is more capable of taking decisions for the family. Her position is as a sign for respect towards her.

Family is the unit of production and distribution of resources and also serves many functions like reproduction, socialisation, maintenance of day-to-day household activities and many others. Decision-making at the level of family is also a very important aspect. So here the concept of decision-making especially at the level of family becomes important because attitude and distribution of power at the domestic level becomes the replica at the national level also.

In general decision is the act of making up your mind about something or a position or opinion or judgement reached after consideration. It could also be said as the process of selecting from several choices products or ideas, and taking action. Decision making is also associated with relative rank that an individual holds, this includes one's rights, duties and lifestyles, in a social hierarchy based upon honour or prestige. The role structure and lifestyles of the family as well as society prompts us to examine the decision-making process.

From the area of investigation it is found that majority of male members takes decision related to family issues. In order clear insight both men and women were interviewed to get a comparison between the two genders. For this purpose 25 couples were interviewed and it is shown in a tabular form in Table 9.5 which is as follows:

Thus, from the table, it is clearly visible that majority of the decisions are taken by male members in comparison to the female counterparts.

We as human being cannot live alone and always require a group for continuous interactions. These interactions take place at the level of community. The dictionary meaning of community is- a body of people living in one place or united by origin, interests etc. In other words, it may be said that the community life of a group of people invariably incorporates social interactions and relationships, patterns of social order, and shared cultural ideas.

In the context of the tea garden, an individual's interactions and relationships start from various angles. Under the umbrella of the tea garden community, first of all, the workers are identified as belonging to various tribes and castes groups. Each of these communities has its own ethnic-cultural identity as well as set norms for mutual interactions and establishing temporary or enduring relationships. Secondly, as stated earlier, they reside in different lines that are generally shared by labourers with hetero-ethnic affiliations. Thus, the immediate neighbourhood

Table 9.5: Distribution of Respondents according to their decision making capacity.

Decision	*Male*	*Female*	*Both*
Maintenance of Household Expenditure	31	16	03
Allocation of work in the Family	35	05	10
Construction and Renovations of Houses	48	00	02
Health of the children and aged	25	18	07
Education of the children	20	18	12
Choice of the occupation of children	44	02	04
Selection of groom or bride for the children	20	10	20
Expenditure to be incurred during marriage	31	02	17
Purchase of Household items and gifts etc	05	19	26
Observance of rituals and functions in the households	27	08	15

of a household, by and large, consists of fellow members belonging to different cultural and religious groups. Beyond all these, they belong to a larger community known as the tea labour community based on many similarities and differences (Kaniampady, 2007).

In this study, beyond their familial context, the labourers relate themselves to their immediate neighbourhood in their respective lines. Social feasts when organised by any of the households, generally all the members of the line equally participate by giving their assistance in the functions. As regard to the womenfolk they generally enjoy within their own age groups by visiting certain places especially during Sundays or in holidays. Outside interaction for the women folks who are most of the time generally remain confined to the plantation and household works takes place during the weekly market. In the Tamul Bari Tea Estate the weekly market sets in very Saturday of the week. The market generally sits in an open field within the garden or adjacent to it.

This is the highly awaited day for tea garden labourers, both men and women as well as children go there to buy various items. This is not only a place of buying and selling, but also an occasion of interaction, meeting friends and other people. It is also the occasion of relaxation from their routine work. For female and especially for young girls it is a very important moment where they come out with full make up and beautiful dresses. It could also be called as a meeting place for young girls and boys.

Apart from this we do not find any other organisation especially for women from this line of the tea estate. Earlier some self help groups were formed but it could not run successfully due to lack of time on the part of women due to double burden of work, lack of unity among the females and also lack of leadership quality among them.

Moving further from the community level to mainstream politics it is found that womenfolk have a very little knowledge about the day-to-day politics in comparison to their male counterparts. When they were interviewed about their opinion at the time of casting vote during election, they say that it is kind of festive occasion for them and they cast votes according to interactions given to them. Their opinion is represented in a tabular form as shown in the Table 9.6 which is as follows:

Table 9.6: Showing the opinion of the respondents regarding casting of vote at the time of election. (n=100)

Sl No.	*Casting of vote during the election*	*Male*	*Female*	*Total*
1.	Actively participate	43	39	82
2.	Do not participate	07	11	18
3.	**Total**	**50**	**50**	**100**

Thus, from the above table it is clear that male takes active participation in casting votes at the time of election but the percentage of female is also not very low. They participate without any knowledge of the political scenario just in the name of vote banks.

Interpretation

Women are considered as the backbone of society therefore the study of identity and status becomes very important in the present scenario. The tea labourer women are considered as an asset in tea plantation work. Generally, it is believed that economic independence raises the status of an individual but among tea labourer women under study, it is partially correct.

In the context of social life they perform various roles and duties. In the family they are associated with domestic work, upbringing of children and in the socialisation process of their children etc. At the time of a birth of a child majority of the parents give preference to the male child for the continuation of their lineage and they will take care of them during their old days. It is found that females are more worried because they are to be blamed if they give birth to female child especially the in-laws. Though the females of the tea garden are considered as very active and self dependent but still are living with traditional mindset of patriarchal society.

After marriage a girl experience a radical change in comparison to their male counterparts. The changes are visible with their change in residence, responsibilities and duties assigned to them, expectations to perform multipurpose roles etc. The most important feature is observed among female is that they subsequently loss their individual identity and now they are recognised only by their husbands identity. Regarding remarriage of a widow the society shows a positive response in one hand but if they are not willing to marry, the society in some instances tries to defame the females.

In the scenario of economic life it is observed that both male and female are engaged in the earning for the family but female have no right on the expenditure of their own income. Though day-to-day requirements are done by them, some do it freely whereas some take the consent of their husband. But they cannot do other expenditure without the prior permission from their husbands. The females have to perform dual work i.e. in the plantation and also in the household work. But in case of males it is not the same. It is not compulsory for them to perform the household work; they can do it if they desire so. The study shows that the society follows the traditional division of labour inspite of earning equally for the family.

The political life also shows the same scenario. It is divided into three levels starting from family to community life and then to mainstream politics. At the family level mostly the eldest male member are considered as the head and majority of the decision related to family affairs are taken by male because females consider themselves as less knowledgeable and less confident in comparison to the females. They were also of the opinion that since their childhood they are treated that girls are associated with domestic work and marriage it is their duty to obey their in-laws and husband. Though here also some variation is observed most of try to follow the traditional norms. In the community life much difference is not observed. Both male and female equally enjoys the festive occasion. In the mainstream politics women has no major role to play but they are ever ready to cast votes. They are considered as good vote bank for the political parties.

References

1. Davis, K, *Human Society*, Surjeet Publication, Delhi, 2007.
2. Jha, M, *An Introduction to Social Anthropology*, Vishal Publishing House Pvt Ltd, New Delhi, 1994.
3. Phadke, S, *Women's Status in North East India*, Descent Books, New Delhi, 2008.
4. Kaniampandy, E, *Status of Women Working in Tea Plantations*, Akansha Publishing House, New Delhi, 2003.
5. Roy, S, *Women in Contemporary India*, Akansha Publishing House, New Delhi, 2010.

10

Social Inclusion of Tribal Women through Social Development: A Study of Tribal Women Empowerment in Assam

Lakhimi Nath

Introduction

The tribal population is an integral part of India's society. Tribals are popularly known as a symbol of self-assertion, comprise of around 8.6 per cent of India's total population as per census 2011. The tribal populations are concentrated mostly in the central belt of India and parts of the North-East. The population of tribal communities scheduled in the Constitution of India and known as Scheduled Tribes (STs) was 104,281,034 as per 2011 census and accounts for 8.6 per cent of the total population. Tribal populations have traditionally lived in about 15 per cent of the country's geographical areas, mainly forests, hills and undulating inaccessible terrain in plateau areas, rich in natural resources. They have lived as isolated entities for centuries, largely untouched by the society around them. This seclusion has been responsible for the slower growth, dissimilar pattern of their socio-economic and cultural development and inability to negotiate and this results in involuntary integration into mainstream society and economy.

The status of women in a society is a significant reflection of the level of social justice in that society. Women's status is often described in terms of their level of income, employment, education, health and fertility as well as their roles within the family, the community and society. In tribal society the role of women is substantial and crucial. In tribal society women are more important than in other social groups, because they work harder and the family economy and management depends on them. Even after industrialisation and the resultant commercialisation started in the tribal economy, women continued to play a significant role. Collection of minor forest produce is done mostly by women and children. Many also work as labourers in industries, households and construction, contributing to their family income. Despite exploitation by contractors and managers, tribals are more sincere and honest than non-tribals. However, tribal women face problems and challenges in getting a sustainable livelihood and a decent life due to environmental degradation and the interference of outsiders. The strategy for tribal development, and specially women, needs improvement, betterment, development and upliftment to affect their empowerment. Tribal women have adjusted themselves to live a traditional life style in the local environment and follow occupations based on natural resources. Undoubtedly, the programmes implemented towards the empowerment of tribal women have improved their socio-economic conditions and status. However, there are wide variations across regions and tribes in terms of work participation, sex ratio, economic productivity and social life. Therefore, the impact of development planning should be evaluated in terms of desired needs and priority of the tribal population. The present paper makes an attempt to study the empowerment of tribal women in Assam. In this regards the paper emphasises the social inclusion of tribal women through their social development.

Since tribal populations are mostly located in North East part of India, Assam is a state where as per census 2011 out of total population 31205576, 3884371 are belonging to tribal population. There are more than fifteen tribal community found in Assam. Despite of having a huge amount, the tribals have not yet received sufficient facilities and programmes for their development. It is important to note that tribal is such a class which always remains untouchable by the upper class people. In case of tribal women, they are one of the largest socially suppressed and discriminated groups. Tribal women are placed at the absolute bottom of the society as they face systemic and structural discrimination three-fold: as tribal, as poor, and as women. It means tribal women experience multiple discrimination, i.e. as they are treated as untouchable they face caste discrimination, as women they face gender discrimination and as poor they face class discrimination. Tribal women generally face certain kinds of domestic violence and social exclusion. So it is very important to undertake several steps to bring about positive changes in the lives of tribal women. Empowerment of women is a concept that has developed in connection with improving their status. Empowerment includes higher literacy levels, education, better healthcare, equal ownership of productive resources, increased participation in economic activities, awareness of rights and responsibilities, improved standards of living, self-reliance, self-esteem and self-confidence.

Methodology

The present study is a review based study and it is based on secondary data. In this paper, all the information have been collected from different books, research studies, journals and also from internet. Here an attempt is made to highlight the concept of social inclusion, social sector and social development and how this social development through social inclusion and social sector can impact on the empowerment of tribal women in Assam.

Meaning of Social Inclusion

To remove the problem of social exclusion from the society a new concept was put forwarded which is known as social inclusion. The term social inclusion was originated in French social policy in the 1970s. It came into play in the 1980s economic crisis when state sponsored republican tradition of solidarity was in vogue. By the year 1990 the term was theorised by scholars like Bourdieu and Luhmann. The latter clarified the concept in the following terms: The concept of inclusion means the encompassing of the entire population in the performances of the individual function systems. On the one hand, this concerns access to these benefits and, on the other, dependence of individual modes of living on them. To the extent that inclusion is achieved, groups disappear that do not or only marginally participate in social living. With this adoption, social exclusion moved on to the political agenda in Europe in the 1990s.

The United Nations concept on social inclusion speaks as follows:

"An inclusive society must be based on respect for all human rights and fundamental freedoms, cultural and religious diversity, social justice and the special needs of vulnerable and disadvantaged groups, democratic participation and the rule of law". It is to note that the concept of social inclusion is based on subjective understanding of what 'right' or 'fair' is. This notion or understanding differs across countries, societies and individuals. Thus, there is no uniformity in the use of the term social inclusion. There are also certain issues related to it. For some, inclusion and exclusion works simultaneously. An individual or a society may be included in one desired area but may be excluded in another important area. This may be as a consequence of the inclusion or as a norm etc.

Social inclusion is based on the belief that we all fare better when no one is left to fall too far behind and the economy works for everyone. Social inclusion simultaneously incorporates multiple dimensions of well-being. It is achieved when all have the opportunity and resources necessary to participate fully in economic, social, and cultural activities which are considered the societal norm. Poverty divides us. Social inclusion can unite us. Whenever too many fall too far behind the rest, our whole society is diminished. Inclusion demands goals and policies that avoid separating us. Inclusion calls on us to strive for a nation in which everyone lives with purpose, dignity, and satisfaction. Indicators based on social inclusion would assess the extent to which low-paid workers fall behind the rest of the workforce, not only in terms of wages and income, but in a variety of dimensions, including health, education, housing, skills, advancement, and opportunity. Unlike poverty, social inclusion is something positive to support, not something negative to oppose. Social inclusion has considerable potential to improve our understanding of social issues and policies. A serious effort should be made to introduce the concept in the United States. A social-inclusion goal addresses multiple concerns. It addresses whether everyone can meet basic needs, as well as rising wage and income inequality, the erosion of middle-class jobs, and pressures that many families face in balancing work and other pursuits. In the United Kingdom, the rest of Europe, and many other well-off nations, social inclusion is an overarching framework for addressing a myriad of social policy issues, including income inequality, skill levels, education, health inequalities, housing affordability, and work-life balance. Social inclusion is now part of the framework laws of the European Union and several nations. The precise boundaries of the concept are far from determinate, and countries have different definitions, but at its core, social inclusion involves including everyone in social institutions and relations in ways that matter for well-being.

Social Sector

Social sector activities are often considered to be those which emphasise improvement in quality of life by offering education, health and sanitation and employment facilities to the population, who are less privileged and who suffer from malnutrition, high death rates and decease, low income and lack of education and who live below the poverty level. Therefore, the social sector development has two important aspects: firstly, it involves improvement of "quality of life" related activities; and secondly, these activities are directed towards a certain section of the population, namely, the Scheduled Tribes.

A vast majority of Assam's tribal population are living in rural and backward areas. The core problems of widespread poverty, growing inequality, rising unemployment find their origin in the stagnation and often retrogression of economic life in rural areas. Tribals experience violence, discrimination and social exclusion on the day-to-day life. Tribals are traditionally the lower caste people who are treated as "untouchable" and are socially, economically and politically discriminated. Similarly, tribal women are placed at the absolute bottom of the society as they face systemic and structural discrimination in the society. Discrimination and violence have systematically deprived them from opportunities, choices and freedoms in all spheres of life. This underestimates not only their dignity and self-respect, but also their rights to equality and development. Since tribal women are most deprived, socially excluded, less literate, absentee of property rights, and less empowered both socially and economically, therefore they are ignorant about women entrepreneurship. To tackle these problems the social sector allocations and expenditure needs to be increased and the strategy of tribal women empowerment has to be routed through social sector development.

Meaning of Social Development

As a working definition, social development can be described as the process of increasing

- The assets and capabilities of individuals to improve their wellbeing.
- The capacity of social groups to exercise agency, transform their relationships with other groups, and participate in development processes.
- The ability of society to reconcile the interests of its constituent elements, governs itself peacefully, and manages change.

Though the use of the term "development" is usually confined to economic progress, in reality the term applies to political, social and technological progress as well. All these various sectors of society are so intertwined that it is difficult to neatly separate them. Development in all these sectors is governed by the same principles and laws and therefore the term can be applied uniformly to all these fields.

The original definition of "social development" during the 1960s and 1970s was mainly the social infrastructure to support economic development. This corresponds with the mainstream "development" during this period focusing on economic development. The conceptualisation of human development in the 1990s, to broaden the choices of people, is also closely related to the foundation of the social development concept. The 1995 Copenhagen Social Summit emphasised "social development" as a global imperative. In the Report of the World Summit for Social Development, definition of "social development" can be read from the following passage: We gather here to commit ourselves, our governments and our nations to enhancing social development through the world so that all men and women, especially those living in poverty, may exercise the rights, utilise the resources and share the responsibilities that enable them to lead satisfying lives and to contribute to the well-being of their families, their communities and human kind. To support and promote these efforts must be the overriding goals of the international community, especially with respect to people suffering from poverty, unemployment and social exclusion. The objectives of social development can be summarised as ensuring poverty eradication, full employment, and social integration.

In 1995, the World Summit on Social Development (WSSD) put the agendas related to social development such as education, health, employment, and involvement of civil societies as global priorities (UN, 1995).

Development can be broadly defined in a manner applicable to all societies' at all historical periods as an upward ascending movement featuring greater levels of energy, efficiency, quality, productivity, complexity, comprehension, creativity, mastery, enjoyment and accomplishment. Development is a process of social change, not merely a set of policies and programmes instituted for some specific results. This process has been going on since the dawn of history. But during the last five centuries it has picked up in speed and intensity, and during the last five decades has witnessed a marked surge in acceleration. The basic mechanism driving social change is increasing awareness leading to better organisation. Life evolves by consciousness and consciousness in turn progresses by organisation. When society senses new and better opportunities for progress it accordingly develops new forms of organisation to exploit these new openings successfully. The new forms of organisation are better able to harness the available social energies and skills and resources to use the opportunities to get the intended results. Development is governed by many factors that influence the results of developmental efforts. There must be a motive that drives the social change and essential preconditions for that change to occur. The motive must be powerful enough to overcome obstructions that impede that change from occurring. Development also needs resources such as capital and technology and the availability of supporting infrastructures.

Empowerment of Tribal Women in Assam

Assam has the largest number of tribes within their variety in tradition, culture, dresses, and exotic way of life. Most tribes have their own languages. Bodo (or Kachari), Karbi, Kosh-Rajbanshi, Miri/Mishing, Mishimi, Rabha, Dimasa, Tiwa, Deori are some of these tribes exhibiting variety in tradition, culture, dresses, and exotic way of life. The Government of Assam has taken some initiatives, adopted some policies, scheme, project and many other programme time-to-time to empower the tribal women in the society as well as in the entire state as a whole. Of course, the plan and policies adopted by the central government are equally being implemented in the state unlike the others. Assam is the largest state in terms of population and second to Arunachal Pradesh in geographical area in North East India. In spite of her rich natural resources and culture the state is lagging behind the rest of the country. The socioeconomic set up of the state has not been conducive to overall development. Since it is a multiethnic state with heterogeneous cultural backgrounds, it has been experiencing insurgency and ethnic strife for the last three decades because of which not only its economy but also the social fabric is under threat. The worst victims in the process are the tribal women. Though the entire North East region including Assam is free from some of the social evils like dowry, sati *pratha,* female foeticide and infanticide because of the prevalence of tribal and indigenous culture, other forms of gender discrimination do exist as revealed in various gender gap studies. It is the general perception that tribal women of Assam are more disadvantageous than the tribal women in rest of the country. In certain aspects the position of tribal women in Assam is weaker than the average women of the state. The percentage of tribal women employees to total employees in the state in the government services is very low. Tribal women enjoy autonomy at their household level, especially in social aspects and enjoy equal rights along with their husbands in economic matters but their community participation is passive and autonomy level is very low. The major reason behind this is low literacy rate and unemployment. The development of tribal community cannot be accelerated without women participation. Therefore, the government should focus on developing the literacy rate among the tribal women which would facilitate their economic upliftment. This would surely result in their qualitative participation and decision-making among all aspects of their living. Tribal women empowerment is a very imperative concern in the present day society. Women empowerment is an essential element in national development. Since tribals constitute more than the half of the total population of Assam there can be no development unless the needs and interests of tribal women are fully taken into account. In fact, empowered women are a nation's strength. Since development means improvement in the living condition of the society, as a whole, it is logical to accept that this also mean improved status of tribal women. The effective management and development of women's resources, their capabilities, interests, skills and potentialities are of paramount importance for the mobilisation of human resources.

To empower the tribal women in the society various development policies and programmes should be introduced. In this case the government should also adopt necessary steps for proper implementation of those policies. Because in many cases it is found that government introduces many policies but they are not properly implemented. In order to increase the female workforce participation among tribal women, innovativeness and awareness about business prospects and proper training programmes should be provided to them.

Beside this, weaving industry is very much popular among tribal women in Assam. Most of tribal women select weaving industry as their livelihood option. As the tribal women contributes significantly in socio-economic development of rural sector through weaving industry, the tribal women should be provided proper training programme and financial and technological supports for development of weaving industry.

A large number of tribal women have missed education at different stages and in order to empower them there is a great need of providing opportunities so as to enable them to assume leadership qualities for socio-economic self-reliance and even social transformation. Therefore, adequate educational opportunities should to be provided to them so that they get motivated to participate, support and also ultimately learn to initiate their own programmes of development. The main aim of education should be to change the cultural norms and patterns of life of tribal women to make them economically independent, to organise themselves to form strong groups so as to analyse their situations and conditions of living, understand their rights and responsibilities and to enable them to participate and contribute to the development of women and the entire society.

Microfinance is emerging as a powerful tool for poverty alleviation and gender empowerment in the economy. Microfinance programmes like the Self-Help Bank Linkage Programme (SHG) in Assam has been increasingly hailed for their positive economic impact on the empowerment of women. SHGs serve as agent for the purpose of savings, credit, production, employment and thus create a situation of economic security among tribal women. It also introduces several training programmes for the poor women with the help of which tribal women are able to get self employment. Moreover, participation within SHGs by tribal women helps in reduction of different kinds of evils experienced by them. In this sense, we can say that SHGs programme is an important instrument to bring about remarkable changes in lives of tribal women and thus help to achieve empowerment among them. SHGs have become platform for tribal women for human resource development including overall personality development.

Tribal women are more likely to engage in forest activities for their livelihood. The tribal women spend considerable time in collection of vegetables, roots, firewood, cattle feed, honey, silk cocoon, medicinal herbs and fruits as part of their domestic chore and also for commercial purpose. Tribal women are found to be deprived of in most development indicators and therefore their occupations largely depend on agriculture. Their integration with the forest-related economic activities is very low and there is in need of modernisation of their manufacturing enterprises. These shortfalls can be filled up through proper training on business and sustainable forestry on one hand and on the other hand sensitisation of the markets and their negotiation process. This can strengthen the relation between forest and tribal women in the sense of empowering them. This will also mean to reduce their high level of dependence on agriculture.

Conclusion

Tribal women play a major role in the management of their natural, social, economic resources and agricultural development including crop production, livestock production, sericulture, and horticulture and harvest operations. But still they remain backward due to traditional values, illiteracy, superstitions, and dominant roles in decision-making, social evils and many other cultural factors. As a state of India, Assam is suffering from lack of women empowerment especially in tribal areas. Though the government has initiated number of steps in this regard, but practically these are least implemented in the society till. So, awareness should be generated among the people to establish gender equality and to provide empowerment of tribal women in the society. This will only possible when the tribal women will be able to come out from the perimeter of social exclusions i.e. the prejudicial bindings of other societies. But on the other hand they must be given chances to be engaged in various social works. In this case the social sectors of various types will also have to take meaningful and important roles. When the tribal women will enjoy all the facilities according to their needs, they will socially, economically and politically be developed and the empowerment of tribal women will by this way be effective in real sense.

References

1. Awais, Mohammad, Alam, Tasib and Begum, Mirseth. "Socio-Economic Empowerment of Tribal Women:An Indian Perspective." *International Journal of Rural Studies* 16, no. 1 (2009).
2. Roy, Burman. "Status of Tribal Women in India." *Mainstream Weekly* L, no. 12 (2012).
3. Rani, Sandhya, Rajani, N. and Neeraja, P. "An Analysis of Tribal Women Education in India", *International Conference on Social Science and Humanity*, IPEDR, Vol. 5, IACSIT Press, Singapore, 2011.
4. Das, Sanjay Kanti. "Women Empowerment and Self-Help Group: An Analytical Study of Constraints in Karbi Anglong District of Assam" *Journal of North East India Studies* 1, no. 1 (2011):1-22.
5. Talukdar, Ritul. "Women Education and Rural Economic Development of the Bodo Community of Assam" *International Journal of Science, Environment* 1, no. 1 (2012):41-48.
6. Tribal Profile At A Glance, May, 2013.
7. Das, Madhushree, "Pattern of Social Change and Development Among the Tribal Women in Assam, India", *The Clarion* 2, no. 1 (2013):115-128.

8. Devi, Ambiga, Gandhimathi, S. and Begum, Mirseth. "Social Inclusion through Financial Inclusion – An Empirical Study on SHG Women in India" *EXCEL International Journal of Multidisciplinary Management Studies,* 2 Issue 4 (2012):59-68.
9. Das Gupta, M. "Selective Discrimination against Female Children in Rural Punjab, India." *Population and Development Review* 13, no. 1 (1987):77-100.
10. Gopalan, S. *Towards Equality – The Unfinished Agenda – Status of Women in India 2001,* National Commission for Women, Government of India, 2002.
11. Soni, J. K.*Women Empowerment -The Substantial Challenges,* Authors Press, Delhi, 2008.
12. Gupta, N.*Women's Education Through Ages,* Concept Publication Co, New Delhi, 2003.
13. Rao, R. K. *Women and Education,*Kalpaz Publications, Delhi, 2001.
14. Pandya, R.*Women in Changing India*, Serials Publications, Delhi, 2008.
15. Sahay S.*Women and Empowerment- Approach and Strategies,* Discovery Publishing House, Delhi, 1998.
16. Devi, Mridula. "Women Empowerment by way of Muga Silk Industry", *Global Research Methodology Journal* 2 , issue- 8 (2013).
17. Boro, Sakasing and Basumatary, Rupon. "Women Empowerment through Self Help Groups (SHGs): A Case Study of Bodo Women under Udalguri District, Btad", *International Journal of Social Science Tomorrow* 1 No. 9 (2012).

11

Going Beyond the Confines of Her Class, Caste and Gender: The Character of Sanichari in *Rudali*

Devastuti Sharma

"Rudali is about... how to survive... bread and mouth."

– **Mahasweta Devi**

Mahasweta Devi (1926) is an Indian writer and social activist born in erstwhile East Pakistan who writes primarily in Bengali. A recipient of the prestigious awards of Padma Vibhushan and Jnanpith, she works for and writes about the incessant struggles faced by the tribes and 'low castes' in the states of West Bengal, Bihar and Chhattisgarh. She is also known for championing causes like women's empowerment and eradication of rural poverty. Her first work is *The Queen of Jhansi* (1956). In the subsequent years, she has published over twenty collections of short stories and close to a hundred novels. Her famous works include *Aranyer Adhikar* (1977) (*The Occupation of the Forest*) - a novel which won her the Sahitya Akademi award), *Agnigarbha* (*The Womb of Fire*) (1978), *Breast Stories* and the short fiction *Rudali* (1979).

Rudali (1979), first published in *Nairitey Megh*, is a short but powerful story that touches over multiple sensitive socio-economic realities of rural India. At the heart of *Rudali* is Sanichari, a woman born on and named after the 'accursed' Saturday (*Shanivaar*). She lives in the village of Tahad where the majority of the inhabitants belonged to 'lowly' *Ganju* and *Dushad* castes. She is a victim of a tripartite Marginalisation involving gender, caste and class. Sanichari is, simultaneously, a woman, a low caste Ganju and belongs to the subordinate class of bonded labour. Sanichari is not individuated but is historicised. She is representative of an entire community of socio-economic Others. The story places her in a historical situation, provides a socio-economic context and emphasises that her problems are not hers alone; but are common to her class, caste and gender. "Like the other villagers, her life too was lived in desperate poverty."[1] The current paper argues that Sanichari strategically makes use of the gender roles imposed on her to assert her identity not only as a woman, but also as a Ganju labourer who is more than just capable of fending for herself.

Spivak, in her essay, *Can the Subaltern Speak?* makes a valid statement: "*... the subaltern as female is even more deeply in the shadow*."[2] *Rudali* is about Sanichari's journey from these shadows towards agency and empowerment. What sets Sanichari apart from other Others is the fact that she is not just another muted and silenced Subaltern, but is a potentially subversive agent in the phallogocentric order of Brahmanichal patriarchy. The turning point in her life comes when Dulan coerces her to take up the occupation of being a *rudali* (professional mourner). She evolves from being a hapless, poverty-stricken, lonely widow to being a liberated individual capable not only of fending for herself but also of leading the socio-economic community she represents.

The profession being a *rudali* involves a 'commodification of grief'. It is the ultimate perversion imposed by the socio-cultural constructs of caste, class and gender. "*Low caste*" women and "*whores*" are forced to feign sorrow and wail over the corpses of rich, upper caste males. This humiliating act highlights the fact that the Brahmanic patriarchy not only has control over the economic status of the Subaltern; but also exerts power over the bodily and emotional domains of the gendered Subaltern. Sanichari however metamorphoses the degraded profession into a lucrative one. "...Sanichari thought that perhaps her tears had been reserved for a time when she would have to feed herself by selling them."[3] She rises to the occasion and seises the opportunity by making her profession an act of revenge and an expression of historical dissent. She manipulates the very system that seeks to oppress her, moulds it to her advantage and works her way to emancipation; and in doing so, she reclaims the space that has traditionally been denied to her on account of her being a poor *ganju* woman.

An attempt has been made to elucidate how Sanichari counter-exploits the exploitative and oppressive forces of caste, class and gender-based hegemony and thereby destabilises the three levels of otherisation and marginalisation that she has been subjected to.

The primary conflict in the story arises out of the economic determinism leading to a class based stratification in the society. The inhumane squalor received from the social superiors and feudal lords along with class oppression and financial misery is a recurrent part of the narrative text. The ganjus and dushads of the Tahad village work as bonded labours in the fields of Ramavatar Singh and the other Malik-Mahajans. Debts are repaid with exorbitant interests. According to the feudal lords, "It was not the amount that mattered... What mattered was the yoke, the burden of debt that kept the (dushads and ganjus) labouring like cattle."[4] The Malik Mahajans led lavish lives. Even the death of a kin is an occasion for establishing their honour and supremacy vis-à-vis their fiscal status. Expensive *kriya* ceremonies are held, rudalis are hired and the race for being the most lavish spender ensues: "When someone died in a Malik Mahajan household dies, the amount of money spent of death ceremonies immediately raises the prestige of the family... The price for these was paid by the dushads, dhobis, ganjus and kols from the hides of whom the overlords extracted the sums they had overspent."[5] Sanichari too belongs to the economically marginalised group of Subaltern bonded labours. When Sanichari and Bikhni are hired as rudalis, they strike hard bargains with their customers. Their business prospered because the two women learnt to take advantage of the war of prestige that prevailed among the feudal lords:

"Just for wailing, one kind of rate. Wailing and rolling on the ground, five rupees one sikka. Wailing, rolling on the ground and beating one's head, five rupees two sikka. Wailing and beating one's breast, accompanying the corpse to the cremation ground, rolling around on the ground there – for that the charge is six rupees. At the *kriya* ceremony, we want cloth... you people are like kings, can't you spare some dal, salt and oil with the rice? And Sanichari will sing your praises wherever she goes."[6]

Plagued by their need for competition, the Malik-Mahajan households had to give in to the demands of the rudalis. Thus, Sanichari manoeuvres the discourse of class-based hegemony. It is not the Malik Mahajans but the rudalis who are in charge; for their stature in the society is retained only when the rudalis acquiesce to professionally mourn their unmourned deads. And the rates charged by the rudalis are determined not by the mahajans but by the 'accursed' rudalis.

The second layer of Otherisation imposed on Sanichari has its roots in casteism. Paralleling the economic stranglehold of the malik-mahajans is the social repression of a religious system which controls through fear and superstitions. Like any other rural Indian society, the Tahad village too is in the clutches of Hindu Brahmanic system of caste division. The 'low castes' of the village are treated with apathy by those who stand higher on the caste-based hierarchy. When Sanichari's son, Budhua, falls ill and Sanichari rushes to the village vaid (doctor) for aid, the valid makes a rather callous and appalling statement. He says, *"You lower castes have no patience, no ability to bear up."* [7] Besides this disdain and contempt, the lower castes are also subjected to economic exploitation through the influence of religious and caste-based discriminatory practices. When Budhua's father dies, a widowed and penniless Sanichari is forced to bring upon yourself the burden of a financial loan in order to honour the customs dictated by the priests: "On his (the Tohri priest) insistence, she spent a precious rupee and a quarter on a Spartan offering of sand and sattu which Budhua offered as panda-daan... Mohanlal, the priest of Ramavatar's presiding deity, was scoffed... In order to appease Mohanlal, she was forced into debt to Ramavatar; she received Rs 20 and put her thumbprint on a paper stating that she would repay Rs 50 through bonded labour on his fields over the next five years."[8]

In the later course of the narrative when Sanichari is a Rudali, she makes strategic use of these superstitious beliefs and customs for her livelihood. Besides, when she is in the upper caste households, she often feigns an air of innocence and makes sarcastic and ironic statements that strike Brahmanic patriarchy at the heart.

"... But I heard that the upper castes never got smallpox? That it was a disease of the poor and the low castes? That's why we take the government vaccination as well as appease the gods."[9]

Thus, Sanichari, a 'low caste' rudali, turns her profession into a weapon used to undermine the masternarratives created by the traditional caste system.

Though Mahasweta Devi refuses to categorise Rudali as explicitly feminist text or a text concerned with gender, the gendered innuendos of the story cannot be overlooked. Intertwined with the socio-economic context of the story is the dimension of gender. India, by and large, is a patriarchic nation and the village of Tahad is no exception. Circumscribed by the endless class oppression and material depravity is the gendered subaltern who is at the bottom of the hierarchy. Sanichari is not just economically downtrodden and a low-caste but is a poor and low caste woman. And it is by virtue of being a woman that she becomes a rudali and subsequently an empowered being. Besides the class and caste-based Otherisation, there is another level of otherisation at play in the society- the level in which the women of the hamlet are sexually exploited by the Malik-Mahahjan. "Young women who work for him (Ramavatar Singh) never return."[10] It is the caste lords who create whores and wailers. The word 'whore' is used multiple times in the text perhaps to implicate the fact that the tag 'whore' has been socially forced upon the lower caste women. The community of whores is created and maintained to retain hegemonic control over the gendered Subaltern. Whores are not just made but are kept, preserved and rated according to the commodity price index. Thereafter, the descent of 'out of business' prostitutes are led to form a separate community of rudalis. Though Sanichari adopts her profession, she is seen to empathise with the prostitutes who were forced to become rudalis. She calls for unity. "It is the women who are ruined by the malik-mahajans who turn into whores. Nonsense, they are a separate caste."[11] After her initial qualms about her profession, Sanichari ardently adopts it. And, after the death of her companion Bikhni, she takes on the leadership. She goes to the randipatti or the whore-street to gather a large group of rudalis to wail at Gambhir Singh's funeral. In this moment, Sanichari takes her final lead towards agency. She not just fends for herself but leads the community she represents and paves their way towards empowerement:

"Gambhir Singh has died; by wailing for him and taking their money, you'll be running salt in their wounds. Don't hold back. Take whatever you can... All of you come. When you grow old, you'll have to do this anyway. So while I am still around, let me initiate you."[12]

The closing image of Mahasweta Devi's text, set in Gambhir Singh's funeral, an organised band of women, comprised of the marginalised and the outcast, subvert the solemn hypocrisy of a man's funeral. The funeral is a metonymy for the patriarchal, exploitative system.

Usha Ganguli's play *Rudali* (1992) and Kalpana Lajmi's movie *Rudaali* (1993), are both adaptations of Mahasweta Devi's short story *Rudali* (1979). Rudali is a story about a woman, written by a woman, brought on stage by another woman and also cinmatised by a woman. In that sense, it is a woman's text. It however does not represent the woman alone, but is representative of the society on the whole. The Sanichari we encounter in the end all the three versions of the story is very different from the stoic, long suffering, repressed woman we see in the beginning of the narrative. She is a true matriarch in a patriarchal setup and sets healthy precedents for others to follow. She, in course of her life, she articulates the larger questions of the community of people who are erased from the discourses of mainstream narratives, and in doing so, she asserts her identity as a 'subaltern' capable of toppling the Self/Other dichotomy. She and the community she belongs to is not the Other, but is the mighty and dynamic self. In a situation that is not conducive for climbing up the socio-economic ladder, Sanichari does magnificiently climbs up and overthrows the forces that pull her down. She speaks, she survives. She proves that the Subaltern can indeed speak when they flourish economically and socially.

Bibliography

1. Afsher, Haleh, ed. *Women and Politics in the Third World*. New York: Routledge, 1996.

2. Chandra, Joseph and Samy, K.S. Anthony. *Classical to Contemporary Literary Theory: A Demystified Approach*. New Delhi: Atlantic Publishers. 2012.
3. Katyal, Anjum. *Rudali: From Fiction to Performance*. Calcutta: Seagull Books, 1997.
4. Mcleod, John. *The Beginning of Postcolonialism*. New Delhi: Viva Books, 2010.
5. Murfin, Ross and Ray, Supriya M. *The Bedford Glossary of Critical and Literary Terms*. Boston: Bedford, 2009.
6. Spivak, Gayatri C. Introduction, *Breast Stories* by Mahasweta Devi, Calcutta: Seagull, 1992.

References

1. Anjum Katyal, *Rudali: From Fiction to Performance* (Calcutta: Seagull Books, 1997) p. 4.
2. John Mcleod, *The Beginning of Postcolonialism* (New Delhi: Viva Books, 2010) p. 193.
3. Anjum Katyal, *Rudali: From Fiction to Performance* (Calcutta: Seagull Books, 1997) p. 93.
4. *Ibid.*, p. 76.
5. *Ibid.*, p. 97.
6. Anjum Katyal, *Rudali: From Fiction to Performance* (Calcutta: Seagull Books, 1997) p. 97.
7. *Ibid.*, p. 90.
8. *Ibid.*, p. 75
9. Anjum Katyal, *Rudali: From Fiction to Performance* (Calcutta: Seagull Books, 1997) p. 101.
10. *Ibid.*, p. 79.
11. *Ibid.*, p. 103.
12. Anjum Katyal, *Rudali: From Fiction to Performance* (Calcutta: Seagull Books, 1997) p. 117.

IV

Literature, Language and Marginality

12

Parallel Struggles; Paralleling Identities: A Reading of Two Native Novels

David Jeyaraj Franklin T

Native literature can be defined as the creative output of the lived experience of the world's oldest communities, hitherto expressed and transmitted over generations through the oral mode. What makes Native Literature a compelling reading is the plight of these first nations. Whether it is the case of the Native Americans of the North and South Americas or the primitive tribes of Africa or the Aborigines of Australia or the nomadic prehistoric settlers of Europe or the Adivasis of the Indian subcontinent, they have certain things in common: their identities, their struggles, their cultural constructs, and their very existence in the heavily urbanised, commercialised, Europeanised world that seeks pleasure out of plundering the vitality of Mother Earth. Native literature does not glorify native existence nor does it talk about the mainstreamed lives of its community members; it rather talks in detail about the idea of being 'abnormal' in the world view. It also talks about the painful existence of the native as an alien, outcaste, and the museum monument in the same land that he roamed in assonance with other members of the natural order. Native literature documents the lives of the living survivors.

Among the plethora of fiction writing from among the native writers stand out two texts of great importance – Native

American writer of Chippewa heritage Louise Erdrich's *Tracks* and Adivasi Indian writer of the Mala-Arayan tribe Narayan's debut novel *Kocharethi*.

Tracks (1988) documents the plight of the Chippewa tribe in the early decades of the twentieth century when the Natives tried to come to terms with the reality of government legislations and epidemic diseases. The novel documents the struggles between tradition and modernity, native and white cultures, and native religion and Christianity. The story is told in the form of a duelling narrative – two narrators taking very subjective, opposing standpoints to look at events as they unfold. *Tracks* has been used to illustrate Native American Literature by Martin Padget in Helena Grace's *Beginning Ethnic American Literatures*. It also finds an important place in Greg Garrard's new critical idiom series book titled *Ecocriticism*.

Kocharethi, on the other hand, is a humble first text. Often alluded to as the first south Indian tribal novel, this Malayalam novel by Narayan of the Mala-Arayan tribe discusses the pangs of being a native in the twentieth century, especially in the decades that preceded and followed the birth of independent India. The original Malayalam text was completed in 1988; published in Malayalam in 1998, and saw the light in English and other Indian languages in the year 2011. The focus of the novel is on the issue of cultural change, subtly brought out by the lives of Kunjipennu and Kochuraman, the protagonists of the text. This Kerala Sahitya Akademi Award winning novel, though often criticised for lack of style, is a poignant tale that has set a new trend among Adivasi writers.

Land loss

Pulitzer Prize winning Native American author Scott Momaday puts the native perception of land in simple terms:

> (The Native) is deeply involved in the earth, committed to it both in his consciousness and in his instinct. In him the sense of place is paramount. Only in reference to the earth can he persist in his true identity.[1]

The focus of the novel *Tracks* is landloss. For the natives, the land upon which their lives were lived symbolised a bond that could not be gauged in monetary terms. The entire period of action in *Tracks* documents the process and the aftermath of this plaguing issue of landloss.

The various policies and regulations of successive white governments forced the Native Americans away from their forests and into the chequered squares of the reservations. These reservations are borne out the long-drawn process of Native American resettlement. The Westward Ho resulted in a comprehensive change in the lifestyles of the natives. The hunters were forced to take up farming to be labelled 'civilised' and be entitled to land ownership rights. These resettlement clusters were called Reservations, managed by the Bureau of Indian Affairs.

When the mandatory retainership period expired, huge parcels of land were sold to non-natives, especially white settlers. Later policies of the government that attempted to make the natives pay taxes to the federal government proved detrimental to their welfare.

The narrator Nanapush warns the young Eli Kashpaw against selling the land. He reminds him that he would one day "wake with no place to put (his) foot down".[2] The novel also documents how disease and poverty made the natives sell their lands for pittances, faster than anyone could even imagine. The narrators record how land was sold in exchange for a bag of flour or for a paltry sum of a few dollars. The hurry with which this was done is expressed in Nanapush's words: "Some signed their land away with thumbs and crosses."[3]

Right from the beginning of the novel, he demonstrates what can be best described as the native fury over the tricky Dawes Act.

> I spoke aloud the words of the government treaty, and refused to sign the settlement papers that would take away our woods and lake.[4]

As the process of resettlement and white encroachments into native lands increased, Nanapush decides to take upon himself the role of a leader and spokesperson for his community. He calls government treaties as 'baits' that lured the native away from his own soil.

> We stumbled toward the government bait, never looking down, never noticing how the land was snatched from under us at every step.[5]

The novel ends with a majority of the land being sold as even those who wanted to keep the land could not do so since they did not have the expertise in commercial agriculture, which the government wanted them to take up.

Narayan's *Kocharethi*, as the translator Catherine Thankamma argues, is a "chronicle of a community."[6] It documents the Arayars struggle to keep the land they owned and loved to themselves. Though not threatened to the extent of the Native Americans, the Arayars' livelihood is threatened by the goons of the state. In her detailed Introduction titled 'Adivasi Rachana: Life, Land and Language', G.S. Jayasree notes that "the novel maps the adivasi's changing perceptions of land and its ownership."[7] She also traces the origins of logging and deforestation to the colonial days.

> Large quantities of teak were required for shipbuilding and the laying of railway lines. For this, great stretches of land were forcefully taken from the Malayarayars and leased out to European planters. . . land (was) obtained by evicting the adivasis.[8]

Lumbering and agricultural practices entered, thus ending centuries of self-sustained man-nature relationship based on food, yielding to the advancement of cash and commercial crops.

Narayan even takes up the activist role when he dedicated his 2008 collection *Nissahayante Nilavali* (The Wail of the Helpless) to 'those Adivasi brethren who have died, are dying, and are yet to die, fighting for their right over a piece of land'.[9]

The native's absolute dependence on the forests is revealed as Narayan discusses the food practices of the community.

The Arayan's crop of rice was so meagre it would barely suffice to make *kashayam.* Only the forest could guarantee freedom from hunger.[10] As the protagonist Kochuraman attempts to make a deal with the government officials, he is seen pleading for a bit of the land that was their own. The Kaanikaran behaves benevolent but is corrupt as Kochuraman announces, "if Eecharan Kaani gets arrack and meat he'll let you clear the entire hill".[11] At the annual inspection, the head guard stamps his authority over the forest and the dwellers.

Ironically, it is he who preaches to the tribe as to how to live in the forests. Even the Arayars acknowledge how they have been overpowered when it comes to land ownership. A discussion among two of them reveals the poignancy of the situation.

> 'Why? They're all things (forest produce) lying about in the forest'
> 'Eda, the entire forest belongs to the precious king'[12]

Even when the Arayars try to sell the farm produce to the merchants, it becomes a sordid tale of cheating by the people of the mainland.

The other argument that hindered the peaceful existence of the community was their subjugation in the form of religious beliefs. Even land becomes a commodity to which the ultimate owner is God.

> The hills and forests were Lord Ayyappan's garden. The Arayar and Uralies were destroying the forests so they must pay compensation for it . . . If they did not, both God and king would be displeased – displeasure that took the form of rowdies hired by Kunjunni.[13]

When Sankaran runs to the contractor to stop the men from cutting down trees that are destroying the cash crops, the contractor jerks out loud.

The contractor burst out laughing as though he has heard a joke. 'Your yard? Eda Araya, a-aall this is government land, not yours.' ... Who gave you permission to plant coconut trees in government land?[14]

When the Arayars keep hearing that about the land, they feel that "their hearts (have become) heavy with the awareness that the land they stood on was not theirs". Their reaction borders on nihilism:

> They won't allow any of us to live in these hills. They think we are some cursed tribe that came from god knows where and settled down in their forest and hills ... we won't perish either. It would be nice if small-pox wiped us out![15]

Things become worse when the Arayars and the businessmen come to blows. The Arayars are arrested but a few of them consult a *Tahsildar* through a lawyer to bail the seventeen arrested brethren. Only then do they realise that they have a 'royal decree' to use the land for agriculture without any need to pay any taxes to the head man.

Community Living and Politics

Nanapush laments about his pitiable position as a lonely elder at a relatively young age of around fifty. The series of diseases, namely pox, fever, and consumption devastated the tribe as "the old and new are taken".[16] Later as he recounts the lost community life, he draws a dark picture:

> I stood in a birch forest of tall straight trees. I was one among many in a shelter of strength and beauty. Suddenly a loud report, thunder and they toppled down like match sticks, all flattened around me in an instant. I was the only one left standing. And now, as I weakened, I swayed and bent nearer to the earth.[17]

Towards the end of the novel, Nanapush realises that the long-held community life of the natives is coming to an end. The leaders of the tribe were no longer chieftains but bureaucrats, namely officers of the federal government. The entire tribe is now forced to follow the regulations imposed on them by these officers.

> We were becoming ... a tribe of file cabinets and triplicates, a tribe of single-space documents, directives, policy. A tribe of pressed trees. A tribe of chicken –scratch that can be scattered by a wind, diminished to ashes by one struck match.[18]

Nanapush, recounting the disintegration of the Native American community life, compares the decline to that of a forest losing its trees. The strong connection between the native's life and the natural environment is being highlighted in his lament. Furthermore, the narrator explains the problem with the situation itself that provides no meaning or end to the travails of the native communities. He also describes the lives of the native beings as something that is defined, described, and determined by the idiotically huge volume of papers, easily lending itself to be contrasted with the pre-colonial days:

> Once the bureaucrats sink their barbed pens into the lives of Indians, the paper starts flying, a blizzard of legal forms, a waste of ink by the gallon, a correspondence to which there is no end or reason.[19]

One of the biggest casualties of the entire process of reservation and removal was the Native American family system. Just like the community life, it is another of the many identities borne by the native over a period of centuries. The kinship pattern of the Chippewa was described as bifurcate merging kinship system. Under this system, siblings and cousins are considered on an equal footing with both parties enjoying certain inalienable benefits over this form of bonding. Just as the Native American maintained the presumed relationship between the spirits of the past and the realities of the future, the family is an integral part of the native's family life.

In *Tracks,* the familial disintegration is poignantly expressed while discussing the separation of Lulu from her mother Fleur. Lulu was sent to the government run home, where she was taught the white ways of life. The entire narration of Nanapush is aimed at informing Lulu about the reasons behind her being sent to the hostel, away from her mother Fleur, who mysteriously continued to live in the forests where she lost her entire family to disease earlier. Nanapush expresses the pain of losing Lulu to government ways when he says, "So you were sent away, another piece cut from the heart".[20] The process of sending Lulu away and the pain endured by the doting mother Fleur is also expressed with a keen sense of observation:

> She sent you to the government school, it is true, but you must understand there were reasons: there would be no place for you, no safety on this reservation, no hiding from government papers.[21]

Another key aspect of Native American life along with the well maintained social institutions is the reaction of the characters to issues related to governance and politics. Nanapush in *Tracks* is introduced as an elder at a relatively young age of fifty, the novel concludes with the same elder contesting successfully in federal elections for the native councils. Between this transformation from being an elder to being a politician in the contemporary sense of the word, Nanapush stands as an classic instance of the changing social scenario.

Tracks begins with the natives' refusal to accept the norms set by the federal government. Peterson notes that the opening scene of the novel as well as the elegiac introduction to it by Nanapush himself "is revisionist because it defamiliarises the popular narrative of American history as progress by showing the cost of the "progress" to native peoples".[22] Nanapush moves from the traditionally native-used pronoun "we" in the beginning of the narration to the more individualistic "I" towards the end of it. This change in pronoun marks the beginning of the shift of the native community from a comprehensive, all-inclusive self-governing mode to a more individual centric mode of democracy.

> We started dying before the snow ... we signed the treaty, and then a wind from the east, bringing exile in a storm of government papers ... In the years I'd passed, I saw more change than in a hundred upon a hundred before".[23]

Nanapush sees himself being transformed into a government agent and interpreter – his Jesuit education making him eligible to become one. But despite wearing the government's colours, he makes sure that the native welfare is taken care of, even at the cost of his own job.

> As a young man, I had made my reputation as a government interpreter, that is, until Beauchamp Treaty signing, in which I said to Rift-In-A-Cloud, "Don't put your thumb in the ink." One of the officials understood and I lost my job.[24]

We also find Nanapush getting authorised as the designated authority to receive the postal letters addressed to members of the native community much against his own as well as the community's hatred towards the system that had "words in envelopes".[25]

Nanapush's hatred for the American government system is soon overcome by the need for the community to have one of their more responsible men to stand up and be counted for the sake of his community. Nanapush contests elections, just to save his community from being wiped out of their lands.

For I did stand for tribal chairman, as you (Lulu) know, defeating Pukwan in that last year. To become a bureaucrat myself was then only way that I could wade through the letters, the reports, the only place where I could find a ledge to kneel on, to reach through the loophole and draw you home.[26]

L.W. Gross in his assessment of *Tracks* identifies a similar trend in the politics of Nanapush and Margaret. The strategies they employ for survival and adaptation involve participating in the ways of the white world while maintaining their Anishinaabe culture. Despite her violent and passionate protests and refusals to surrender to the law of the land, Fleur is only able to make her exit felt, but not impossible. But, at the same time, through careful manoeuvrings, Nanapush becomes the chief of the tribe while Margaret is able to keep her land as well as her identity that she is proud of.

Kocharethi, on the other hand, documents the community living of the Arayars, who followed the matrilineal tradition still followed by some communities of Kerala. Even the property belonged to the woman and the children belonged to the 'illam' of the woman. They had strict codes regarding marriage between the illams, pointing out to the community as the family at large.

The community as such stands for any individual, especially when faced with the task of protecting him or his family from the attacks of wild animals or outsiders. When Kochuraman attempts to build his house all by himself, his brother-in-law Kunjadichan gets angry for not letting him help with the work. He asks, "Is there a man on this hill who can claim he can fend for himself?"[27]

The community also faces the problem of untouchability. They are neither allowed inside the houses of the caste Hindus living in the plains nor were they allowed to participate in the temple festival, to which they contribute with their produce. When they were told that the Maharaja has declared that the Arayans can participate in the temple festival, they themselves could not believe that.

The community comes into the firing line when they protest illegal looting and cheating by the mainlanders. Many of them end up in prison and only at this point of time, they realise the need for a better and united struggle.

> The Arayar had to unite or they would be destroyed one by one. Every heart ached for such unity.[28]

The novel ends with the Arayar community breaking into pieces with the advent of religion into the hills. Politics is another element instrumental in the breaking down of the community life. The Arayars are found to be loitering in the cities and towns of modernised Kerala looking for jobs and livelihood. The protagonists Kochuraman and Kunjipennu are found devastated with the community breakdown, alcoholism, and the young Arayar generation's willingness to be absorbed into the mainstream.

Religion

In *Tracks,* religion is a key issue. The main narrator-characters Nanapush and Pauline stand as representatives of the two sides of the argument. The Aninishinaabe religion that

Nanapush practices and protects is a faith system that is constructed out of belief in spirits. Pauline, on the other hand, despite not warming up to the idea of following Christianity very much, jumps on to the bandwagon and becomes a nun with the Catholic Church.

During her description of the community life at Argus, the small town where she and Fleur work with a butcher, Pauline describes the commodified Christianity that put more number of churches than provision stores.

> Two stores competed for the trade of the three hundred citizens, and three churches quarrelled with one another for their souls. There was a frame building for the Lutherans, a heavy brick one for the Episcopalians, and a long narrow shingle Catholic church.[29]

Nanapush himself was trained in the Catholic ways before he came back to the woods. "I had a Jesuit education in the halls of Saint John before I ran back to the woods and forgot all my prayers".[30] He also recounts another incident when Mrs. Bijiu used her cross to ward off a spirit in the form of a dog that blocked the family's way. Margaret steals Fleur's baby when the mother was asleep and tries to get it baptised by Father Damien when it was interrupted by Fleur's arrival. The baptism hung in the balance without the naming being completed. Nanapush gives her the name Lulu and adds his name as surname to the child whose father remains unknown to the society as well as the readers.

When Father Damien sermonises to Nanapush saying that God "enters the soul through the humblest parts of our anatomies", Nanapush retorts by saying, "A god who enters through the rear door ... is no better than a thief" (110). After experiencing the church service for a little time, the trickster Nanapush decides to go back to his ancestors' religion:

> I felt no great presence (at the church) either, and decided that the old gods were better, the Anishinabe who were not exactly perfect but at least did not require sitting on hard planks.[31]

Pauline attempts to bring Fleur to Christianity and even says an earnest prayer for her only to find the other person becoming murderously violent.

Later we find even Pauline acknowledging that Christianity is too gentle and powerless for the society that she came from.

> Christ was weak, I saw now, a tame newcomer in this country that has its own devils in the waters of boiling-over kettles. I lifted my hands to my face. ... I knew God had no foothold or sway in this land, or no mercy for the just, or that perhaps, for all my suffering and faith, I was still insignificant. Which seemed impossible.[32]

In desperation to become significant, Pauline takes up self-rejection and self-punishment to gain spirituality at the nunnery. She believes that she was being a pioneer in bringing the masses to Christ.

I was a poor and noble creature now, dressed in earth like Christ... God would love me better as a lily of the field, though no such flower as I had yet appeared on reservation ground. ... I will be the bride and Christ will take me as wife, without death.[33]

Later, we find her as Sister Leopolda, on her way to sainthood, while Nanapush continues with the magical religion of the woods, probably as one of the last members of his tribe not to be carried away by the sweeping changes brought in by Europeanisation that included Christianity. As Roy observes, most of the Chippewa today follow either Roman Catholicism or Protestant Episcopalism and only a few followers of the Anishinaabe religion remain.

Kocharethi documents nearly three decades of religious change happening in the hills of the Arayars. Jayashree quotes Narayan in her introduction to the novel:

> The Christians came and started English Medium schools. They said worshipping stones and trees was wrong. Then the Rashtriya Swayamsevak Sangh (RSS) and Vishwa Hindu Parishad (VHP) came and did the same – replaced Puliambuli and Marutha with Vishnu and Durga; ochre robes replaced the gowns of the priests and nuns. No one was really interested in us as a people.[34]

The community accepts these changes in religion out of the threat to their livelihood. Most members of the community seem to be all the more willing to yield to the pull of 'higher powers' due to political necessities. Jayashree notes,

> Their acceptance of Christianity was a shift towards a more proficient spiritual power that they assumed would help them to negotiate the deep crises of self-belief in their native traditions.[35]

Through the novel, we find the native festivals like Makara Vilakku being mentioned. But when the natives were finally allowed to enter the temple after years of untouchability and marginalisation, they were sceptical as to whether this was a plot to kill them as they entered the temple. They claim, "After all, of what help is their God to us".[36] The belief system also put a lot of emphasis on the *velichapad* and miracle healers more than the hill deities.

The arrival of the 'Aashan' – a Sanskrit scholar-cum-religious propagandist in the hills marks the beginning of the end of native religious practices. He brings with him the mainstream Hinduism, though not the Hindutva kind. Narayan notes that the light of education that Aashan brought to the hills in the form of Saraswathi – both literally and metaphorically – was welcomed by even the elders who had to educate their younger Arayars in order to survive in a highly competitive and commercialised mainstream society.

Presented as a saviour of the hill tribe, Aashan himself is confused as to how to integrate the native practices and rituals into the Hinduism discourse.

Native Medicine

The Chippewa native community also prided itself on its strong medicine system. The medicine men and women were also the priests and priestesses of the community. Roy identifies men, women, and children who played the roles of medicine people-cum-clergy. They even had a systematic method by which a young trainee graduated after systematic training that could last up to 20 years.

Though the characters of *Tracks* and *Love Medicine* do not display the priest roles, we do not find any mention about native priests in both the texts. Fleur, Nanapush, and Margaret in *Tracks* and Nector in *Love Medicine* display their prowess as medicine men and women and also interact with spirits and the monsters of the lake, but they stop short of claiming themselves as priests of the Anishinaabe religion.

Nanapush is a native medicine practitioner, who plays the role of a modern psychiatrist as well when he claims,

> I know certain cure songs, words that throw the sick one into a dream and cause a low dusk to fall across the mind.[37]

His fascination and firm belief in the native medicine system is also reflected in his rejection of the regular doctor, particularly the one that Father Damien brought into the community.

Father Damien also brought another something I did not want, the off-reservation doctor who I could not trust ... this doctor was known to refuse Indians to our face but did not dare say no to a priest.[38]

Nanapush claims that the European medicine system would kill a person when he advises Lulu, "saving you the doctor's way would kill you".[39] He also uses his magical powers to track Eli Kashpaw who was mysteriously lost in the woods.

In my fist I had a lump of charcoal, with which I blackened my face. I placed my otter bag upon my chest, my rattle near. I began to sing slowly, calling on my helpers, until the words came from my mouth but were not mine, until the rattle started, the song sang itself, and there in the deep bright drifts, I saw the tracks of Eli's snowshoes clearly.[40]

Tracks ends with the climactic apocalypse brought about by the power of Fleur and in the words of Nanapush become a fantasy of sorts with nature taking its own sweet revenge on the lumberers.

The falling trees and Fleur's own cabin crush the men and the horses while Fluer and Nanapush remain unharmed. Fleur leaves the place and the Matchimanito Lake that she dearly loved, not before bringing those trees down in revenge and making the forest level with the lake and the road.

Kocharethi is the story of a traditional medicine man, Kochuraman, the self-taught *vaijyan* (doctor) of the Arayar community. The novel opens with Valyamundan, the senior medicine man, failing to save his own daughter-in-law Chirutha and later himself dying with the pain of the realisation that his magical medicinal powers have eroded. But Kochuraman marks a new beginning. As Jayashree argues, he "represents the next generation of the adivasis with a more sophisticated method of offering medication".[41]

Kochuraman seemed to know quick effective remedies for various illnesses – wounds, diarrhea, and migraine. Whatever the illness he was always willing to attempt a cure. 'Let me try ...'[42]

It was Kochuraman's medicinal abilities that brought him close to Kunjipennu and their marriage breaks the traditional laws of clan-mixing. Later, as the novel progresses and the external forces of the mainland dominate and erode the native practices, Kochuraman falls prey to the evils of alcoholism, spoils his health and becomes bedridden. The much respected vaidyan is now forced to take up treatment in a government hospital at Thiruvananthapuram. The irony reaches a peak when fearing a mortal 'operashun', Kochuraman and Kunjipennu run out of the hospital into a dark alley, representing the grim prospect of survival for a tribal in the modern world.

Summing Up

Despite separated in term of space, culture, and many other external factors, these two communities represented through the novels *Tracks* and *Kocharethi* face similar struggles, ranging across various issues and differing in terms of the intensity of the problems and their impact on their communities bringing them closer in their ceaseless struggle for unique identities. These two texts also help establish the unique thread of unrelated and unconnected native communities experiencing the same pain at an interestingly same period of historical time.

Works Cited

1. Erdrich, Louise. *Tracks*. New York: Henry Holt, 1988.
2. Momaday, Scott. "I Am Alive." In *The World of the American Indian,* edited by Billie W. Kapp, 11-26.Washington DC: National Geographic Society, 1989.
3. Narayan. *Kocharethi: The Araya Woman.* New Delhi: OUP, 2011.
4. Peterson, Nancy J. *Against Amnesia: Contemporary Women Writers and the Crises of Historical Memory.* Philadelphia: University of Pennsylvania Press, 2001.

References

1. Scott Momaday, "I Am Alive," In *The World of the American Indian,* ed. Billie W. Kapp, (Washington DC: National Geographic Society, 1989), p. 14.
2. Louise Erdrich, *Tracks* (New York: Henry Holt, 1988), p. 98.
3. *Ibid.*, p. 99.
4. *Ibid.*, p. 2.
5. Louise Erdrich, *Tracks* (New York: Henry Holt, 1988), p. 2.

6. Narayan, *Kocharethi: The Araya Woman* (New Delhi: OUP, 2011), p. x.
7. *Ibid*, p. xvi.
8. *Ibid*, p. xxv.
9. *Ibid*, p. xxviii.
10. *Ibid*, p. vi.
11. *Ibid*, p. 86.
12. Narayan, *Kocharethi: The Araya Woman*, p. 90.
13. *Ibid*, p. 116.
14. *Ibid*, p. 122.
15. *Ibid*, p. 126.
16. Erdrich, *Tracks*, p. 2.
17. Erdrich, *Tracks*, p. 127.
18. *Ibid*, p. 225.
19. *Ibid*, p. 225.
20. Erdrich, *Tracks*, p. 219.
21. Erdrich, *Tracks*, p. 219.
22. Nancy J. Peterson, *Against Amnesia: Contemporary Women Writers and the Crises of Historical Memory* (Philadelphia: University of Pennsylvania Press, 2001), p. 23.
23. Erdrich, *Tracks*, pp. 1-2.
24. *Ibid*, p. 100
25. *Ibid*, p. 97.
26. Erdrich, *Tracks*, p. 225.
27. Narayan, *Kocharethi: The Araya Woman*, p. 70.
28. *Ibid*, p. 133.
29. Erdrich, *Tracks*, p. 13.
30. *Ibid*, p. 33.
31. *Ibid*, p. 110.
32. Erdrich, *Tracks*, p. 192.
33. *Ibid*, pp. 203-204.
34. Narayan, *Kocharethi: The Araya Woman*, p. xvii.
35. *Ibid*, p. xxv.
36. Narayan, *Kocharethi: The Araya Woman*, p. 120.
37. Erdrich, *Tracks*, p. 167.
38. *Ibid*, pp. 167-168.
39. Erdrich, *Tracks*, p. 168.
40. *Ibid*, p. 101.
41. Narayan, *Kocharethi: The Araya Woman*, p. xxiii.
42. *Ibid*, p. 6.

13

Fluid Identity and Floating Societies in Amitav Ghosh's *The Hungry Tide*

R. Senthil Kumar

The conflict of the 'self' and the 'other' is evident be it in immigrant situations or within Nation. Owing to the changed economic and social conditions, the world has become a global village. Piya, an American cetologist, finds herself amidst the refugees in West Bengal and calls it her home. Though distance has been conquered, technology is playing the role of leveller in a big way, the division between the 'self' and the 'other' has grown deeper and more subtle.

Amitav Ghosh's *The Hungry Tide* is a novel that deals with a plethora of characters who are rendered homeless. Even the so-called privileged in society admit the fact that behind the façade of their translated world of titles and designations, the emptiness of loss of home linger on. While they could negotiate their space in the postcolonial world by their political connections and bribes, the really disadvantaged such as the Dalit settlers, the Muslim Minority and the refugees fail miserably to make the State keep its election promises and become mute players in the drama of colonial brutality which is continued in different shades.

On the other hand, the marginalised evince a strong sense of self-respect and identity and at times it is a total role reversal of the 'other' and the 'self'. Fakir feels ashamed when Moyna received money from Piya for the help he rendered. Needy, yet has the courage to refuse. In comparison, the charity of the NGOs with foreign funds amounts insignificant. Thus, identity is not fixed, but emerging and fluid.These Fluid identities in *The Hungry Tide* are observed at three levels: in nature, among people and with the State.

In Nature,we observe the Orcella dolphins versus the crabs in the Sunderbans. It had its connection to Kolkata as these were spotted earlier also but mistaken.The Dolphins are privileged. These were sought after by the cetologists, taken on flights, kept warm using huge air conditioners. Even the river water of their habitat was carried across globe for their (dolphins') use and such researches were funded liberally. After Piya spotting these in the Sunderbans and the death of Fokir in the process, it gained further popularity and received huge financial support to start a research project on dolphins under Badabon trust. These creatures were already worshipped in the tide country. These were known as the messengers of Bon Bibi by the locals. Their presence was revered by the tribal here. The Dolphins are big, swift, and noticed in the crowd like Kanai spots Piya in the flood of humanity in Kolkata railway platform.

In contrast, we have the depiction of the 'other', the crabs, which were always there but did not matter. In the words of Piya:

> They (Crabs) were a sanitation department and a janitorial team rolled into one: they kept the mangroves alive by removing their leaves and litter; without them the trees would choke on their own debris. Didn't they represent some fantastically large proportion of the system's biomass? Didn't they outweigh even the trees and the leaves? Hadn't someone said that intertidal forests should be named after crabs rather than mangroves since it was they – certainly not the crocodile or the tiger or the dolphin – who were the keystone species of the entire ecosystem?"[1]

Mulk Raj Anand's *Untouchable,* explains the above predicament in its central message 'They think we are mere dirt because we clean their dirt.'[2] These are the marginalised voices whose toil fails to reach their day light. History is indifferent as stated by Gandhi:

> "And History, in Ghosh's understanding, is almost always pathologised as a chronic condition of poor or bad visibility. Thus, the "grand designs" of historicist narrativity conceal from view "the barely discernible traces that ordinary people leave upon the world" (16, 17); individuals "vanish" into the "anonymity of History" (353). Moreover, and as the Imam Ibrahim conveys, historicism gathers all variety, all colour, into an undifferentiated monochrome."[3]

The above analogy of dolphins versus crabs can be extended to a set of human characters who try to construct their identities by doing things which are based either on their personal aspirations or societal demands. Though the elites sympathise with the downtrodden, they fail to walk the distance to be 'the other'. Their actions sometimes prove to be more of hindrance than help to the settlers here. Sir Daniel Hamilton who started human settlement in the tide country by teaching them what people can do in these islands by taming nature and rising above human barriers of caste and creed had a noble intention. He started the school for their education but his experiment cast a doubt that Fokir who is an illiterate knows more than the cetologist Piya with her foreign education and the state of art technology. We witness the conflict between Moyna and Fokir on money. Moyna aspires to become a nurse and wants Fokir to earn money even if it is given the way Piya does in her house making him invisible and unworthy. The wisdom of our perceived sense of development by mass education is defeated before the raw genius in Fokir. He stuns us out of our wits when he confronts the well-read Kanai on the sublime matters such as being fearless and honest. It surmises us on how many such geniuses we trample every day in the name of literacy and formal education.

Fokir has an instinct for the river. He has shown a brilliant understanding of the way the Dolphins behave. Piya is immensely helped by him in her study of the Orcellaand the way he understands the pictures at the first instant, his help in conducting a study on the deep water pool near Gorjantala, his alertness in spotting the Dolphins in the second expedition when Piya hired Horen's Bhotboti through the complex routes show that he has an in-depth knowledge of these mammals. Piya adored him for his exceptional skills and nobility. Whereas, his image was never allowed to grow beyond the level of the poor illiterate fisherman by others. Kanai is sympathetic more with Moyna than with Fokir. Moyna's ambition to study and learn to become a nurse in the hospital run by the Badabon Trust and her decisiveness in giving education to her son Tutul is similar to the mundane aspirations of Kanai or Piya's father who settled in the USA. Success is defined by personal aspiration of getting employment and getting steady income. With the newly assumed roles, People get newer identities with social approvals which are less threatened.

Piya surmises at this kind of the treatment meted out to Fokir, the 'other' by the Indian Community which is ambitious and judgemental:

"Piya understood too that this was a looking-glass in which a man like Fokir could never be anything other than a figure glimpsed through a rear-view mirror, a rapidly diminishing presence, a ghost from the perpetual past that was Lusibari. But she guessed also that despite its newness and energy, the country Kanai inhabited was full of these ghosts, these unseen presences whose murmurings could never quite be silenced no matter how loud you spoke."[4]

Though he is an illiterate, he is able to recite the legend of Bon Bibi fully which was translated by Kanai later which is an irony.

Kanai's worldly wisdom and education fail when he faces Fokir on his territory i.e. Gorjontala. He makes him face the ordeal of fear experienced by the 'other'.

> "Even in that moment of distraction, Kanai noticed – so tenacious were the habits of his profession- that Fokir was using a different form of address with him now. From the respectful *apni*[5] that he had been using before, he had now switched to the same familiar *tui*[6] Kanai had used in addressing him; it was as though in stepping on the island, the authority of their positions had been suddenly reversed."[7]

The author proves that though the educated tend to be careful in treating the marginalised, at trying circumstances, they fail to hide their deep-rooted antagonism towards them. Kanai abuses Fokir with his mouthful.

> "His anger came welling up with an atavistic explosiveness, rising from sources whose very existence he would have denied: the master's suspicion of the menial; the pride of the caste; the townman's mistrust of the rustic; the city's antagonism to the village. He had thought that he had cleansed himself of these sentiments of the past, but the violence with which they came spewing out of him now suggested that they had only been compacted in to an explosive and highly volatile reserve."[8]

The ruling elite continue to harbour the hegemony which keeps flashing out at different occasions when they are off guard. Thus, however modernised we are, the discrimination or hypocrisy of dealing with the 'other' creates open revolt.

The marginalised begin to show tendencies of insurgency and hatred towards the ruling class.

> "Kanai, but a great host of people – a double for the outside world, someone standing in for the men who had destroyed Fokir's village, burnt his home and killed his mother; he had become a token for a vision of human beings in which a man such as Fokir counted for nothing, a man whose value was less than that of an animal."[9]

That they have the courage to take on the brutal steps of the government to put down their efforts is worth a study. It comes out of deep-rooted idealism connected to their cultural practices. Fokir was submissive all along but act very differently when he was on the Gorjontala Island. His mother Kusum was a revolutionary and fought till her last breath for the cause of the settlers of Morichapi. Thus, the reverse is also true that there is a hidden reserve of revolution for taking vengeance on the ruling class for all the sufferings meted out to them behind the cold exterior of people like Fokir. The display of the same is found in naxalism or other demands for States based on ethnic identities.

The concept of fluid identity may further be seen by the way Home and habitats are often discussed in *The Hungry Tide.* The Dolphins give this subtle message as they migrate and adopt themselves in new habitats. This is the typical postmodern view of identity in contrast to the essentialist view of identity. Emerging identity is simply the space one has in the place s/he dwells. Place and Space or Self and Home are in constant interaction with each other in an active process behind emerging identity. *The Hungry Tide* is a metaphor in this aspect as to how the concept of self and home gets redefined by the interactions that life offers which make the concept of identity formative and not fixed.

The concept of home is very interesting as Piya says, "for me (Piya) home is where the Orcella are: so there's no reason why this couldn't be."[10] Her growing intimacy with Fokir despite the difference in class, language and education is a proof that identity is emerging from that closeness rather than remaining a fixed, water tight compartment of social strata. Her intimacy become much deeper during their journey to track the dolphins, and grew to the level of Piya admiring him very much. She was with him on the tree branch tied to the trunk of the tree to save her life and in saving her he breathed his last. Piya feels indebted to him and provides for the future of Fokir's wife and son. In fact, she, in a sense, finds her home and meaning in serving the family. Thus, it proves that identity is evolved from a researcher of dolphins to an intense human being who loves Fokir and his family. The conflict between the 'self' and the 'other' is resolved in love, though Fokir has paid his life for it. She returns to Lusibari to continue her research through the Badabon Trust naming it after Fokir. It is symbolic of giving recognition to the 'other' for their merit. The crab that combed the riverbed of the Sunderbans was recognised over the elite Dolphins in a symbolic way.

Neelima says, "home is wherever I can brew a pot of good tea". But we know she had to leave her cosy Kolkata home for the sake of love and Badabon Trust is what she made out of the place she went to reside that earned her identity, 'Moshima'. Nilima is rooted to her place and fixed to her own routine that binds her to Lusibari. She is practical and be satisfied with her NGO project in Lusibari doing social service to people. The condescending attitude of Kanai when he invites Piya to Lusibari needs attention. He says that Piya has to say, 'Mashima' on reaching Lusibari and anyone can take her there. When Nilima was waiting for Kanai in Canning Railway station, there was a group around 'Mashima' which marked her different from the 'other'. Despite working for the betterment of these underprivileged people, the people could not identify her as one of them. Whereas, when the settlers of Morichjhopi was arranging the feast for the visitors from Kolkata to mobilise public opinion, Nirmal was asked by Kusum to join the feast. But Nirmal identifies with the settlers and wants Kusum to feed them. In fact, the visitors from outside felt he was one among the settlers rather than able to find out that he did not belong to the tide country. This is reformist and transcendental. Nilima was doing social service through her NGO, whereas Nirmal was involved in a social revolution to fight against the injustice caused to the settlers.

Nirmal, the school teacher, who was inspired by the cause of the refugees identifies totally with them. He uses 'we' rather than I and be inclusive and does not treat the settlers, the 'other'. He says:

> "Who indeed, are we? Where do we belong? And as I listened to the sound of those syllables, it was as if I were hearing the deepest uncertainties of my heart being spoken to the rivers and the tides. Who was I? Where did I belong? In Kolkata or in the tide country? In India or across the border? In prose or in poetry? ..... Standing on the deck of the bhotbhoti, I was struck by the beauty of this. Where else could you belong, except in the place you refused to leave?"[11]

Nirmal is fighting against the aggression meted out to the settlers of Morichjhapi. He leaves from his familial boundaries and finds his identity in joining the struggle of the settlers. We can notice in this the familiar theme of Ghosh as a writer who has larger vision beyond the shadow lines. This message of an emerging identity for those who strive, seek and refuse to leave the place they belong no matter what part of world it is located is seminal. If we deconstruct the power struggle, one can understand that while Piya and Nilima have their place and space based on their choice, there are others represented by Nirmal, Kusum and the thousands who lost their lives in Morichjhapi massacre who fail to negotiate between the two. There were brave and fought till the end for their place and space but could not withstand the onslaught of the police atrocities that sealed food and water, and clamped Section 144. These police were brutal and much worse than the tigers and the tides that took off their lives. The government machinery let loose cheap tactics of using thugs to destroy their settlement and dishonour their womenfolk. There was total anarchy, vandalism and genocide. These settlers were vanquished and left with loss of identity and the entire incident was buried as if nothing had happened. The louder narrative of the national discourse in the name of reserve forest silenced these feeble voices. It is this hegemony and the unjustified onslaught on the marginalised that Ghosh wants to expose. His way of digging at the silenced aspects of the 'other' in the history, giving voice to the mute, the vanquished and exposing the aggressor and the imperialist are the empowerment of such downtrodden people and the refugees who have no place to go.

Also this is an outcome of how Ghosh brings in plug-ins to the established history regarding the untold, the forgotten and the context of the historical text which has given a new identity to his way of storytelling combining history with fiction. The problem of refugees is still an on-going one which needs humane treatment. Saji, M remarks in his essay 'Multiculturalism in Amitav Ghosh's *The Hungry Tide*':

> "The strength of this community (Tide People) is that the members are naturally bound together through shared human values. The community is devoid of ideological and physical violence. The progress and emancipation of human beings is delineated not in material or corporal forms, but in ethical terms. Ghosh's vision and perception of the modern world viewed from Tide presents the possibility of a human world, irrespective of class, colour and creed."[12]

These little narratives get subsumed in the larger narratives of climate, ecology, trade and tourism at the global level for which knowingly or unknowingly people such as Piya, Kanai and Nilima toe the line of Hamilton. Their acts were rightly differentiated by Nirmal as 'social service' not 'revolution'. The giver and the given, the benefactor and the benefitted, the identities of the 'self' and the 'other' are not annihilated. Thus, the divide in the second category is prominent.

Thirdly, the State which treats organised opposition as the 'other' and hence asserts its anti-role of the 'self'. The Morichjhapi massacre was executed by the Left government in Bengal for making a Tiger Reserve. While the State may term such oppositions as insurgency and sedition, there may be the other side to this where justice has taken a severe beating and the victims are rendered mute as their voices fell in deaf ears as that of Kusum's for example:

> "Every day, sitting here, with hunger gnawing at our bellies, we would listen to these words, over and over again. Who are these people, I wondered, who love animals so much that they are willing to kill us for them? Do they know what is being done in their names? Where do they live, these people, do they have children, do they have mothers, fathers? As I thought of these things it seemed to me that this whole world has become a place of animals, and our fault, our crime, was that we were just human beings, trying to live as human beings always have, from the water and the soil. No human being could think this a crime unless they have forgotten that this is how humans have always lived – by fishing, by clearing land and by planting the soil."[13]

Displacement of humans for building dams, making special economic zones and building corporate houses or real estates is an on-going issue in our country. The problems are similar to the tribal or farmers where ever they are. The cries of the settlers of the Morichjhapi may be heard from Kusum's voice above, that at what cost we want economic prosperity or civilisation if human rights are compromised or even humans themselves are sacrificed.

With regard to resettlement and compensation, it is not as simple as the town people think. These settlers who depend on forest, rivers or lands possess certain skills which make them highly intelligent and efficient on their traditional work. The townspeople will appear stupid if they try their hands in any of these as Kanai did with Fokir in the island. But when their homes are displaced, they lose their strength and identity. They become helpless and lost.

While it is perceived as a nationalist discourse against a small marginalised group of refugees, the reasons for the State treating it as a threat could be because of its emerging identity of a Dalit nation. Annu Jalais[14] in her historical findings states that about 30,000 SC refugees sailed to Morichjhapi and set up a settlement there. Nirmal admires the way the refugees run administration which seems to be superior to the Indian Union. The island has been divided into five zones. The family of each settler have been given five acres for farming. There were wards and a group looked after the essential activities of these wards. Thus, they had tube wells, boat building units, saltpans and fishing that started the economic growth. The administration of Morichjhapi was ideal and far superior to the poverty stricken Indian Union then. Such type of independence created an identity that they are nation within the Indian Union. Unlike the dependent wards elsewhere whose leaders were pleading the powerful Indian union for grants, electricity and schools, playing the submissive 'other' so that the 'self' identity of the State was not threatened.

As Sukanta Das observes in his essay 'Towards an Alternative Identity: Amitav Ghosh's *The Hungry Tide*' that

> "The postmodern critics of identity disclaim the concept by discounting the possibility of objective knowledge since the world is to be interpreted only through the ever-indeterminate nature of language. Moreover, the recognition and acknowledgement of identity involves the implicit working of the structure of power involved in the production and sustenance of identity."[15]

The tide country is shaped and reshaped by the will of the tides which symbolises that it is beyond the power of corrupt and selfish brokers who sustain the contest of the 'self' and the 'other' for their petty gains. The relentless voices of the tides keep reminding us that Language will be the key to keep pluralism and inclusiveness in cartography.

References

1. Amitav Ghosh, *The Hungry Tide* (Noida: Harper Collins, 2011), p. 142.
2. Mulk Raj Anand, *Untouchable* (New Delhi: Penguin Classics, 2014), p. 67.
3. Leela Gandhi, "A Choice of Histories: GhoshVs Hegel in *An Antique Land*," *New Literatures Review* 40, (2003): p. 28.
4. Ghosh, *The Hungry Tide*, p. 220.
5. 'You' in Bengali when used with respect.
6. 'You' in Bengali when used with equals and people below your age.

7. Ghosh, *The Hungry Tide,* p. 325.
8. Ghosh, *The Hungry Tide,* p. 326.
9. Ghosh, *The Hungry Tide,* p. 327.
10. Ghosh, *The Hungry Tide,* p. 400.
11. Ghosh, *The Hungry Tide,* p. 254.
12. M. Saji, "Multiculturalism in Amitav Ghosh's *The Hungry Tide,*" *The Quest* (2011): pp. 103-107.
13. Ghosh, *The Hungry Tide,* p. 262.
14. Authentic source of Morichjhapi massacre. No formal historical records found on this.
15. Sukanta Das, "Towards an Alternative Identity: Amitav Ghosh's *The Hungry Tide,*" *The Atlantic Literary Review* 8, no.1 (2007): p. 107.

Works Cited

Anand, Mulk Raj. *Untouchable.* New Dehi: Penguin, 2014.

Das, Sukanta. "Towards an Alternative Identity: Amitav Ghosh's The Hungry Tide." *The Atlantic Literary Review.* 8, no. 1 (2007): pp. 106-113.

Gandhi, Leela. "A Choice of Histories: Ghosh vs Hegel in An Antique Land." *New Literatures Review* 40 (2003): pp. 17-32.

Ghosh, Amitav. *The Hungry Tide.* Noida: Harper Collins, 2011.

Saji, M. "Multiculturalism in Amitav Ghosh's The Hungry Tide." *The Quest,* 2011: pp. 103-107.

14

The Voice of the 'Other': Situating Sahityarathi Lakshminath Bezbaroa's Subalterns at Sambalpur

Bishnu Charan Dash

Derived from the French word' '*autrui*', the term 'other' signifies 'someone else' other than the 'self' and has been conceptualised by such philosophers as Hegel, Husserl, Sartre, Emmanuel Levinias, Derrida, Foucault, Lacan, Said and Bhabha. Though the dichotomy between being and becoming, between odd and even, attraction and repulsion has been integral to Greek thought since Pre-Socratic period, Hegel was rather more convincing in concretising the idea of the other as a constituent in self-consciousness precisely because the self requires the other to define itself. Husserl, the founder of Phenomenology, also used the idea of the other as the basis for inter-subjectivity, whereas Sartre dwelt upon the dialectics of being and nothingness to show how the world orients itself around the other.

The French philosopher Levinas was perhaps the first to theorise 'ethics of the other' against the ontological view of 'Infinite Other' as 'superior' or 'prior' to the self. Since God exists eternally, Ontology tends to describe the Absolute in terms of the infinite and unknowable Other and hence cannot be made available to the self as an object. Levinas is critical about the ontological view of the 'absolute Other' which is conceptually associated with totalitarian ideology of infinity and exclusiveness rather than inclusiveness and assimilation into the fabric of the other. In *Totality and Infinity* (1969:21), he criticises the terms like Infinity, the Other and Being that are indicative of subordination and hegemonic outlook of the imperialists and colonial masters. The notion of totality, according to Levinas, curtails the freedom of the other, and freedom in true sense of the term is "the mode of remaining the same in the midst of the other" (1969:45).While associating the philosophy of Ontology with the philosophy of power, Levinas forwards his ethics of the other on the basis of assimilation and ethical relation of 'I' with the other and this relation is characterised by responsibility, hospitality and ethical conversation as well. In both *Totality and Infinity and Otherwise than Being or Beyond Essence* (1981), he also emphasises the role of language in establishing ethical relation between the self and the world of the other precisely because discourse is the site of relationality. In Otherwise than Being (159), he clearly states: "My relationship with the other as neighbour gives meaning to my relations with all the others".

Significantly, Levinasian ethics of the other is echoed in Derrida's emphasis on 'the ethics of the ear'-the ear of the other and the voice of the other. At the same time, Derrida's discussion on memory that takes us away from the present to remember the other on the ground that the self has obligation to honour the "voice and the signature of the other" can be taken as a clue to understand the other voice and the cultural other. Derrida too dwells upon Levinasian logic of the ethical encounter of the self with the other in which the other is revealed in its 'alterity'. While so doing, he fortifies his deconstructionist reading of the western system of knowledge, colonialism and sovereignty in *The Monolingualism of the Other* (1998) wherein he offers an ethical critique of the sovereign language and undermines the coloniser's erroneous claim to possess 'his language' thereby rejecting the language and culture of the other. Following Levinas, Derrida separates politics from ethics and problematises in his *The Other Heading* (1992) the conception of European hegemony and forwards his idea of democracy as an ethical critique of totalitarianism with a message that democracy cannot be thought of without the community of friends, and without the calculation of majorities- all being equal (The Politics of Friendship,1997:22). The philosophy of the other has been further highlighted by Michel Foucault, who, in his *The Archaeology of Knowledge* (2001) and *Power\Knowledge* (1980), argues that the process of othering is related to power and knowledge through which the dominant culture tends to otherise the historiographies of other cultures. While elaborating on Foucault's representation of the West as the site of power', Edward Said in *Orientalism* (1995:2) shows how the West has constructed the Orient as 'the Other'- a sort of surrogate and dominated self characteristic of the 'colonised other', the subjugated voices reduced to silence under the cruel clutches of colonial hegemony. In *Culture and Imperialism* (1993), Said interrogates Eurocentric discourse and the dominance of grand narrative, and addresses the question of active resistance by the natives to the cultural hegemony of the colonial masters. Imperialism as such is associated with a system of building empires based on the domination and subordination of the territory, economy and culture of the other living in the margin. In Said's scheme of things, othering is then associated with the politics of subordination/marginalisation of any racial, ethnic, religious or geographically defined category of people. One is here reminded of the master-slave dialectic of Hegel which is extended by Feminist critics like Simon de Beavour (*The Second Sex*) to portray the female as the helpless other under the male hegemony.

It was the Italian Marxist Antonio Gramsci who developed the concept of hegemony not exactly/exclusively on the basis of economy, but as a complex socio-political-cultural construct reared through structures of domination. While commenting on the subjugation of Italian peasantry and the injustice of colonial exploitation, Gramsci felt it imperative that there is a necessity for the exploited class to come together and posit a spirited resistance. It is in this context that Gramsci used the term Subaltern to name a subjugated social category-people of 'inferior rank', who are marginalised in the hegemonic power structure of the colonial set-up.

In India, Subaltern Studies surfaced in the1980s in the hands of a group of academicians under the leadership of Ranjit Guha who tended to contest the traditional historiography and forwarded the new method by interrogating the 'colonialist elitism' and 'bourgeoise national elitism'- both being the result of British colonialism. The subaltern group tended to highlight the insurgency of Indian peasantry and agrarian economy, tribal unrest and the onslaught of casteism by forwarding a new model of historiography writing that involves history, politics, economics, anthropology and ethnicity. At the same time, they also contested the colonial imposition of grand narrative and narrativised the margins and their invisible or feeble voices. In this respect, Gayatri Chakravarty Spivak's 'Can the Subaltern Speak?' can be forwarded as a manifesto of the marginalised. Here, it is significant to note that the subaltern consciousness is prompted by what Edward Said used 'a spirit of resistance' rather than a mere passive outlook of bearing oppression and exploitation with reticence. Another important objective of Subaltern imagination is to look 'contextually' (Ludden,1) which means focusing various topical issues in micro level. What the Subalternists tend to realise is the empowerment of the marginalised voices that have been silenced for long. At the same time, they endeavour to bring to the fore their suppressed feelings, anxiety and angst, by narrativising them. In the essay "Cast and Subaltern Consciousness" (SS,vi:169-209), Partha Chatterjee highlights the religious beliefs and practices of subordinate caste groups, and states that caste constitutes an important aspect of subaltern consciousness in India: No matter, how we choose to characterise it, subaltern consciousness in the specific cultural context of India cannot but contain caste as a central element in its constitution" (169). Chatterjee argues how the voices of the Chandalas, Dom, Hadi, Namasudra, Fakir, Bauls and Sahajias have been left out as unheard voices in the mainstream of Indian society and by narrativising one Balaram Hadi, an untouchable, of Meherpur in the district of Nadiya in West Bengal, he tells us how an innocent watchman like Balaram was branded as a thief suspected to have stolen some valuable jewellery from the house of Malik, the Vaidya Zamindar of Meherpur, and was finally declared a social outcaste and driven away. In the light of the above discussion on the post-colonial concept of the other and Subalternian urge for narrativising and bringing to the fore the voiceless voice of the people languishing in the margin, the present paper attempts to situate the Subalterns of Sambalpur in the writings of Sahityarathi Lakshminath Bezbaroa.

Sambalpur, the glorious city that upholds the rich cultural heritage of West Odisha, was a tiny town, socially cast-ridden, educationally backward, economically moth eaten but politically conscious and vibrant in the backdrop of the two World Wars. Lakshminath Bezbaroa, the Sahityarathi of Assam, had to stay at Sambalpur for nearly two decades (1917-1937) initially as the Supervisor of Bird and Company and later on as an independent businessman at a time when the whole of India was under the colonial hegemony of the British on the one hand, and the economic threats of the two great Wars and political upheavals/ protests for freedom from the bondage of the colonial hegemony on the other. The language agitation of Sambalpur demanding replacement of Hindi by Odiya as official/court language, the movement for a separate political identity for Odisha championed by Utkal Sammilani under the leadership of Madhusudan Das and Gopabandhu Das, the Sambalpur Session of the Sammilani held in 1915 under the chairmanship of Chandrasekhar Behera, and the active participation of Sambalpur in the National Movement championed by the Indian National Congress with special emphasis on the Non-Cooperation Movement, Salt Satyagraha, use of Swadeshi/home spun clothes and Charkha Movement, Gandhi's double visit, movement against untouchability and Civil Disobedience Movement-all these were some of the very topical issues that made the Sahityarathi realistically sensitive to the issues and problems of the common men and women, the simple tribals and peasants of Sambalpur. Since literature is the mirror of the society in which it is produced, Sambalpur saw Bezbaroa as a hardcore realist faithfully representing the misery and sufferings of the peasants and tribals-the Kolhas, Gondas and Mundas- the oppressed and marginalised people who were reduced to suffering by double marginalisation-of the colonial hegemony on the one hand and the hegemony of the local Zamindars and the upper caste people on the other. Though he was born in a high class Hindu family, Bezbaroa was however opposed to all sorts of social evils such as casteism, communalism, narrow chauvinism and colonial oppression and injustice meted out by capitalism represented by the local Zamindars and moneylenders of Odisha, who used to lend out money with exorbitant interest finally forcing the peasants and rustics to part with their land. By the time Bezbaroa reached

Odisha, Fakirmohan Senapati had already narrativised the peasants groaning with poverty under the hegemony of the local Zamindars. The Poignant story of Bhagia and Saria in Senapati's magnum opus "Chhamana Athaguntha" is a classic in modern odia fiction in which the land and even the cow of Bhagia were taken away by the Zamindar Ramachandra Mangaraj. Bezbaroa can be rightly compared with Senapati as both of them are considered to be the father of the modern Assamese and Odia fiction, besides protecting their mother tongue which was almost on the verge of extermination under the cultural hegemony. As the champion of the poor and the marginalised section of the society, Bezbaroa, like Wordsworth forwarded his literary Manifesto in the Dhubri Session of Assam Sahitya Sabha that literature should be written on common men and in the language of the common men. Bezbaroa's humanitarian outlook and his silken sympathy for the simple tribals and peasants is evident from the services he rendered to\for them by acting as the representive of the poor in Sambalpur Municipality and by supplying medicines to the poor villagers of Sambalpur in the evening. Charity begins at home, and Bezbaroa proved it by keeping tribals and peasants at his Sambalpur and Jharsuguda house and by sympathising with them in their hours of distress and suffering. For instance, he had a Muslim cook at Sambalpur named Golap whose children Sona and Gora were his disciples at the Music Association of Sambalpur. His love for the tonga driver Adi, for his travelling assistant Bhalu, for his gardeners like Sadananda and Bhaira and his fan-puller Dasmantar is unparalleled. Though Sabaltern Studies and Postcolonial theories were yet to be born when Bezbaroa was at Sambalpur, it would be highly profitable to see Bezbaroa's narrativisation of the oppressed and suppressed class by poviding them with a voice to protest against the bondage of colonialism which Zamindari system inherited from British colonialism and cultural imperialism.

Bezbaroa's poignant story "Ratan Munda", can be interpreted in the light of Subaltern imagination. The eighteen year old Kolh boy Ratan, the son of Benga Munda, works with his father in a bell-metal store day and night to earn his livelihood, and this realistic background of the story brings to the fore the misery and suffering, the economic hardship and even exploitation of many young tribal peasants of Sambalpur and Bargarh districts who work at bell-metal stores with nameless popularity. Though bell-metal products are famous in the Western Odishan markets, the socio-political systems hardly take note of the sufferings of the young boys who put in their labour and earn their livelihood honestly by the sweat of their brow. Besides bell-metal products, Ratan and Benga have also made necessary arrangement for supplying various decorative ornaments to customers on the occasion of the Magh festival. Here, Bezbaroa has become a subtle-souled psychologist to dive deep into the mind and heart of the tribal subalterns, who also know how to dream of a future with romance and cheerfulness at least on the occasion of the Magh festival, which constitutes an indispensable component of Kolh culture. Reminiscent of the Assamese Magh Bihu, Magh festival is observed by the Kolh tribe for three days with dance, music and song, and the tribal boys and girls of Sambalpur feel free and forget for three days the fever and the fret of their prosaic daily life of hardship and suffering. Behind the veil of their dull and dreary life, the Sahityarathi presents the psychology of three Kolh girls, i.e., Kamini, Junjuni and Budhuni who have made their tinkling ornaments ready for dance on the occasion of the festival. But unfortunately, financial hardship stands on the way of the Subaltern heroine Jumuri's preparation for the festival, as her father is not in a position to buy a pair of tinkling ornament (nepur) for her feet. Through this narrative of the marginalised people, the story writer realistically presents the physical and mental suffering of the tribal girls, who under the back stroke of the stringent financial circumstances of the war-prone society of Sambalpur, keep on accumulating money for protecting their culture by regularly selling firewood. In the present story, we are told that Junjuni has come forward to help Jumuri with eight paise for buying 'nepur' that stands for the dignity of Kolh culture. Bezbaroa has satisfactorily brought the Kolh mind that values friendship far above petty monetary considerations. Ratan's love for Jumuri at the first sight at the bell-metal store in the absence of his father and his fitting of a pair of tinkling ornament on Jumuri's feet adds romance to reality which does not last long. Benga's visit to Jumuri's house with a proposal after the Magh festival and the demand of her father for a cow, a pair of oxe and seven rupees as the bride price (dawa) breaking the marriage proposal there-suddenly give a romantic twist to the narrative that finally tends to a tragic end. Ratan Munda is an aggrieved subaltern who lodges only ideological protest by interrogating the ugly practice of bride price/dowry which is an onslaught on pristine human relationship. And the narrative is silent about his revolutinary outlook of Balaram Hadi of Partha Chatterjee's Subaltern narrative. No doubt, being beaten black and blue by the people of the Zamindar of Meherpur and socially derecognised my the Maithili brahmin-priests, Balaram left the society for twenty years and finally took a solid revenge through resistance and by forwarding a popular religion in the forest which was embraced by many. Balaram, as the very name suggests, is a revolutionary subaltern in action. But, in Bezbaroa's story, Ratan's voice is invisible precisely because he left the society along with a passive protest- a protest that could not exercise any tangible impact on the tribal psyche, and the hegemonic outlook epitomised by 'dawa' and dowry which still eat into the vitals of the Indian society. Ratan's death in the flowing fountain and Jumuri's heart-rending cry in the forest symbolically points to the helpless suffering of a subaltern woman marginalised by her own society. Thanks to the timely arrival of the Deputy Commissioner of Chainbacha who took the trouble of carrying her to her father- a stony father representing the dominant male hegemony. The father otherised her own daughter by calling her a spirit, and refused to take her back, whereas the Deputy Commissioner symbolising absolute power of a district remained a silent spectator. The powerful also became powerless and otherised her in the sense that he did not return her the rights of being a daughter and a daughter-in-law of Benga Munda as well. Here is a case of triple marginalisation experienced by Jumuri- the daughter, the daughter-in-law and the helpless woman played upon by masculine hegemony as a second sex and also by the helpless administration. However, the Sahityarathi, being a powerful painter of the condition of the women in the contemporary society (as in Bhadari, Malati, Seuti etc), has kept a 'small space' for Jumuri, because she will have to live on after all despite all humiliation and acts of otherisation. The Commissionor finally admits her into the Christian missionary of Chaibacha to let her live a life of 'the other' under the hegemony of administration/politics and religion.

"Dasmantar" is yet another poignant story of character in which he presents the miserable life of another Kolh boy crushed by the cruel and oppressive hegemony \ritual of torture unleased by the then Sambalpur society ridden with superstitions, blind beliefs like witch-hunting and the cancerous scar of untouchability. The story, fit for being interpreted as a subaltern narrative, is grounded upon the real life and experiences of Dusmanta, whose identity as a name has been threatened by the language of subordination, and hence Dusmanta has been linguistically/hegemonically distorted as Dasmantar. His only identity is that he is an orphan right from his very childhood left to the care and nourishment of his ninety year old grandmother, who begs from door to door to feed him. Bezbaroa's description of the emaciated old women deserves mention:

"I saw an old woman of about eighty or ninety years coming tottering in faltering steps with the help of a stick. Her back has a hump; her steps are unsteady; the skin of her face is wrinkled and folded; her hair is as white as jute; her face is pale; but her two eyes dazzle prominently" (A.C. Hazarika:777).

This ill-fated old women who has lost her son and daughter-in-law lives on begging and occasionally selling egg, pumpkin and brinjal borrowed from others. After the death of her son, the Gaian people of Sambalpur do not allow her to live in peace; the leg of her only female goat was broken, and her dream of feeding Dasmantar with goat-milk remained a dream. Following the quarrel of Dasmantar with a boy of Ganda caste, the wicked Gaians once again entrapped her and declared her a social outcaste- a fact which vindicates Partha Chatterjee's contention that in certain specific cultural conditions, the question of caste consciousness is crucial to Subaltern Studies. They were accused of having violated the caste rules, and in the name of purification, the Gaians demanded twenty rupees as charges for repentance and spiritual punishment, and the story brings to the fore the ugly practices of casteism, economic exploitation, and religion as a powerful weapon of hegemony. Following the double visit of Gandhi to Sambalpur, the caste question figured as a topical issue, and Chandrasekhar Behera who championed the Gandhian Movement in Sambalpur came as a savior to the people of inferior rank by launching a vigorous tirade against untouchability, evils of casteism, dowry and oppression and exploitation of the underpriviledged (harijan) class, of which, Bezbaroa's Sadananda, an untouchable worker in his Sambalpur garden is the prototype. Sadananda has been narrativised in Bezbaroa's story "Barichowa" (1932) together with another untouchable of the Ganda class. Bezbaroa, like Behera, with whom he worked in Sambalpur Municipality for the uplift of the poor, disapproved of the caste question and criticised the high class people of Sambalpur as highly rigid (pitpitia) and strict, and called upon them to be rather strict in discharging their duties and responsibilities for the development of the society (Hajarika:780). In "Bhaira", the Sahityarathi has narrativised another subaltern, the gardener of his own house at Jharsuguda. Like Wordsworth's rustics and peasants, who epitomise the concept of innocence, purity and noble savage, Bhaira is heard of hearing and for him work is worship and duty is God. Pride and pretence, jealousy and exploitation can hardly touch him even though he is branded as untouchable by the Society of Sambalpur. For him, ignorant is bliss, and knowledge is curse. Far away from the madding croud, Bhira signalises the birth of a new subaltern.

In "Maganiyar Buddha", we find another subaltern otherised to the level of madness under the cruel clutches of colonial hegemony of the Zamindars and Gauntias of Sambalpur. Here is a pathetic story of an old beggar of Ganda caste, who has been reduced to poverty and madness under the conspiracy of the wicked village head Braja Gauntia who in the name of collecting revenue grabbed his lands through forgery. The lands of this Ganda peasant finally fell into the hands of Braja and Bimbadhar Teli, representing a class called oilman (teli) in Odisha who are famous for lending out money with exorbitant interest. Through the Characters of Braja and Bimbadhara, Bezbaroa has exposed the ugly face of the money lenders and swindlers who played a powerful role in strengthening the capitalistic structure to otherise innocent people. Even the political centres of power like the office of the Tahasildar has been misused to deprive the subaltern of his land. Four of his sons have died, yet the Ganda protagonist lives in a state of madness on Shasan Railway station and cries, like an 'aggrieved subaltern', for justice to the poor and punishment for the wicked who reduced him to the state of the other.

Works Cited

1. Levinas, Emmanuel, 1969, *Totality and Infinity: An Essay on Exteriority*, A. Lingis (trans), Pittsburgh, PA, Duquesne Press. 1981, *Otherwise than Being or Beyond Essence*, A. Lingis (trans) The Hague: Martinus Nijhoff.
2. Derrida, J. 1998, *The Monolingualism of the Other, or the Prosthesis of Origin*, P. Mensah (trans), Palo Alto, CA, Stanford University Press.
3. The Politics of Friendship, G. Collins (trans), London, Verso.
4. Said, Edward, 1995, *Orientalism: Western Conceptions of the Orient*, Harmondsmith: Penguin.
5. Gramsci, A. 1971, *Selections from Prison Notebooks*, Q. Hoarse and G.N. Smith (trans), London: Lawrence and Wishart.
6. Guha, R. 1982, *Subaltern Studies,* Vol. 1-8, Delhi; Oxford University Press, 1997, Dominance Without Hegemony: History and Power in Colonial India.
7. Spivak, G. 1988, "Can the Subaltern Speak?" *In Marxism and the Introduction of Culture*, C. Nelson and L. Grossberg (eds), 271-313, Urbana: University of Illionois Press.
8. Ludden, David, 2010: *Reading Subaltern Studies*, Orient Longman, Delhi.
9. Hazarika, A.C. (ed.), 1988, *Completer Works of Sahityarathi Lakshminath Bezbaroa, Sahitya Prakash*, Guwahati.

15

Language Loss Among the Thangal Tribe of Manipur

Maibam Monoranjan Singh

"Our language is like a pearl inside a shell. The shell is like the people that carry the language. If our language is taken away, then that would be like a pearl that is gone. We would be like an empty oyster shell."

—Yurranydjil Dhurrkay

Introduction

Without language, human culture would be wholly impossible. Language is learned and it is a special system of communication that is specifically oral and symbolic (Hoebel and Frost, 1979). According to the United Nations (2012), "Language is an essential part of, and intrinsically linked to, indigenous peoples' ways of life, culture and identities. Languages embody many indigenous values and concepts and contain indigenous peoples' histories and development. They are fundamental markers of indigenous peoples' distinctiveness and cohesiveness as peoples" (p. 8). Language change is a natural phenomenon which results from the differential propagation of linguistic variants distributed among the linguistic repertoires of communicatively interacting individuals in a given community. From this it follows that language change is socially mediated in two important ways. First, since language change is a social-epidemiological process that takes place by propagating some aspect of communicative practice across a socially-structured network, the organisation of the social group in question can affect how a variant propagates. It is known, for example, that densely connected social networks tend to be resistant to innovations, where as more sparsely connected ones are more open to them. Second, social and cultural factors, such as language ideologies, can encourage the propagation of particular variants at the expense of others in particular contexts, likewise contributing to language change (Michael, 2014). As shown by Kloss (1966), Fishman (1980) and Dorian (1982), it is believed that language and cultural shift is the by-product of the interaction of a number of socio-linguistic, cultural, and affective variables that work together to affect one's choice or use of one language over another.

"For centuries people have speculated about the causes of language change. The problem is not one of thinking up possible causes, but of deciding which to take seriously. We can begin by dividing proposed causes of change into two broad categories. On the one hand, there are external socio-linguistic factors—that is, social factors outside the language system. On the other hand, there are internal psycholinguistic ones—that is, linguistic and psychological factors which reside in the structure of the language and the minds of the speakers." (Aitchison, 2001).

"There are many factors influencing the rate at which language changes, including the attitudes of the speakers toward borrowing and change. When most members of a speech community value novelty, for example, their language will change more quickly. When most members of a speech community value stability, then their language will change more slowly.

When a particular pronunciation or word or grammatical form or turn of phrase is regarded as more desirable, or marks its users as more important or powerful, then it will be adopted and imitated more rapidly than otherwise..... The important thing to remember about change is that, as long as people are using a language, that language will undergo some change" (Ottenheimer, 2009).

During the last century, the phenomenon of language loss is considered as a side effect of linguistic change over time by the linguists (Fromkin and Rodman, 1998; Greenberg, 1968; Hall, 1959). Rottet (2001), the noted French linguist, asserts language loss (shift) is "a community's transition from predominant use of one language to predominant use of another". It implies to the process where group of people speaking a particular language change, or shift, to the use of another language and language loss can led to language death, where no living speakers of the original language exist. Crystal (2000) opines that dead language may continue to have existence in a recorded form, of course - traditionally in writing, more recently as part of sound or video archive (and it does in a sense "live on" in this way) -but unless it has fluent speakers one would not talk of it as a 'living language'. Rottet (2001) further explains that language loss and death can occur in two ways either suddenly, or gradually over time. Incidence of language loss or death suddenly is rare and can occur as a result of natural disasters or the genocide that kill an entire population or group. Gradual language loss or death is more probable and occurs when the language comes into contact with a dominant group that has no interest in maintaining the native language (Dorian, 1981; Rottet, 2001).

But how do we assess or recognise language loss or shift? Crawford (2007) opines that the obvious sign of a language under threat is the decline in the number of its speakers. Some other symptoms may be:

- the aged are more fluent in the language in comparison to the younger generations as they prefer to speak another (usually the dominant societal) tongue;
- decline in usage in "domains" such as churches, cultural observances, schools, and most important, the home where the language was once secure;
- increasing numbers of parents fail to teach the language to their children.

Experience of language endangerment is felt over the world. According to Crystal (2000), 96 per cent of the world's languages are spoken by only 4 per cent of the population; a quarter by less than 1000 people; and well over half by less than 10,000. Lewis *et al.* (2015) accounted 7,102 known living languages in the world. It is believed that 80 per cent of the American languages are not growing and 50 per cent of the existing languages in today's world are threatened. About 90 per cent of the world's languages may be extinct in the next century, to be superseded by the English, Spanish, Chinese, etc. The danger of language extinction and of the loss of linguistic diversity parallels and exceeds the severity of the decline of plants and animal on our earth (Cantoni, 2007, p. vii). Out of 196 endangered Indian languages listed by UNESCO, 89 languages are located in North Eastern region, but it failed to give a clear picture of the endangered region (Singh, 2013). Tarao, Paomei and Kharam in Manipur may be identified as little less than falling in the endangered language category (*ibid*).

Aims of the study

This study aims to discover whether there is a difference in terms of language use between age groups. As language loss/shift is caused both by internal and external factors and can take place both at macro and micro levels, the present paper tries to highlight the factors responsible for shift of Thangal language to a new *lingua franca*. It also attempts to examine if there is a different perception towards factors linked with language shift as found in other studies. In this age of sending children to English medium schools, imposition on use of English in the institutions draws the children closer to it. The study further tries to find out if the children are more accustomed to use of English terms in their day-to-day activities.

Hypotheses

- Loss/shift of Thangal language is caused by demographic factors like intermarriage.
- Absence of established market centers and employment opportunity in the village compelled the people to come in contact with other groups with whom they remain in constant interaction.
- English as medium of instruction in educational institutions restricts usage and understanding of the native language.

Significance of the study

In Manipur, extensive linguistic research on various communities of the state have been undertaken but researches on threatened language of the small indigenous groups are lacking. Language loss/shift occurs due to several factors which go undetected till the stage when acute endangerment is felt. People in Thangal Surung, Makeng and Tumnoupokpi villages are still fluent in the indigenous language while signs of decline are felt in the remaining Thangal villages such as Ningthoupham where the study was carried out. The emergence of a mixed dialect called *lamjan / ching-gee-lon / chinglon* as the *lingua franca* can pose a threat to the native language. There is dearth of literature on language loss in Manipur and such a study is singularly lacking among the Thangal. This study seeks to fill that gap with a hope to provide a small step towards a better understanding of the language situation among the Thangals in terms of their acculturation strategies, attitudes to the host and source cultures, ethnic identity, and language maintenance and/ or shift patterns. Timely revitalisation is possible only when the factors of change are detected early.

Limitations of the study

The smallness of the sample size and the selection of only one village limit generalisation of data. More villages and more individuals need to be included in such a study to arrive at a more concrete conclusion.

The Thangal

Thangal is the name of the language as well as the people who speak the language. It is also a common practice to use the term as a suffix to their names. They are found in the hilly state of Manipur, which is situated on the eastern frontier of Indian subcontinent. It is bounded on the east by Myanmar, on the north by the State of Nagaland, on the west by the state of Assam and on the south by the state of Mizoram and Myanmar. Manipur, though landlocked by hill ranges, has some important routes that serves as a transit between Gangetic valley and China and South-East Asia. Despite the difficult geographical, it has favoured the movements of people from different regions mainly from Myanmar and India for many centuries and merged with the local people through miscegenation, a process which still continues. Historical accounts also reveal the influx of migrant populations in successive waves at different periods in these routes and they merged with the aboriginal people of Manipur (Singh, 2001; Roy, 1973). In short "the mass people in Manipur is a composite one to which the Dravidians, Mongolians, Aryans, Pongs, Chinese, Siamese, etc. were contributory" (Kriti, 1980). The movements have made Manipur the homeland of various ethnic groups such as the Meiteis (the major community), the

Manipuri Muslims (Meitei Pangal), seven Scheduled Castes, thirty-nine Scheduled Tribes inhibiting the hilly areas and a small percentage of other communities coming from different parts of India.

The Thangal, formerly identified as Koirao, is a small indigenous Scheduled Tribe of Manipur, India. The etymological meaning and origin of the term 'Thangal' is still obscure and the views of the people are varied. According to H. Khangba (ex-President of Thangal Naga Union, Manipur), the Thangals represent one of the Naga tribes who are found on the southernmost part of Manipur. They are referred to as "*Thangkaimi*" (meaning the southernmost people) by the other Naga tribes. The name 'Thangal' is believed to have been derived from this term. K. Lengkham, the present Chief of Thangal Surung village, on the other hand, opines that the name 'Thangal' has been derived from the name of a Thangal king named 'Thangkaba' meaning 'most superior'. The people of the valley called him "Thanggraba". Rev. Th. Thangmi, Ex Executive Secretary of the Thangal Naga Baptist Association (TNBA), is of the opinion that "Thangal Hill range is so long that it was commonly known as 'Thangkan' in the olden days. Under the jurisdiction of Thangal Surung village, there are two Kuki villages, namely, Thangkanphai and Thangkan Thanglunpa. Having extracted some portion of the village names, the word 'Thangkan' has been coined in naming their village. The neighbouring Kuki villagers used to call the people of Thangal Surung village as 'Thangkan'. This could be one of the reasons of popularising the term 'Thangal' to mean their people (Thangmi, 2012, p. 56).

Physically, they are indistinguishable from the neighbouring indigenous tribes who are of Mongoloid stock. The 2001 Census of India reports that the population of Koirao now identified as Thangal is 2348 individuals comprising of 1191 males and 1157 females and it made up 0.32 per cent of the state tribal population. The Thangals believed themselves to be indigenous to their area of settlement. According to their mythological account, they originated from a place called Makhel located in Maram area in Senapati District of Manipur. From Makhel the Thangals moved southward to settle at Angkaipang and dispersed to different places (Singh, 2008). All of them are now clustered in 11 villages in Senapati District of Manipur. In the wake of the Naga-Kuki inter-ethnic clash of 1990s that spread like a wildfire throughout the state of Manipur, the villagers of Makeng deserted the village and took shelter at safer places. At present, they have clustered in three newly established villages, namely Makeng Taphou, Katomei Makeng and Katomei Makeng Chajinba. Table 15.1 shows all the existing Thangal villages and their approximate distance from Imphal, the capital of Manipur.

Table 15.1
List of Thangal villages and their approximate distances from Imphal

Sl.No.	*Village Name*	*Distance from Imphal (in Kms.)*
1.	Angkailongdi	60
2.	Katomei Makeng Chajinba	66
3.	Makeng Chajinba	66
4.	Makeng (Taphou)	58
5.	Mapao Thangal	15
6.	Mayangkhang	54
7.	Mayangkhang Ningthoupham	53
8.	Thangal Surung	31
9.	Tumnoupokpi	40
10.	Tumuyon Khunou(Yaikongpao)	41
11.	Tumuyon Khullen	52

(*Source*: Singh, 2008)

The Thangals are patriarchal, patrilineal and patrilocal. The household head in a Thangal family is generally the seniormost male member and follow ultimomogeniture system of inheritance. Altogether there are sixteen exogamous clans among the Thangals. Monogamy is the general rule in the society. In the olden times marriage among the Thangals were prohibited as all the Thangals are regarded as brothers and sisters. Nowadays marriage among the Thangals is allowed while strictly maintaining clan exogamy. However, the long tradition of Thangal male acquiring mates from the other tribe is still in vogue, on the other hand many non-Thangal men who took temporary refuge at various Thangal villages have in time married Thangal women. Some of them have become permanent residents while some are taking temporary shelter. Those who have become permanent residents have been inducted into the Thangal society with a proper clan name and hence treated as full-fledged Thangal men.

As mentioned above, Thangal is the name of the tribe as well as the language. It is known by alternate names like Khoirao, Khoirao Naga, Koirao, Kolya, Mayangkhang, Miyang-Khang, Ngari, Thangal, Thanggal, Tukaimi (Lewis *et al.*, 2015). Dr Grierson (1987) considered Thangal (Koirao) language as belonging to the Naga-Bodo sub-group having close affinity with Kabui and Kacha Naga languages. The language code of the Thangal language is ISO 639-3 and it has been classified under Sino-Tibetan as shown below.

Sino-Tibetan
Tibeto-Burman
Sal
Kuki-Chin-Naga
Zeme
Naga, Thangal

The Thangals are multilingual and communicate with non-Thangal people primarily in Manipuri and use Roman script in writing their language. There is no regular radio or doordarshan programme in the language except for some occasional cultural programmes. Though it is a recognised language, it is neither included in the curriculum of the formal education nor taught in the school as the number of speakers of the language is few. It has limited published works with only the holy Bible and a few song books in Thangal as a result of revitalisation started by a section of dedicated social workers.

Agriculture undoubtedly is the main occupation of the Thangal while some have either taken up various governmental services or have started small scale business like grocery shops, hotels, etc. There is no permanent or weekly market in the village. To procure essential commodities or sell or exchange agricultural products the people go either to the market place at Senapati (the district headquarter) or Imphal where communication is possible only in Manipuri.

Methodology

Data used in this study were collected though questionnaires, interview and observation supported by data from secondary sources. The questionnaire was prepared and designed to elucidate socio-demographic and socio-linguistic background of the subject including use, proficiency and attitude of the subject towards Thangal language. The questionnaire was prepared in English but Manipuri was used during interaction. The body of the questionnaire consists of three sections. The first section consists of nine questions to ascertain socio-demographic backgrounds, like name, age, sex, occupation, education and the language they speak, etc. The second section contains questions related with language use to examine the language they use in their day-to-day life. The third section contains questions on knowledge of language, proficiency and attitude towards the local dialect. The survey was conducted in January-February 2015. The subjects were made to fill up the questionnaire by themselves and whenever necessary they were assisted by the researcher and his co-workers. While collecting data on the questionnaires, direct observations were made on language use, language attitude and language.

Ningthoupham village located in Senapati District of Manipur was selected as indications of language shift in the village were observed by the researcher during his earlier investigation among the Thangal. Moreover, the President of the Thangal Naga Union, the apex body of the tribe also claims that use of the native language is most reduced in this village. Data were collected from 48 respondents of both sexes and from different age groups. Analysis was carried out after proper sorting of data.

Results

The demographic details of the respondents are presented in Tables 15.2, 15.3, 15.4 and 15.5. Forty-eight Thangal individuals (26 male and 22 female) belonging 15 to 75 years of age participated in this study. 52.08 per cent are married and 47.91 per cent unmarried (Table 15.3). Five (10.42 per cent) of the participants are graduate, seven (14.58 per cent) undergraduate. Except for 6 (12.5 per cent) all the participants are literate. Eleven participants are employed in the Government (10.42 per cent) or Private sector firm (16.66 per cent), 13 (27.08 per cent) are students and 12 (25 per cent) are farmers.

Table 15.2
Age and sex-wise distribution of the participants

Age Group	*Male*		*Female*		*Total*	
	f	*p.c.*	*f*	*p.c.*	*f*	*p.c.*
15-29	13	50.00	14	63.64	27	56.25
30-44	2	7.69	6	27.27	8	16.66
45-59	8	30.76	1	4.54	9	18.75
60 +	3	11.54	1	4.54	4	8.33
	26	99.99	22	99.99	48	99.99

Table 15.3
Marital Status of the participants

Marital Status	*Male*		*Female*		*Total*	
	f	*p.c.*	*f*	*p.c.*	*f*	*p.c.*
Married	14	53.84	11	50	25	52.08
Unmarried	12	46.15	11	50	23	47.91
	26	99.99	22	100	48	99.99

Table 15.4
Educational level of the participants

Educational level	*Male*		*Female*		*Total*	
	f	*p.c.*	*f*	*p.c.*	*f*	*p.c.*
Graduate	3	11.54	2	9.09	5	10.42
Under Graduate	5	19.23	2	9.09	7	14.58
Secondary completed	6	23.07	5	22.72	11	22.92
Secondary incomplete	7	26.92	6	27.27	13	27.08
Literate	3	11.54	3	13.64	6	12.50
Illiterate	2	7.69	4	18.18	6	12.50
	26	99.99	22	99.99	48	100.00

Table 15.5
Occupation

Age Group	*Male*		*Female*		*Total*	
	f	*p.c.*	*f*	*p.c.*	*f*	*p.c.*
Govt. Employee	2	7.69	1	4.54	3	6.25
Employee at Private firm	2	7.69	6	27.27	8	16.66
Farmer	4	15.38	8	36.36	12	25.00
Small scale business	1	3.84	0	0	1	2.08
Student	10	38.46	3	13.64	13	27.08
Jobless	2	7.69	1	4.54	3	6.25
Too old to work	2	7.69	1	4.54	3	6.25
Others	3	11.54	2	9.09	5	10.42
	26	99.98	22	99.98	48	99.99

Summarising Tables 15.6 and 15.7, it is seen that inter-tribal marriage far exceeds marriage within the tribe. Marriage between Thangal man and woman is 44 per cent, 36 per cent between Thangal men and women from other tribes and 20 per cent between men from other tribes who took refuge in Thangal villages and Thangal women. This shows that acquisition of non-Thangal speaking mates is higher than the Thangal speaking mates (Table 15.6). Table 15.7 shows that maximum number of bride is from Maram tribe as compared to others. This finding is in agreement with the study conducted by Thangmi (2012).

Table 15.6
Inter-tribal marital relationship

Tribal affiliations of the married couples	*Frequency*	*Percentage*
Thangal men marrying Thangal women	11	44.00
Thangal men marrying women from other tribes	9	36.00
Tribes other than Thangal marrying Thangal women and taking residence in Thangal villages	5	20.00
TOTAL:	**25**	**100.00**

Table 15.7
Tribal affiliations of the marriage partners of Thangal men

Tribal affiliations of the partners	*Frequency*	*Percentage*
Thangal male with Thangal woman	11	44.00
Thangal male with Maram woman	4	16.00
Thangal male with Mao woman	1	4.00
Thangal male with Poumai woman	2	8.00
Thangal male with Rongmei woman	2	8.00
Maring male with Thangal woman	1	4.00
Maram male with Thangal woman	2	8.00
Rongmei male with Thangal woman	2	8.00
Total:	**25**	**100.00**

Table 15.8 which shows the multilingual status of the Thangals reveals that accept for one monolingual individual

Table 15.8
Language(s) understood /spoken

Language(s) Understand/Speak	*Male*		*Female*		*Total*	
	f	*p.c.*	*f*	*p.c.*	*f*	*p.c.*
Thangal, Lamjan	1	3.84	2	9.09	3	6.25
Thangal, Manipuri	0	0	1	4.54	1	2.08
Thangal, Manipuri, English	0	0	1	4.54	1	2.08
Thangal, Lamjan, Manipuri, English	8	30.76	1	4.54	9	18.75
Thangal, Lamjan, Manipuri, Others	5	19.23	6	27.27	11	22.92
Thangal, Lamjan, Manipuri, English, Others	7	26.92	8	36.36	15	31.25
Lamjan only	1	3.84	0	0	1	2.08
Lamjan, Maram, Manipuri,	1	3.84	1	4.54	2	4.16
Lamjan, Maram, Manipuri, English	3	11.54	2	9.09	5	10.42
Total	**26**	**99.97**	**22**	**99.97**	**48**	**99.99**

(2.08 per cent) all the Thangals are bilingual suggesting co-existence of minor language with a major one which is an indication initiation or precursor of language shift. Table 15.9 displays the language better spoken by Thangals and an overwhelming majority (66.66 per cent) choose *Lamjan* as the most convenient language for them. The findings affirm the informal observation of the people where they in most social domains use *Lamjan*, even among themselves, much more often than Thangal.

Table 15.9
Language better spoken

Language	*Male*		*Female*		*Total*	
	f	*p.c.*	*f*	*p.c.*	*f*	*p.c.*
Thangal	9	34.61	5	22.72	14	29.16
Lamjan	16	61.53	16	72.72	32	66.66
Others	1	3.84	1	4.54	2	4.16
Total	**26**	**99.98**	**22**	**99.98**	**48**	**99.98**

Table 15.10 displays the types of name among the participants. Thangal name is more popular in male than the females. But as a whole use of non Thangal name (56.25 per cent) is more than the Thangal name (43.75 per cent).

Table 15.10
Type of names

Name	*Male*		*Female*		*Total*	
	f	*p.c.*	*f*	*p.c.*	*f*	*p.c.*
Thangal name	13	50.00	8	36.36	21	43.75
English / Biblical name	12	46.15	8	36.36	20	41.66
Others	1	3.84	6	27.27	7	14.58
Total	**26**	**99.99**	**22**	**99.99**	**48**	**99.99**

The use of Thangal language at home, as seen in Table 15.11, has declined remarkably. Nearly 60 per cent of the participant never use Thangal at home, 20.83 per cent hardly speak while only 21 per cent speak Thangal regularly at home. It is also obvious that nonspeaking of Thangal is noticed in large numbers

Table 15.11
Age-wise speaking of Thangal language at home

Speaking Thangal at home	*Male*				*Female*				*Total*	
	15-30 yrs		*30 yrs and above*		*15-30 yrs*		*30 yrs and above*			
	f	*p.c.*	*f*	*p.c.*	*f*	*p.c.*	*f*	*p.c.*	*f*	*p.c.*
Never	10	76.92	7	53.84	8	57.14	3	37.50	28	58.33
Sometimes	2	15.38	3	23.07	2	14.28	3	37.50	10	20.83
Yes	1	7.69	3	23.07	4	28.57	2	25.00	10	20.83
	13	99.99	13	99.98	14	99.99	8	100.00	48	99.99

Table 15.12
Age-wise understanding of Thangal conversation

Understand Thangal conversation	*Male*				*Female*				*Total*	
	15-30 yrs		*30 yrs and above*		*15-30 yrs*		*30 yrs and above*			
	f	*p.c.*	*f*	*p.c.*	*f*	*p.c.*	*f*	*p.c.*	*f*	*p.c.*
No	4	30.76	1	7.69	3	21.42	1	12.50	9	18.75
Yes	9	69.23	12	92.30	11	78.57	7	87.50	39	81.25
	13	99.99	13	99.99	14	99.99	8	100.00	48	100.00

Table 15.13
Language skill

Language Skill	*Yes*	*No*	*Total*
Are you always able to understand jokes and proverbs in Thangal ?	31 (64.58%)	17 (35.41%)	48 (100%)
Are you always able to understand heated arguments in Thangal ?	29 (60.41%)	19 (39.58%)	48 (100%)
Can you always find the right words to express your thought in Thangal ?	24 (50.00%)	24 (50.00%)	48 (100%)

in the younger generation. On the other hand, Table 15.12, 15.13 and 15.14 demonstrates overwhelming majority (81.25 per cent), including the younger generation, could understand Thangal conversation (Table 15.12) and have the capacity to use the local dialect. This contradictory view where non-speaking or not using of local dialect on one hand despite having the knowledge of it, indicates Thangal is witnessing the sign of language loss and the finding is in agreement with Crawford (2007).

Negligence of local dialect leads to lack of cognitive knowledge of the local dialect in the mindset of the people. Non-usage of original language leads to its decline. Test of various items listed in Table 15.15 shows that overwhelming majority of the people does not know the original language. Not a single individual can answer correctly all the items listed, no individual can spell out the Thangal equivalent of the months of the year. They use predominantly non local terms in various day to day activities listed in Table 15.16 and the average percentage is around 70 per cent in all categories. Of all the items, use of local language is highest in singing (47.91 per cent).

Discussion

A number of research studies show that exogamous marriages are influential in shaping the linguistics environment at home. The Thangal being an exogamous group choose marriage partners from outside the group. Traditionally wives were given to and taken from the Liangmei and Maram tribes. This is one of the factors which lead to language shift among the Thangal.

Table 15.14
Language used in different domains

Language used in different domains	*Thangal*	*Lamjan*	*Manipuri*	*Total*
Which language(s) did you Speak at home as a child?	15 (31.25%)	26 (54.16%)	7 (14.58%)	48 (100%)
In which language(s) did your parents speak to each other?	12 (25.00%)	29 (60.41%)	7 (14.58%)	48 (100%)
What language do you use on Thangal occasions?	33 (68.75)	9 (18.75%)	6 (12.5%)	48 (100%)
What language do you use when you meet Thangal friends away from home?	21 (43.75)	13 (27.08)	14 (29.16%)	48 (100%)
Which name do you prefer to give to your newly born children?	30 (62.5%)	6 (12.5)	12 (25.0%)	48 (100%)

Table 15.15
Knowledge of Thangal Language

Thangal equivalent	*Yes*	*A little*	*No Knowledge*	*Total*
Seasons in a year	1 (2.08%)	9 (18.75%)	38 (79.16%)	48 (100%)
Days of the week	11 (22.91%)	4 (8.33%)	33 (68.75%)	48 (100%)
Months of the year	0	3 (6.25)	45 (93.75)	48 (100%)
Heavenly bodies	15 (31.25%)	14 (29.16%)	19 (39.58%)	48 (100%)
Flora and fauna	12 (25.0%)	16 (33.33%)	20 (41.66%)	48 (100%)
Parts of the body	8 (16.66%)	20 (41.66%)	20 (41.66%)	48 (100%)
Kinship terms	7 (14.58%)	31 (64.58%)	10 (20.83)	48 (100%)

Table 15.16
Language use in different activities

Activities	*Thangal per cent*	*Lamjan / Others per cent*
To think	22.91	77.08
To play	29.16	70.83
To curse	25.00	75.00
To joke	25.00	75.00
To scold	29.16	70.83
To sing	47.91	52.08
To dream	29.16	70.83
To count	27.08	72.91
To abuse	22.91	77.09
To perform rituals	37.50	72.50
To pray	31.25	68.75

This finding is in agreement with the studies conducted by Borberly (2000); David (2008) and Martin. In situations where spouses come from different linguistic background, there is a clear need to establish a common language for the home. In some situations, a linguistic compromise is made which often does not include the use of either spouse's mother tongue. In other situations, one of them will adopt the spouse's language if it is the dominant one in the society. Both situations involve a lack of mother tongue usage which discourages the maintenance of such language (Lasimbang, 1996). Such a situation is also observed in the studied population which supports the first hypothesis.

Except for some petty shops and tea stalls, no market center is found in the village. Commodities are purchased from market centers either at Imphal (53 kms from study site) or at Senapati Bazar (6 kms from study site) where Manipuri is used as a medium for communication. As economic activity is an intrinsic part of life, the people are compelled to come in contact with other groups with who they remain in constant interaction. The study also found 50 per cent of the working group engaged in occupations other than farming (see Table 15.5). Medium of communication at work places again is Manipuri. The overall frequency of use of Manipuri is higher than use of Thangal in the daily schedule of the population under study by virtue of the number of hours spent at the work places. A shift in the occupation from the traditional to the modern also influences the level of knowledge on the elements of traditional life among the younger generation. In support of this finding, Kershaw (1992), who conducted a study on the Dusuns in Brunei, attributed language shift to the changes in the socioeconomic landscape of a speech community. His study revealed that today's younger generation is not exposed to the "elements" which require the use of the native language. These elements include an agrarian atmosphere in which agricultural occupation was the norm. With more career choices, many Dusuns in Brunei have progressed from being farmers to civil servants. The success of the pioneering Dusuns in 'upgrading' their lives is an encouragement to others to follow in their footsteps.

Maximum numbers of students included in the present study are reading at Mt. Everest School which is approximately 3 kms from the study site. Medium of instruction in this institution is English with Manipuri or Alternative English as the second language. Non-inclusion of Thangal as the third language restricts its usage and understanding among the school going children. The medium of instructions in educational institutions attract the efforts of non-native speakers to acquire it. The motivation for such behavior is obvious--to succeed in academics. Based on a study done in Sabah where the medium of instruction in school is BM (Bahasa Malaysia), Lasimbang (1997) reported that parents, in efforts to ensure that their children will do well in schools, have resorted to communicating to their children in BM as a way to assist them master the language. Martin (2005) observed the same phenomenon in Brunei. Many parents admitted that they used Malay at home instead of their own mother tongue because Malay is the medium of instruction in schools. Other studies concur with this finding (Anonby, 1999; Borbely, 2000; David, 2008). In similar trend, the declining popularity of the language among a vibrant section of the society has resulted in difficulty in maintenance of the original language.

Conclusion

A high degree of language shift is observed among the Thangal which can pose a threat to the identity of the group in the long run if timely steps to revitalise it are not taken at the earliest. As Imtiaz Hasnain (1997) points out, the signs of growth or decline in the use of mother tongue not only indicate vacillation but marks nexus between language and identity. There does exist an underlying relationship between language and identity. Another factor that determines the sociolinguistic status of these tribal languages is the process of urbanisation and industrialisation. There is an inverse correlation between levels of industrialisation or urbanisation, and the maintenance of tribal language as mother tongues (Abbi, 1997:135). As observed in this study, a very low percentage of the participants are monolingual due to constant interaction with other groups for various reasons. A gradual adoption of a non-tribal language as mother tongue presents a classic case of language shift. Theoretically, these symptoms are considered diagnostic of potential language death (*ibid*).

This study has established three facts regarding the accelerating decline in the use of the Thangal language. The traditional practice of group exogamy has not only led to miscegenation but also to a high degree of mixture in language. A shift from the native Thangal to a new lingua franca called Lamjan in the study area is a distinct sign of language shift. This has to be checked with well formulated policies. Unless the Thangals are ready to spend the time and effort required to learn and promote Thangal, it is expected that their language will be lost completely in a few decades.

Secondly, the choice of a language other than the mother tongue for initial and academic literacy is also likely to have a long term disempowering and disabling influence on the mother tongue. The data presented here provide valuable information regarding home language loss in young children as day-to-day conversation with family and friends is done with a lot of words borrowed from other languages. There are signs of preference of languages other than their mother tongue. Even among the aged, the unchecked use of words borrowed from other languages have led them to forget the original and many were found to take time in giving responses to certain terms, names and words at the time of investigation. This is yet another sign of decrease in fluent speakers of Thangal.

Lastly, the shift in occupation from the traditional farming to the modern and compulsion to acquire commodities from outside the village is a change which cannot be stopped. But language loss due to such an inevitable change cannot be allowed. The native/original/indigenous language should be made to exist despite agents of change acting upon the society.

Recommendation

To check the adoption of a common language for communication in families with spouses belonging to different groups, attempts have been made by the TNBA (Thangal Naga Baptist Association) to revitalise the language by translating and printing the Holy Bible and gospels in Thangal, compulsory use of Thangal in Church services and Thangal gatherings. The effort is yet to bear fruit as the present study found very low percentage of individuals who are fluent in the native language. Other means of revitalisation in the form of organising literary competitions in Thangal among the children and youth would ignite a search for the correct form of writing and speaking. Inclusion of radio programmes in Thangal on regular basis would not only popularise it but also motivate the people to master it for flawless presentations over the radio.

References

Abbi, Anvita. Languages of Tribal and Indigenous Peoples of India: The Ethnic Space 8. New Delhi: Motilal Banarasidass, 1997.

Aitcheson, Jean. Language Change: Progress or Decay?. Cambridge: Cambridge Univ. Press, 2001.

Anonby, Stan J. "Reversing language shift: Can Kwak'wala be revived?" In Revitalising indigenous languages edited by Jon Reyhner, Gina Cantoni, Robert N. St. Clair and Evangeline P. Yazzie, 33-52. Flagstaff, AZ: Northern Arizona University, 1999, http://jan.ucc.nau.edu/~jar/RIL_4.html: (Accessed on February 29, 2015).

Borbely, Anna. The process and the factors of language shift and maintenance: a sociolinguistic research in the Romanian minority in Hungary. Praha: Research Support Scheme, 2000. http://rss.archives.ceu.hu/archive/00001155/01/167.pdf.

Cantoni, Gina. "Introduction." In Stabilising Indigenous Languages edited by Gina Cantoni, Flagstaff : Northern Arizona University. 2007, http://www.afn.ca/uploads/files/ education2/stabilising_ indigenous_ languages, center_ for_excellence_ in_education, _2007. pdf.

Crawford, James. "Seven Hypotheses on Language Loss Causes and Cures." In Stabilising Indigenous Languages, edited by Gina Cantoni, 45-60. Flagstaff: Northern Arizona University, 2007.

Crystal, David. Language Death. Cambridge: Cambridge University Press, 2000.

David, Maya Khemlani. "Language choice of urban sino-Indians in Kuala Lumpur, Malaysia." Migracijske i etnicke teme 3 (2008):217–233, http://hrcak. srce.hr/index. php?show=clanak& id_clanak_jezik= 48622(2008): (Accessed on February 20, 2015).

Dorian, Nancy. Language Death: The Life Cycle of a Scottish Gaelic Dialect. Philadelphia: University of Pennsylvania Press, 1981.

Dorian, Nancy. "Language loss and maintenance in language contact situations." In The Loss of Language Skills edited by Richard D. Lambert and Barbara F. Freed, 44–59. Rowley: Newbury House Publishers, 1982.

Fishman, Joshua Aaron. "Bilingualism and biculturalism as individual and societal phenomena." Journal of Multilingual and Multicultural Development 1 (1980): 1–13.

Fromkin, Victoria and Robert Rodman. An Introduction to Language. Florida: Harcourt Brace & Company, 1998.

Greenberg, Joseph Harold. Anthropological Linguistics: An Introduction. New York: Random House, 1968.

Grierson, George Abraham. Linguistic Survey of India 111, no. II and III. Delhi : Motilal Banarsidas, 1987.

Hall, Edward Twitchell. The Silent Language. Doubleday: Anchor Books, 1959.

Hasnain, S. Imtiaz. "New Economic Policy and the fate of minority languages." In Translation and Multilingualism: Postcolonial Context, edited by S. Ramakrishna. Delhi : Pencraft International, 1997.

Hoebel, Edward Adamson, and Lloyd E. Frost. Cultural and Social Anthropology. New Delhi: Tata McGraw-Hill Publishing Company Limited, 1979.

Kershaw, Ethel M. "Final shifts: some why's and how's of Brunei-Dusun convergence on Malay." In Papers from the second bi-ennial international conference 3 edited by P. W. Martin, pp. 179-194. Virginia: The Borneo Research Council, Inc., 1992.

Kloss, Heinz. "German-American language maintenance efforts." In Language Loyalty in the United States, edited Joshua A. Fishman, 206–252. Mouton : The Hague, 1966.

Lasimbang, Rita. "Situatsi bahasa Kadazandusun masa kini" [The Kadazandusun language situation]. Paper presented at the Seminar Pendidik Kadazandusun [Seminar for Kadazandusun Educators], Malaysia, July, 1997.

Lewis, M. Paul, Simons, Gary F., and Fennig, Charles D., eds. Ethnologue: Languages of the World. Dallas, Texas: SIL International, 2015.

Martin, Paul W. "Language shift and code-mixing: a case study from Northern Borneo." Australian Journal of Linguistics 25 (2005), no. 1: pp. 109 – 125.

Michael, Lev D. "Social dimensions of language change." In Handbook of Historical Linguistics edited by Claire Bowern and Bethwyn Evans. London: Routledge, 2014.

Ottenheimer, Harriet Joseph. The Anthropology of Language: An Introduction to Linguistic Anthropology, 2nd ed. Boston:Wadsworth, 2009.

Rottet, J. Kevin. 2001. Language Shift in the Coastal Marshes of Louisiana 8. Pieterlen : Peter Lang – International Academic Publishers, 2001.

Roy, Jyotirmoy. History of Manipur. Calcutta: East Light Book House, 1973.

Singh, Kh. Dhiren. "A Sociolinguistic Study of Kharam." Language in India 13, no.9 (2013): pp. 172-184. www. languageinindia.com.

Singh, Maibam Monoranjan. Bio Anthropological Study Among the Koirao Tribe of Manipur (Unpublished Ph.D. thesis). Manipur University, 2008.

Singh, R.K. Jhalajit. A Short History of Manipur, Yaiskul, Imphal: author, 2001.

Thangmi, Chand Anth. The Thangal Naga Tribe of North East India. New Delhi: Mittal Publications, 2012.

United Nations. "Expert Mechanism on the Rights of Indigenous Peoples: Study on the role of languages and culture in the promotion and protection of the rights and identity of indigenous peoples." Our Land Our Languages. United Nations General Assembly paper, fifth session, 2012. http://www.ohchr.org/EN/Issues/IPeoples/EMRIP/Pages/EMRIPIndex.aspx. (accessed February 10, 2015).

16

English Medium Education and Dalit Emancipation: Some Reflections

Indira Priyanka Veernala

Introduction

English medium education in India is the vital aspect for upholding the equality, particularly for Dalits' in the Indian social context.[1] English is the Language of freedom and emancipation for Dalits both in the arena of academia and the public sphere. Dr B. R. Ambedkar expressed the prominence of English education in the typical Indian context by stating *'English as a milk of lioness. One, who drinks it, can roar'*. The upper castes have been handling the contradiction between English and mother tongue language quite carefully. But when it comes to teaching English to the Dalits, they have been arguing that English is the responsible for the obliterating of the mother tongue in India. But, till recent times, it has not been proved in reality. Eventually, the so called upper caste people's children study in the foreign universities by ignoring the mother tongue languages to occupy the superior positions in social, economic and political systems in India.

The Dalit societies are incredibly devoted to allow their children to study in English medium in the recent scenario. This transformation has come to Dalits from their efforts to overcome the discrimination in the typical Indian caste system, where the downtrodden sections have been facing lot of discrimination, inequity and bias in their lives. English education from primary education level is proved that the Dalit's liberation in overcoming the rare opportunities in the globalization. They also believe that the English education as a significant aspect for their societal strengths, particularly to conquer against the subjugation of Dalits to climb up the social and economic ladder in the biased culture of Indian caste system.

In this context, this paper critically analyses various aspects of English education and its impact in emancipating the Dalits by transforming them towards egalitarian society.

Scope of Dalits and the Impact of English

The scope of Dalits from the very beginning is interconnected with the development of English education in India. English education among Dalits in Southern India in general and Andhra Pradesh in particular was first propagated by British Missionaries and later by the enormous leaders of our freedom movement. Dr B. R. Ambedkar evaluated English as "the milk of the lioness, and said those who drink it become stronger."[2] This shows us that the prominence of English in India was recognised from 1930s for the true emancipation of Dalits and the discrimination of deprived sections of the society in India. Mr Chandrabanu Prasad also states that "If your child learns English it's as if he or she has inherited 100 acres of fertile land". Therefore, the scope for the development and smooth survival of Dalits in all parts of the country was started from pre-independence India.

Later, Britishers embarked on English education from the initiation of their administration to run the elementary education system. This system focuses both on regional language as a medium of instruction till fifth standard. However, they introduced English as a subject from the sixth standard in their system which in fact initiated the fundamental step for the implementation of English education in the pre-independent India. The elementary education system which was initiated by Britishers was given the scope for all the communities in the country. However, the downtrodden sections in the country could not reach up to these elementary schools due to their relentless poverty and untouchability in then existing society. Therefore, the effort of elementary education was completely monopolised by the upper caste societies in the country.

Later on, the prominence of English education for Dalits to abolish the poverty, discrimination, inequality and untouchability was increasing due to the efforts of some eminent scholars in the country. According to D. Syam Babu, a Dalit scholar who opined that "English is no longer just a language-it's a skill. Without it we will remain as unskilled labourers." This idea reverberates today particularly due to the alliance of English with India's upcoming technology boom.

After the Independence of India in1947, the general education turned into the obligatory for everyone in the country under the age group of 16 in government run schools. However, the scope for the Dalits was still regulated due to the monopoly of private schools from the upper classes which were initiating the English medium in the country. On the other hand, the majority of the schools which were established in the rural and remote areas in the country were still under caste discrimination.

The Role of Christian Missionaries in the Propagation of English Education: A View in Andhra Pradesh

The noticeable effort for the development of Dalits and marginalised sections in the country were encouraged by the Christian Missionaries in the Indian sub-continent. One of the early arrivals of Britishers in India was in Southern part of the country. They first arrived in coastal area of Andhra Pradesh to trade with the Indian people in 1830s. Later, they established their administration and started the social service with the establishment of the Christian Missionaries. In fact, the Britishers initially understood the intensity of the discrimination towards the marginalised sections of the country.

Afterwards, they initiated the English education in missionaries for the deprived sections of the society and encouraged them to learn English with the purpose of eradicating the untouchability and emancipating the Dalits in Southern India and in Andhra Pradesh.

However, the missionaries were also occupied by the upper classes by using the weapon of conversions for their outstanding development in the society. In this context I would like to estimate the efforts initiated by Missionaries for enlightening Dalits in AP by their constant efforts with support of missionaries which initiated the English education for the emancipation of Dalits.

Although the very purpose of the inception of missionaries in AP for the emancipation of Dalits, they were predominantly occupied by the upper classes. There was a less representation from the scheduled castes whereas the majority captured by the upper classes. Most of the teachers in missionaries were the Brahmins, who were the highest caste in the hierarchy.

Christian Missionaries did a lot of effort to develop and attract the Indian underprivileged sections who were under so called Hindu fold. In the process, they tried to indianise themselves to attract them towards to Christianity. They wore Saffron dresses and ate vegetarian food, learnt Sanskrit for converting Indian marginalised sections towards the Christianity. They were called 'Roman Sanyasulu' (Rome Saints).

Dalits were impressed by Missionaries campaign against untouchability and their non-discrimination among different communities. Initially these missionaries propagated Christianity through Telugu medium schools. They later started schools where English was the medium of instruction and hospitals where English as medium for communication in the administration. Initially Dalits were apprehensive of English medium education, but later on, they started joining the schools. The reasons for their rejection of joining schools were their willing of their four fathers professions. However, later on, they realised the importance of English education and joined the English medium schools and enormously promoted from it towards the emancipation of their social status. Afterwards, they became enlighten souls who later fought against upper caste domination in social life.

The Significance of English in the Present Scenario

English education for Dalits became very significant for the empowerment of the deprived sections of the country. English became a tool for their social emancipation. Many voices came out to raise the issues of Dalits and downtrodden section by highlighting the discrimination towards them in the English media. Dalit ideology developed because of the English education and its impact in the modern India. English not only influenced the lives of the Dalits but also changed their fate in the social milieu. For the true emancipation of Dalits, English education became a prominent strength.

An English medium education system in the pre-and post-independent India influenced the fate of Dalits towards the development in the society. The whole phenomenon of the education system in India has been changing rapidly because of the impact of English education. The knowledge of English is required in many fields, professions, and occupations to sustain in various fields. Many states decided to establish English educational institutions because of its prominence in each and everything of the life. To sustain the existing competition, again Dalits should learn English language. English made the downtrodden sections upright in the society.

On the other hand, Learning English has become mandatory because of the impact of the globalisation, where maximum communication of the globe is happening in English. English became part of the life of the modern world. Moreover, maximum information of the entire globe on various subject is stored in the computers is in English. English has become a part in the lives of various professionals, students, businessmen and every one across the globe which is connecting successfully. The whole world is running after English and the life without English became pathetic in the academics of the whole world. The societal recognition as an intellectual is also based on English in the present scenario of India.

Most importantly, English skills for the people from marginalised communities in India are making them socially upward and their social status has been recognising and increasing because of the English education for them. This shows us the importance of the English education in overcoming the discrimination, inequality and the exploitation in the so called society for the Dalits in this country.

English Medium Education and a Contemporary Outlook of the emancipation of Dalits

The ruling higher castes in India had for many years restricted teaching English in government schools under the guise of preserving culture and heritage of the country. However, the modern attitude of the governments has recently changed about English and some states of the Indian nation have already announced that English will be taught from class one in government schools. While this is acknowledged as foremost step forward for lower castes and for Dalits, who fall outside the caste system, critics fear that the quality of English teaching will be poor. Professor Kancha Ilaiah[3], is calling for the gap to be closed between private English medium schools and the government schools in terms of both infrastructure and teaching methods. He insists on a two-language formula where 50 per cent of the syllabus is taught in English and the other half in the regional languages. Because, the marginalised sections in this country need the English education for their empowerment with the support of their regional language to understand and strengthen the English skills.

In the contemporary skilled world, now-a-days is viewing knowledge revolution, IT uprising and common lingua-franca for the first time in the history of mankind. Globalisation made the country as a hub for the opportunities, especially in India. In view of the new-fangled challenges promising out of globalisation, the youth of the country is having the bountiful of offers. But, the majority of the unemployed youth in India is from the deprived sections. At this juncture, to envision the emancipation of Dalits through the learning of English language is significant. Due to demographic evolution, there is an urgent need of furnishing India's working age populace, especially the Dalits with proficiency in English and essential skills. But the ease of access of English education to the Dalits is a challenging issue. Due to bitter poverty and state's discriminatory attitude towards marginalised sections in the country, Dalits could not afford English education in public schools from the last five decades.

The scenario of English education during the British rule in India was available only for the upper class sections in the country to work and support the British administration. During the transition from initial British administration to the independence of Indian nation, English education to the Indians played pivotal role in inspiring people towards the independence struggle and other transformations to sustain in the world. From this period onwards, English started influencing the Indian nation with wide variety of impacts and influences from various revolutionary ideologies.

At this juncture, the role of Dr Babasaheb Ambedkar both in the struggle for the independence and the emancipation of Dalits inspired many in the country. He became the fundamental for the country's future by writing the Constitution of India, where the future of country projected ideally. He also claimed that the *'Education everyone must have. Means of defence everyone must have. These are the paramount requirements of every man for his self-preservation'.*[4] Here, the means of every Dalit will come out of their education in English.

This representation of modernity and empowerment has global significance. English is the major working language for the entire world which has been influencing the enlightenment of the suppressed and marginal communities across the globe. In Indian scenario, English education always helped for the empowerment of the Dalit communities and their upright in the typical social system of the country. The voice for the Dalits from various sections of the people, organisations and the ideologies approached through the English education, which in fact escorted the Dalits towards the social and political identification in the country.

According to Kancha Ilaiah, Katti Padma Rao, Vulli Dhanaraju who have been the pioneers for the empowerment of Dalits in the recent times, opined that the efforts for the acceleration of English education for the Dalit emancipation shall become legal from the respective governments, organisations and institutions. So that, the inequality, discrimination, exploitation and intolerance towards Dalits from the upper class hegemonic communities can be terminated permanently. However, the recent phenomenon of caste discrimination has changed its face due to the perpetual vigilance of marginal communities and organisations because of the impact of the English education among contemporary activists of the emancipation of Dalits in the existing social milieu.

Jyotiba Phule an educationist and social reformer from Maharashtra, who established the first school for Dalits in Bombay in 1851, was one of the greatest pioneers of Indian Social activists, who indeed sacrificed his life for the egalitarian society in India. He also opined that without English education, the marginalised sections in the country will not develop in India. Furthermore, the influences of Dr B. R. Ambedkar's viewpoint of caste and its annihilation on Dalit activists from various perspectives helped marginalised sections to have their freedom and equal status in the society. This phenomenon had began in the society because of the continuing efforts of Dalit activists across the country by using the weapon i.e. English education.

In the recent scenario, India has another goddess, which is for the Dalits. There's nothing uncommon in that for a nation with bunches of gods, aside from that this is the Goddess 'English'. The goddess is a two-foot tall bronze statue in view of the Statue of Liberty. The imagery is not lost on Dalits, who see the English language as a method for getting away from the destitution and slavery.

Conclusion

English education in India had changed the fate of Dalits and other deprived sections to overcome the discrimination and inequality in the society. English education also encouraged Dalits and downtrodden section to be self respectful in the typical caste hierarchy society in India. It also cleared the way for the empowerment of the Dalits in the existing society. The opportunities in social, political and economical sectors for Dalits accelerated because of the impact of the English education system in India. Today a large proportion of Dalits who were educated in English medium schools and colleges are in higher positions in both the administration of the governments and private sectors across the country. However, there is a lot to do for the upliftment of poor Dalit masses in the rural areas of the country with the conviction towards the empowerment of the Dalits in the society through English education.

References

1. India is fully interconnected with caste system which causes the discrimination, inequality, exploitation and suppression of lower castes in the caste hierarchy.
2. Stated by Chandra Bhan Prasad, a Dalit columnist, researcher and chief promoter of the Pro-English campaign in India.
3. Kancha Ilaish is an eminent Indian writer and activist for Dalit rights. He is also the Director, Center for the Study of Social Exclusion and Inclusive Policy, Moulana Azad National Urdu University, Hyderabad.
4. Dr. B. R. Ambedkar stated in his book 'Annihilation of Caste' (1936), (DBAWAS Vol. 1, p. 62).

Bibliography

1. Ambedkar, BR. (2007). Annihilation of Caste. New Delhi, Critical Quest.
2. Vulli, Dhanaraju.(2014). English and Medium of Instruction: Dalit Discourse in Indian Education. International Science Congress Association, Assam.
3. Saroja Bala.(2010). English: The Language of Liberation for Dalits, Delhi.
4. Ilaiah, K. (1996). Why I Am Not a Hindu. Calcutta. Mandira Sen For Samaya.
5. Ilaiah, K. (2007). 'English Empowers' (Excerpted from What Kind Of Education Do Dalit-Bahujan Children Need'. Tehelka.
6. Reddy, PG. (2013). Telugu Prânta Sri Sabha; nâdu-nçdu. Telugu Bharati. Hyderabad.
7. Dr. Joseph, Ravela, (2003). A History of the Telugu Baptist Churches: Sri Kalanjali Graphics, Hyderabad.
8. King Robert D. (1998). Nehru and the Language Politics of India. Oxford University Press, New Delhi.
9. Fr. Mathew, Kunnumpuram, (1983). Origin and Development of Christianity among the Telugu people. An unpublished manuscript, Rome.

17

Othering in Self-Ascription: A Case for the Linguistic 'Selfie'

Suranjana Barua

Introduction

In most academic debates on 'self' and 'other', the latter has been described as something apart from the self. It is the entity which is *not* the self and hence its opposite. This dichotomous relation –antonymic in popular perception – locates the self-other debate in essentialist terms and seldom is the paradigm of difference (which constitutes self-other in other dichotomous terms as 'internal' versus 'external', 'intrinsic' versus 'extrinsic', 'private' versus 'public') ever questioned. But what if, following postmodern conceptualisations, the self-other distinction is questioned with regard to the very essentialist base on which it is premised and what if we learn to see the 'self-other' distinction also as rather fluid? What if the other, instead of being the inverse of the self, is actually thought of as an extension: contiguous to its existence instead of its converse? How will it influence the very theorisation of self-other in socio-psychological, philosophical or cultural terms? This paper is an attempt to look at the linguistic construction of the self from this fluid perspective of otherness – hence the analogy to the 'selfie' in its very title. Just as the present trend in social media is to upload a 'selfie' – a self-clicked photographed presented to the world in which one wants to be seen in a particular way by another's gaze as it were – a linguistic construction of the self, this paper claims, is inevitably presented by a self but structured from an other's perspective. In which case, any claim of clear-cut divergence of the twin perspectives of self versus the other will be misplaced. It is an academic platitude that our socio-psychological identity is inevitably in conjunction with others (we are all related to someone, live somewhere, have affiliations, play multiple social roles etc), and hence our communication processes too would inevitably feature 'others'. In a rather Sartrean vein[1], it can be asserted that just as others exist for our cognition so too, we exist as ourselves for others. From such a perspective, the idea of the self defined in opposition to the other will stand belied owing to the fact that self-other are defined not in opposition but in relation to each other.

Theoretical perspectives

The enmeshed, inter-related nature of self and other has been anticipated by Hollway (1995) when she notes:

> Throughout an individual's history, meaning has been achieved, consciously and unconsciously in relation to others. Since infancy, we have used significant others as vehicles for containing some of the ambivalent feelings which it is difficult to acknowledge in ourselves" (Hollway, 1995: 94).

Before Hollway, Cixous and Clement (1975/86) too have said in the context of this seeming imperative to know oneself through the construction of the Other that "...if there were no other, one would invent it" (*ibid*, p.71). The active involvement of self and other in situations of interloction has also been debated upon extensively by Erving Goffman who conceived verbal communication as a form of *telementation* (Goffman,1981: 80): that is, as a means of conveying to hearers the speaker's mental content – thoughts, feelings, attitudes, ideas. His idea of communicational interaction was organised by two fundamental requirements: *system constraints* and *ritual constraints*. While the former type of constraints organise talk into familiar patterns of dialogue and lead conversationalists to assume that participants' contribution to an ongoing conversation are intended as – and even interpreted as – contributions to the development of a sequential chain, ritual constraints concern the management of feelings in talk. Goffman contends that the source of these feelings lie in the presentation of the self in everyday social world and ritual constraints thus define:

> how each individual ought to handle himself with respect to each of the others, so that he not discredit his own tacit claim to good character or the tacit claim of the others that they are persons of social worth... (Goffman, 1981: 16).

This attention to ritual constraints seems to suggest that when people are engaged in communication, they are not merely concerned with the task of *conveying* their cognitive content/ thoughts to each other, they are also engaging in a form of interpersonal interaction – one in which they lay great emphasis on their *public self images* or what Goffman calls their *face.* An individual's 'face' under this theoretical perspective is characterised as the positive social value that a communicator claims for himself or herself – in other words, face is:

> an *image* of self delineated in terms of *approved social attributes* (Goffman, 1955: 213; italics mine).

While for Goffman, 'face-work' becomes a matter of habitual and standardised practices for the observance of which the participants of the communication situation are morally responsible, for our current purpose what we should understand is that the functional relationship that exists between "the structure of the self and the structure of spoken interaction" (Goffman, 1955: 225) as envisaged in face theory encodes a crucial *self-other dependency*. The public face of the self that is conjured in a situation of interaction is inevitably an *image* (see emphasis in above quoted line from Goffman) that gets delineated in terms of *approved* social attributes – that is, the other is actively engaged in the construction of the self. But then in order for a self to get this social approval of the other for its own construction, there must be a presupposition or a tacit knowledge of the self about which image is *likely* to get such social approval. To put it more clearly, a presentation of the self that is approved and sanctioned by the other would presuppose *an intent* on the part of the self to be presented in a particular manner so as to *elicit* the approval. Such a cognitive intent will scarcely be to the exclusion of language and Goffman himself hints at this manipulative role of language in the self-other interaction:

> In general then, a person determines how he ought to conduct himself during an occasion of talk by testing the potentially symbolic meaning of his acts against the self-images that are being sustained, in doing this however, he incidentally subjects his behaviour to the expressive order that prevails and contributes to the orderly flow of messages. His aim is to save face; his effect is to save the situation. From the point of view of saving face...it is a good thing that spoken interaction has the conventional organisation given it; from the point of view of sustaining an orderly flow of spoken messages, it is a good thing that the self has the ritual structure given it. (Goffman, 1955: 228)

Subjecting one's own behaviour to the prevailing "expressive order", can only entail that the self is expressed in a manner that conforms to specifications of the other – the other in such case is scarcely extrinsic but intrinsic and crucial to the constitution of selfhood itself. In the following section, we shall examine in greater detail how exactly does otherness and othering come to inhabit a discourse on self identity.

A self *of* the other, *by* the other, *for* the other?

Just as communicational interaction is premised on the two fundamental requirements of system constraints and ritual constraints in Goffman's early theory, in his latter work (Goffman, 1983) he posits the Felicity's Condition which deems that it is the responsibility of the speaker to construct their contributions to an ongoing conversation in such a manner that their hearers can work out the intended meaning by drawing on available presuppositions.

> Whatever else, our activity must be addressed to the other's mind, that is, to the other's capacity to read our thoughts and actions for evidence of our feelings, thoughts and intent. This confines what we say and do, but it also allows us to bring to bear all of the world to which the other can catch allusions (Goffman, 1983: 51).

Goffman's interpretation of the Felicity's Condition not only highlights the importance of presuppositions that speakers and hearers might share but should be read for the implications it has on self-other other notion. As noted earlier, given that our (linguistic) activity must be "addressed to the other's mind" or in the other's *capacity* to read our thoughts and actions for "evidence of our feelings, thoughts and intent", we must also realise that this addressing of the other's mind is preceded by the recognition of *our own* capacity to read the other's thoughts and actions. If we want the mirror to stare back at us, we must first direct our stare towards the mirror so that it reflects that stare: by the same analogy, the other's capacity to read our thoughts and actions about ourselves, must necessarily be preceded by our *recognition* of this capacity. To extend this argument, the other's capacity to understand all presuppositions regarding the self must necessarily be *preceded* by the self's own presupposition of how the other would perceive the self: in our case which self-image will find approval from the other[2] would require a prior anticipation of what kind of self-image is most likely to be liked by the other. To take our example of the selfie in a hypothetical context, the thought process would be akin to: 'Let me take a selfie with the sea/ my boyfriend/ the Pyramids in the background, as my friends are likely to like it'. What is put within the frame of the 'pictorial' selfie would be determined by the presupposition of how my friends are likely to react to it. Just as my perspective of my pictorial image is driven by the interpretion that I anticipate my friends to give it, so too Goffman's approach to communicational understanding is driven by interpretational resources whereby interpretation depends on the twin resources of *language* and *presupposition*. For our current purposes it would suffice if we understand that this active involvement of language and presupposition is not only in the context of the other's mind which can interprete our "feelings, thoughts and intent" but necessarily preceded by the self's (or speaker's) own interpretation of the hearer's presuppositions.

The one other communicational rescource that is related to presupposition in Goffman's theory and one that will be also be appropriated for this study of the linguistic selfie is the idea of the *frame*. In Goffman's theory, frame is an interpretational schema that provides the communicators the ability to identiy a particular stretch of conversation as a given type of communicational event. It is the frame that allows for a particular conversational moment to be recognised mutually by both speaker and hearer as, for example, a joke. Further, while the frame does restrict the identification and interpretation of a given conversational moment (a joke may not be construed as sarcasm for example), it accentuates the possibility of a correct negotiation of the face-saving/ maintaining situation of interlocution.

Given the above theoretical concepts, we shall now move to an examination of the talk-in-interaction of young Assamese University speakers to see how their interpretation of their selves are actually *linguistic snap-shots* that are presented for the benefit of, and defined by, others involved in that communicational moment. A subjective self in this examination will be shown to be as mythical as an objectified other and the real posited self, more often than not, will be revealed to be an extension of the other. The basic premise of this idea is laid out in the following section with speech extracts from actual situations of interlocution.

Interpreting the self: From the eyes of the other

One of the first questions usually faced in any job interview is "Tell us something about yourself". This seemingly simple question then becomes an extremely complex one because describing oneself and ascribing attributes and that too for the first time by way of introduction in an extremely contrived and formal setting is actually a very challenging enterprise. More often than not, interviewers look at that answer as an insight into the mind of the interviewee because what one says and in what order may indicate many things such as salience of identity, importance accorded to each such identity etc. The idea for this paper came from reflection of such a seemingly simple task of speaking about oneself. The data presented here was part of research conducted by the author at Tezpur University Assam[3] – and the analysis broadly follows a Conversation Analysis framework[4]. *A total of 17 respondents* (13 females and 4 males), volunteered to take part in the research and they are students of different departments who had signed up for an interdisciplinary course that the author taught. The respondents who volunteered were all in their early twenties and the study required them to take/ give interviews. In the initial questionnaire that the respondents were given, apart from supplying personal information, they had to indicate whether they preferred to be an 'interviewer' or 'interviewee': those who preferred the role of interviewer were then asked to interview any two of the peers who preferred to be interviewees and were themselves interviewed by the author. One of the reasons for structuring the interviews in such a manner was to see the impact of the presence of other people, who were in the role of interviewers, on the interviewees. In other words, role preference became a variable in the study and the type of interviewer as another (whether it was the author who was their teacher or a peer member) was, expectedly, seen to have bearings on the language of the interviewees. In the case of the those who preferred to be interviewers, the author was the only other during the recording whereas any respondent who took the interviewee preference typically had two 'others' during the recording - the peer who interviewed her/ him and the peer who was a fellow interviewee. It is interesting that of the 17 respondents, five wanted to be 'interviewers', 10 wanted to be 'interviewees', only one wanted to be *both* an interviewer and interviewee and one listed an 'either/ or' preference and each respondent gave very interesting reason for choice (this is outside the purview of the current paper).

For this paper we shall be examining only two extracts out of which the first one was on a respondent (R1 below) whose preference was for the role of interviewer: while she was interviewed by the author, the second extract cited is from an interview of three peers one of whom (R2) was a semester senior to the others (R3 and R4). While R2 preferred the role of interviewer, the other two members of that situation preferred to be interviewees. The first question that was asked to all interviewees (whether regardless of whether they were interviewed by the author or by a peer) was "Tell me something about yourself" and respondents typically encoded the other's perspective that we have been speaking of in the previous few section. The data presented is followed by the gloss of each word and a translation of the speech segment and the list of abbreviations in the gloss and symbols in the transcript is provided at the end of the paper. The backchannel communication (that indicates a listerner' approval to continue a speaker's turn) in this case is by the current author who is marked as 'SB'.

Extract 1

[NIM0023][5]

1 R1: *moi eta xadharon suwali* (0.3)
I one simple girl
'I am a simple girl'

®2 SB: *hmm taar: pisot*?
That after
'And then?'

3 R1: (0.2) *gaan xuni bhaal pao*-(.){SB: *hmm*}*ti vi sai bhal pao*-{SB: hmm}
song listen1 good gettv see good get
'I like listening to songs, watching TV...'

4 *logor: lora suwali logot kotha: pa:ti* [*bha:l laage*
peer boy girl with talk lay good get
'I like talking with my peers'

5 SB: [*logor*? peer
6 R1: *lora suwali logot. >LOGOR khini logot<*{SB: *buisu*} *kotha pati bhal pao*
boy girl with peer cl with understand1 talk lay good get
'With the boys and girls – my peers. {SB: I understand}. I like talking (with them)'

7 *FRI: hoi aru. <JUNE BHA-:BEma:ne fri buli.*
free am and. Who think2 means free quot
'I am free. Those who think that I am free'

8 *bohute nabhabe-¯u.xeiye¯.*
Many think-neg. that's all
'Many don't think also. That's all'

What is interesting in the above extract is that R1 gives a single line (of being a simple girl) as an initial response to the question request "Tell me something about yourself". Her laconic reply is followed by a pause (0.3) which prompts a backchannel communication from the interviewer (current author) who asks her to continue and R1 does so after another timed pause of few seconds. She continues by saying that she loves listening to songs, watching TV and talking with her peers. It is noteworthy that when she utters the phrase *lora suwali* which means boys and girls and the interviewer misses it and asks in a clarificatory turn to specify the term used (line 5), R1 replaces the phrase *lora suwali* with a plural classifier *logor khini* (peers). Although the dialogue format continues as per system constraints (Goffman, 1981; discussed above), her substitution of the boys and girls phrase with the neutral plural classifier may be seen as a ritual constraint – one that saves her face and presents her as someone who talks with peers and not '*boys* and girls'. It is important to understand two things here in this interaction: (i) R1 presentation of self required the other's intervention very early on – it was following the current author's backchannel in Line 2 that R1 continued with her turn in Line 3 (ii) R1's substitution of the potentially contentious phrase *lora suwali* with the neutral classifier *khini* can be interpreted as her desire to present an ideal self – she possibly neutralises any negative connotation of being associated with boys. This substitution perhaps marks her attempt to conform to the other's projection of an ideal self. It is because she is communicating with another who is her teacher; her projected self identity was in deference to the self-other identity of student-teacher. The face that she inadvertently projected with the initial silence and the later substitution was an indirect acknowledgment of the presence of another in front of whom she needed herself to be projected in an ideal manner.

Contrast R1's careful choice of words with the following extract where R2 is being interviewed by her peer R3 in the presence of another interview R4 (who does not feature in the extract below). In response to the same question, R2 indeed does start with a measured response where she first states her name, her place of residence and departmental affiliation (not cited below), and she follows this with the first couple of lines cited below (1-2) on when she arrived on campus and that she likes hostel life. It is probably because her interviewer is a senior peer from the same hostel, she is eager to present a face that she quite likes hostel life. An intervention from her interviewer R2 in lines 3-5 act as the frame for her projection of selfhood – she is asked *what she thinks of herself* and more specifically she likes to do. It is because of this other-defined frame within she is expected to present herself that she lists the activities she likes: cooking and household chores like cleaning. Lest this leads to a construal of her (projected) self as too domestic and boring in front of the significantly important other like a senior peer from the same hostel, she ends her turn with line 9 by saying that she likes engaging in *masti* (fun)

Extract 2

[NCD 00:32]

1 R2: *a:: ahibo du - ¯mah hol yat*
coming two month happen here
'I reached here two months ago'

2 *aru::: thike.* ().*bhale-¯i lagise hostel laif*(.)
And right good get hostel life
'And its alright. It's good enough – hostel life'
[NCD00:45]

3 R3: *aru tumi nije nijoke keneke* (.) *ma:ne*(.)
And you self self-acc how means
'And how do you (see)...yourself... means'

4 *mrinmoyi kumar buli kole-<KUN buli koba* (.)*ma:ne>*
Mrinmoyee Kumar quot say who quot say2 means
'Who would you say in Mrinmoyee Kumar[6]?'

5 *>Ki buli kobama:ne<*(.)*NIJOR bixoye ma:ne* (.) *ki bhal pua, ki kora*
What quot say2 means self-of about means what good get what do2
'And what would you say about yourself... means... what do you like? What do you do?'

6 R2: *mur bhal pua kaam- hoi moi KUKING kori bhal pao*
My good get work is I cooking do good get
'What I like doing is I like cooking.'

7 *kuking bhal lage* (.)
cooking good get
'I like cooking'

8 *ghoror ka:m kori eibilak* (.) *sapha saphai bhal lage*
house-of work do these cleaning good get
'Doing household chores – these things – cleaning. I like that'

9 *aru xei-¯. masti kori*
And thatFun do
'And that's it. fun'

As seen from lines 3-5 in Extract 2 above, it is R3's 'frame' that provides R2 with the opportunity to interpret and present her in terms of what she likes to do.

Conclusion

Given the extracts and the discussions in the previous section, it can now be perceived that describing the self and ascribing attributes is a more difficult linguistic endeavour than is generally presumed and talking about oneself is typically in consideration to/of an 'other'. Most often, who we describe ourselves to be are fragments of who we think we are and the description is presented for the benefit of others i.e. they are *public* self-images that Goffman calls 'face': the public self-images that both R1 and R2 present in Extract 1 and 2 respectively showcase a self that is in consideration of the other who is present in the situation of communication. In the case of R1, she presents an ideal self with a taciturn reply that needs prodding from the hearer-cum-interviewer (who is also her teacher). Hence the self that is presented in deferential, waits for proper encouragement before speaking and constructs a face which is perceived by some reported others as 'free' and some others and as not too free. On the other hand, in Extract 2, R2 endeavours to construct her selfhood in terms of her salient identity as a peer of the interviewer who is from the same hostel. Given the frame within which she had to define the contours of her selfhood, she presents a ideal and likeable self who is capable of having fun at the same time. In her case, given that the other present in the situation of interaction is a peer, she even code-mixes her language and lapses into a Hindi term *masti* to be construed as a fun-loving individual. Her peer group culture allows her this privilege of constructing a self that can be seen as conforming and yet fun in her own way.[7] Even the choice of a single code-mixed lexical item can indicate this presentation of an ideal self in consideration of another who acknowledges it as such. As in the case of R1 and R2 in the extracts above, ultimately, all we do is present 'snap-shots' of ourselves in contextual moments of interaction: for all practical purposes then a self-ascription is inevitably a linguistic 'selfie' that we take *of* ourselves, *from* another's perspectives and *for* other others to perceive.

List of symbols and abbreviations used

(.) = untimed pause	<> = slow speech	→ = important segment discussed
↑↓ = pitch variation	>< = fast speech	cl = classifier
: = sound length	[=overlapping speech	CAPS = loud speech
{} = backchannel communication	1/2/3 = first/ second/ third person	neg = negative marker
acc = accusative	quot = quotative	h/ nh = honorific/ non-honorific

References

Atkins, K. (ed.) *Self and Subjectivity*. UK, Blackwell Publishing Ltd. 2005.

Barua, S. (forth.) "Marginalising the marginalised: The feminine narrative voice and/ as exclusionist language". Chapter in forthcoming volume edited by D.P. Nath titled *Women's Narratives from North East India: Writing Lives from the Margins*.

Cixous, H. and Clement, C. *The Newly Born Woman*. Minneapolis, University of Minnesota Press (1975/86).

Goffman, E. "On face-work: An analysis of ritual elements in social interaction". *Psychiatry: Journal of the Study of Interpersonal Processes*, 18, 3. August; 213-31, 1955.

Goffman, E. *The Presentation of Self in Everyday Life*. New York, Anchor Books, 1959.

Goffman, E. *Interaction Ritual*. Pantheon Books, New York, 1967.

Goffman, E. *Frame Analysis*. New York, Harper and Row, 1974.

Goffman, E. *Forms of Talk*. Oxford, Basil Blackwell, 1981.

Goffman, E. "Felicity's condition" in *American Journal of Sociology*, 89, 1. 1-3, 25-51. University of Chicago Press, 1983.

Hollway, W. "Feminist discourses and women's heterosexual desire" in Wilkinson, S. and Kitzinger, C. (eds.) *Feminism and Discourse: Psychological Perspectives*. London, Sage Publications, 1995.

Hutchby, I. and Wooffitt, R. *Conversation Analysis: Principles, Practices and Applications*. Cambridge, Polity Press, 1998.

Notes

1. "Being-seen-by-the-other" is the *truth* of "seeing-the-other" (Sartre; *Being and Nothingness*; cited in Atkins, K. (ed.) *Self and Subjectivity*. UK, Blackwell Publishing Ltd. Atkins 2005: 96): that is, one's existence hinges as much on the acknowledgment from the other as acknowledging the other as a self.
2. Face being an *image* of self which is delineated in terms of "approved social attributes" (Goffman, 1955: 21; cited earlier).
3. At the Centre for Assamese Studies, Tezpur University where the author was previously working.
4. Conversation Analysis in the study of talk-in-interaction and typically uses minutest details of everyday talk to analyse macro phenomenon. While the transcription symbols to be used in the data are explained in the table at the end of the paper, readers may kindly refer to any basic text such as Hutchby, I. and Wooffitt, R. *Conversation Analysis: Principles, Practices and Applications*. Cambridge, Polity Press. 1998 etc. for further elucidation and references on CA.
5. Extract headings indicate author's transcript source.
6. All names that appear in transcript have been changed from original.
7. The influence of peer group on subjectivity has also been explored from the perspective of marginalisation in Barua (forth.)" Marginalising the marginalised: The feminine narrative voice and/ as exclusionist language". Chapter in forthcoming volume edited by D.P. Nath titled *Women's Narratives from North East India: Writing Lives from the Margins*.

Index

U

V

W

Z